P.V18 - Description of planner
PLANNING pp. 116-129
OBJECTIVES TREE 123-12[?]
OBJ. TREE AS BASIS FOR ORG. - 177-179
TASK FORCE ORGANIZATION 179-183
(ie MATRIX BASED ON OBJECTIVES)

SPAN OF CONTROL & ORGANIZATIONAL BLOAT 187

* ON MATCHING PERSON & TASKS AND pp. 204-5
EFFECT ON MOTIVATION

Karloss not necessarily good because he is rigor but because he writes directly, succinctly and assertively. When he hits a nail on the head he hits it square, clean and hard.

P132 'The problem in running any organization is not that people do things wrong — it is that they do the wrong things' ie. they do not plan effectively before they start doing things.

P 208 ' In the absence of a rational set of objectives, this (i.e. setting up a lot of committees) is only an expensive way of bringing together a number of people to share their confusions.'

MAIN THESIS

Management is the process by which resources are converted into value.

REDEFINING THE MANAGER'S JOB

REDEFINING THE MANAGER'S JOB

THE PROACTIVE MANAGER IN A REACTIVE WORLD

MERRITT L. KASTENS

A DIVISION OF AMERICAN MANAGEMENT ASSOCIATIONS

Library of Congress Cataloging in Publication Data

Kastens, Merritt L
  Redefining the manager's job.

  Bibliography: p. 273
  Includes index.
  1. Management. I. Title.
  HD31.K335   658   80-65701
  ISBN 0-8144-5619-7

© 1980 AMACOM
A division of American Management Associations, New York. All rights reserved. Printed in the United States of America.

This publication may not be reproduced, stored in a retrieval system, or transmitted in whole or in part, in any form or by any means, electronic, mechanical, photocopying, recording, or otherwise, without the prior written permission of AMACOM, 135 West 50th Street, New York, N.Y. 10020.

First Printing

This book is dedicated to managers and to the people who hire managers in the hope that it will save them some time and agony, help them make some money, and enable them to understand the so-called management literature.

PREFACE

This is a Utopian book. Like all futures scenarios, it deals with the logical consequences to be expected if certain preconditions are fulfilled. Its major premise is that "management" will eventually surmount the mythology, jargon, and general hocus-pocus that now afflict it and will be pursued as a rational endeavor.

Hope for such a consummation may not be so forlorn as it might first appear. Management, after all, deals with "getting things done." It operates in what Daniel Bell calls the "economizing mode." It is inextricably concerned with the sequence of cause and effect.

Some observers detect an antirational trend in modern society. They may be right, but even if they are, the inherent causality of human enterprise is not negated. Pervasive atheism does not permit religion the option of becoming atheistic. Management has no choice but to try to be logical.

The increasing availability of factual information along with the growing sophistication of devices for logical manipulation of these data permit a rational approach to complex problems that were inaccessible to logical processes in the past. The increasing presence of professional managers relatively free of the emotional complications of proprietorship at least suggests the possibility of the development of a management

PREFACE

technology capable of objective appraisal and reproducible results.

The rapidly expanding scope and complexity of human enterprises along with the suddenly apparent need to be both more precise and more efficient in the use of physical and human resources dictate rapid advances in the skill with which the necessities and the amenities of humankind are provided. The alternatives in social chaos and material decline are only too easily foreseen.

Let us explore, then, the directions these necessary advances might take under, admittedly, idealized circumstances. Utopias, after all, are intended not as forecasts, but as formulations to illuminate the needs and potentialities of the future.

If we are to hypothesize a logical evolution of management practice, we must first clear the miasma of mythology, confusion, and obfuscation that has arisen around this function.* The first part of this book addresses that task.

The second part explores the consequences of substituting rational procedures for some of the prevailing irrational practices of conventional management. Some of the suggestions reflect atypical approaches already used in enterprises with which I am familiar. All honor to those innovators who have had the perception and courage to break with the habitual dogma. I will not identify them, because I do not wish to impose on them my interpretation of their rationales. Some of

---

* Etymologically, "management" has some rather unsavory antecedents. The word stems from the Latin *manus*, hand. "Manage" originally meant to "handle," particularly as in the training of a horse. The dictionary gives us definitions: "to make and keep submissive," "to alter by manipulation." This may explain why some of the prevailing management practices seem so perverse. The practitioners may just be more scholarly linguists. It is tempting to propose a new word, *managology* (*manus* + *logos*, reason), to describe the reasonable or rational handling of complex responsibilities.

PREFACE

the suggestions are purely speculative. They are intended to be provocative.

Since this is not a scholarly work, the text is not encumbered with footnotes. It seemed unnecessary to provide pejorative examples of the unwarranted assumptions and arrant non sequiturs about management that appear in the management literature and the public press. Most readers will have already seen quite enough of such silliness.

Many of the prescriptive ideas explored here have been suggested or confirmed by other authors. However, since I have fragmented and recombined these concepts, I chose to acknowledge my indebtedness to their sources in general rather than to associate them with any specific citation that might be thought out of context. The volumes I have found most thought-provoking are listed in the Bibliography. I recommend them to you.

As with any book, this volume owes its existence in considerable measure to the efforts of editors and typists. I am particularly obliged to Anita Kastens, who not only edited the manuscript but endured the gestation of the ideas over many a martini, and to Audrey Snyder, who typed and retyped the many drafts often at odd hours of the day and night.

Merritt L. Kastens

CONTENTS

PART I

1 What It's All About   3
2 Management Mythology   17
3 Who Manages the Managers?   27
4 The Business of Government   39
5 The Government of Business   53

PART II

6 By Their Fruits Ye Shall Know Them   73
7 The Honor without Profits   86
8 Do You Want to Live Forever?   94
9 Why Not?   106
10 "... Gang Aft Agley"   116
11 Some Notes on Accounting   130
12 How We Can Keep Score   141
13 What Happened to Production Management?   164
14 Begin at the End   175
15 Pavlov Was Right   190
16 The Feast of Reason   213

APPENDIX A: MANUAL SHIFT   231
APPENDIX B: THE CONTRACT SOCIETY   236
APPENDIX C: THE STRATEGY BOARD   244

BIBLIOGRAPHY   273

INDEX   275

I, at least, will not be so willfully wrong, and so ungrateful to nature and to God, that having been gifted with sense and logic, I should voluntarily set less value on such endowments than on the fallacies of a fellow man and blindly and blunderingly believe whatever I hear.

Galileo

PART I
IN WHICH A RATIONALE
IS PROPOSED AS A
FRAMEWORK FOR CONSIDERING
THE FUNCTION OF
MANAGEMENT

1
WHAT IT'S ALL ABOUT

Let us have some plain talk about management. Management is "running the place." More elegantly, management is the assembly, disposition, and exploitation of resources to produce a new value. The manager takes available resources and manipulates them in such a way as to create something of value that did not exist before. The more new value created by the commitment of a given store of resources, the better the management. Beyond that it's all details. Management by results is not only the best kind of management, it is the only kind of management. Without results, management doesn't make any sense at all.

REDEFINING THE MANAGER'S JOB

Whether the new value created is recorded on the bottom line of some document as "Net Income after Taxes" or as "Contribution to Surplus" or in some other convention is of interest primarily to tax people and political philosophers. The function and responsibility of management in making resources productive are not affected by the manner of keeping score. In any human enterprise undertaken for purposeful ends, the function of management is necessary, whether the ends are tangible or intangible, social or commercial. If people at both ends of the political spectrum could get that simple notion through their heads, it would save a lot of foolish rhetoric and not a little individual anguish. If the railroads are badly managed, changing them to public ownership is not going to affect the problem. It is not the ownership that is wrong—the management is bad. Changing the political status of the U.S. Post Office obviously did not solve the management problem. Nationalizing the oil industry will not produce more petroleum.

A NEED FOR NEW CATEGORIES

Centuries of haggling over the "ownership of the means of production" have thoroughly obscured the fact that the most important means of production is management, which nobody owns effectively. A lot of newly independent countries are so preoccupied with who holds nominal title to the bricks and mortar that they ignore the fact that their greatest underdevelopment is in managerial talent. There is a plausible argument that a major cause of the current world food crisis is not the migration of the peasants to the city but the social and economic disincentives that have caused competent managerial talent to migrate from food production enterprises to more rewarding activities.

In some societies profit is related to productivity, but

WHAT IT'S ALL ABOUT

profit is the dependent variable. Being motivated to be productive is not synonymous with "thinking only of profits." It merely means a desire to be useful. The guys who will do anything to make a buck are very seldom good managers.

In discussing management the categories "profit-making enterprise" and "non-profit-making enterprise" are irrelevant. In fact they are becoming increasingly meaningless. As you proceed along the spectrum from the Philadelphia Navy Yard, to the federal nuclear facilities operated by profit-making contractors, to the captive suppliers to the government who get renegotiated if they win but bailed out if they lose, to the heavily regulated utility companies, to the generously subsidized steamship companies and peanut farmers, on further to the multinational oil companies and the beleaguered food companies, and ultimately down to the drug store on the corner—at what point does the profit motive become the dominant determinant? Who can define the functional difference between an SRI International and an Arthur D. Little, Inc., between a "voluntary" and a "private" hospital? For that matter, between AMACOM and McGraw-Hill? Enterprises have in fact changed from one category to the other with no effect perceptible to anyone other than the lawyers and tax accountants.

In international activities the situation is even more ambiguous. You have the formally public companies with large government shareholdings—for example, British Petroleum. You have government/industry joint ventures—in Yugoslavia and Liberia, for instance. You have wholly owned "crown corporations" in thoroughly capitalistic countries. You have aggressive, expansionist government enterprises like ENI in Italy, and slumberous "nationalized" industries in the United Kingdom. And then of course you have the production agencies of the Communist countries that must function in a market economy as soon as they step out of their home territory. Now how does profit motivation fit into all this?

In Sweden, the most socialistic of the democracies, 90

REDEFINING THE MANAGER'S JOB

percent of industry is in private hands. Another 5 percent belongs to co-ops. But, by law, allocations of profits and new fixed investments are subject to collective bargaining with the labor unions. "Communist" Yugoslavia has a national stock exchange.

What is the status of an overseas subsidiary, nominally still owned by its founding, profit-making parent but subject to what amounts to 100 percent corporate income tax? Compare that case with the subsidiary that is nationalized, with or without compensation, but operated under a profitable management contract by its former owners.

The old categories don't work anymore. Their language just does not match up when you try to lay it against the real world out there. Much of the talk about "business morality" and "business practices" and even the regulation of "business" just does not accurately define the subject under discussion. Even such laudatory statements as "Business is predominantly an organ of innovation, the only social institution created for the express purpose of making and managing change" and "Business is the preeminent instrument for getting something done" become meaningless if we don't know where the perimeters of "business" lie. So we must abandon the notion of "business management" as a thing apart. This book will use many examples relating to profit-making enterprises as a convention of convenience and because most managers are still found in "business." But this in no way implies that the concepts being explored are not intended to be applicable to all kinds of productive enterprises no matter where they are situated or how they are institutionalized.

If the responsibilities of management are not related to the legal status of the enterprise, neither are they affected by the particular way in which the human resources involved are related to one another. You do not manage an organization. "Organization" is a technical convenience for implementing

WHAT IT'S ALL ABOUT

the management of resources. The procedures and conventions of the organization must be "administered" to keep the machinery running; but if the mechanisms of the organization become more important than the primary management job of making resources productive, we have what is commonly cursed as "bureaucracy"or, translating literally from the European usage, "officism." A smooth-running organization in itself is no more meaningful than those do-nothing machines you buy at Brentano's. A great many so-called managers, most management theorists, and virtually all government officials don't seem to know this.

WHAT RESOURCES?

What are the resources that constitute the material of management? Money, of course, and its direct descendants: physical plant and equipment and other tangible property. There are the intangible "commercial properties" technology, know-how, product franchises, goodwill, which may or may not appear on the balance sheet. Certainly not recorded on the balance sheet but nonetheless the subject of much conversation are the human resources: the knowledge, the skills, the energy and enthusiasm of the people involved in the enterprise to be managed. Finally, as is being emphasized increasingly, most managers employ certain public resources: the air, the water, and frequently transportation and other more specialized facilities.

Management's job is to arrange and combine these various resources in such a way as to produce a useful result. If this role is to have any meaning, it must be based on the assertion that certain arrangements will produce certain results and that some arrangements will produce more or better results than others. There must be a direct relationship between resource/cause and value-produced/effect; otherwise a manager cannot pretend any special skill in manipulating resources. Any gambler or yogi or a table of random numbers might do just as well. Management must be approached as a causal process or it makes no sense at all. There is no point in indulging in verbal scuffles as to whether it is an "art" or a "science," whatever those words mean. The significant fact is that effective management demands a high facility in relating causes and effects.

What happens to the romantic, venturesome "entrepreneur" if management is to be pursued rationally? It all depends on how you take your industrial mythology. The chief executive who says, "What we need is more entrepreneurial spirit around this place" usually means, "What we need is a couple of *successful* entrepreneurs in the organization." Which may be the same as saying, "If we had a couple of lucky horseplayers on the payroll, it would be a lot easier way to make money than by trying to run this business." In spite of all the documentation available we insist on recognizing as "entrepreneurs" only that small fraction of adventurous souls who start *successful* new enterprises and slough off the myriad of unsuccessful entrants to the limbo of "failed businessmen."

Obviously the entrepreneur is a risk taker, as is any manager, but frequently, either because of personal lifestyle or because it is the only course open to him, he is a long-odds risk taker. He may well be like the day laborer who buys a lottery ticket because that is his only possible way to "make a bundle." It is this tendency to bet against the odds that the president of a large and aggressive conglomerate had in mind when he said, "The last thing I need in my management is more entrepreneurs." He certainly was not rejecting the kind of new venturer who identifies an unfilled need in the market, assembles appropriate resources, and moves in sharply to ride a trend to early success. He probably would not even exclude an avowed "gambler" if he were a "professional" gambler who based his

WHAT IT'S ALL ABOUT

actions on knowledge of the odds and played only when he had a statistical advantage. The professional would know that "you can't win them all," but he would know too that you have to win more than your share if you are going to make a living at it. This successful conglomerateur wants "professional" risk takers who bet only with the odds, not against them.

The folk-figure entrepreneur who, with little knowledge but great determination, "succeeded against all odds" has got to go the way of the "self-sufficient frontiersman" and the Great Blue Ox. If he existed today, he could not long stand the competition in the closely calculated, rapidly modulating current business climate. The entrepreneur as risk taker is still needed, perhaps more than ever as sure bets become more and more scarce in an environment of constantly accelerating change, but risks must be taken coolly and consciously and not in a spirit of bravado or superstition. Management is a rational activity.

RATIONALIZING THE IRRATIONAL

If management is going to be all that rational, does that mean it must act as if it were dealing with entirely rational phenomena? Of course not. To expect all customers, stockholders, employees, competitors, and even regulatory bureaucrats to behave unfailingly in a rational manner would be sophomoric—hence "irrational." The trick is to provide a rational structure within which to accommodate irrational behavior. Abnormal psychology is a rational system for dealing with pathological irrationality. You can provide for irrational factors within a rational system; what you cannot do successfully is deal with rational phenomena with a nonrational system.

Every successful lover knows that if you are trying to arouse an emotional response, an emotional appeal is much

REDEFINING THE MANAGER'S JOB

more likely to be effective than is a well-reasoned argument. Therefore sweet talk becomes a "rational" strategy. However, in a productive enterprise, what is desired is a tangible, orderly, constructive response—which is to say, a primarily "rational" response. It would seem to follow that a rational approach to management is most likely to be effective. At least it should be worth a first try before attempting charismatic or other manipulative forms of leadership.

It is not necessary to pretend that every individual will, every time, respond to a rational appeal. It is sufficient to assume that every individual has a rational faculty to a greater or lesser extent. Man, after all, has been called "The Rational Animal," which reflects the observation that human beings do appear to be able to relate cause and effect in a more orderly fashion than other living creatures. It is further generally assumed that the human being is the only animal that can carry out rational processes with abstract concepts. There is usually a final inference: that since rationality is the *sine qua non* of humanity, the more rational individuals are, the more "human" and less beastlike. In that view a rational management system is ultimately the most "human" system.

This is not to say that instinctive, behavioral factors are not important determinants in human motivations or reactions. It is merely to suggest that it would seem more productive to design a system of management based on an acknowledged common factor that functions in the same way for every individual than to depend on behaviorist-designed parameters that are often poorly understood and that seem to express themselves differently under different circumstances. Why don't we try to appeal to the rational component in people that we think we understand and that we know is there to a greater or a lesser degree rather than attempt to direct a management structure based on emotional factors that most of us admit we have diffi-

WHAT IT'S ALL ABOUT

culty understanding and exploiting. The physicists have a dogma that the right solution will always be a simple one. It should apply in management.

The prevalence of nonrational styles of leadership is undoubtedly an unfortunate legacy from the military establishment, which, after all, has been managing complex enterprises for 5,000 years or more. The simple fact is that there is no rational argument for getting a man to go out and have his head knocked off. So you use the next best technique—you try to manipulate his visceral responses. The preacher who notes in the margin of his sermon, "Pound pulpit, argument weak here," understands this. So does the football coach who does the tearful locker-room scene about doing and dying for him and dear old Siwash. He knows his line is outweighed by 35 pounds per man and his only healthy quarterback stands five feet ten in his cleats. If he could think of some new plays that might work, he would spend the time teaching them. Too often management resorts to that second-best technique without ever trying to exploit the inherent rationality of its position.

RESULTS REVISITED

The primacy of results as a motivator of human effort is in no way extinct. It has been largely institutionalized into impotence by prevailing management systems. When you find someone unhappy with a job, almost always the first comment heard is, "You can't get anything done around here." Then the bitching may continue: "The boss is a bastard," "We are understaffed," "The organization is fouled up," "The equipment is shoddy." This is equally true whether you are talking to an industrial manager, a college professor, or a surprising number of government bureaucrats. The first complaint is a lack of per-

REDEFINING THE MANAGER'S JOB

sonal productivity People do like to accomplish something they recognize as useful, and it is nice if somebody else recognizes it as useful, too.

An extreme form of the syndrome is found among the demi-dropouts of the younger generation who have opted for a "simple" lifestyle. They have rejected a system that obscures the useful results of their efforts in favor of an existence that provides immediate and tangible evidence of their accomplishments. The burgeoning popularity of arts and crafts and "do-it-yourself" generally in all parts of society reflects the need to produce something directly, a need that is often frustrated in contemporary organizations.

There is much comment about "the decline of the work ethic," but, depending on how you define the observation, the evidence does not particularly jibe with the conclusions. It is quite possible that the contemporary population has only about the standard quota of freeloaders. But there are fewer followers of the biblical "sweat of your brow" injunction who believe any work to be a response to holy mandate. That conviction seems destined to follow into the dustbin of history a premise once held as strongly and for a longer period of time: that warfare is the most noble occupation of men. In a more secular formulation, what is being rejected is the notion that "work is what you do so you can afford to do the things you want to do." Increasingly, people want to work at something that produces an identifiable *result* that they recognize as useful and that they can relate directly to the effectiveness of their efforts. This is not the same as rejecting the necessity or even the desirability of work as such.

The behavioral scientists are constantly telling the industrial engineer that his factory workers are so hard to live with because modern industrial processes isolate them from the tangible fruits of their efforts. Job enrichment, production teams, and a number of schemes have been conceived to alle-

WHAT IT'S ALL ABOUT

viate this problem. But what about the poor middle managers? Many of them at headquarters never see anything produced. Most of them never see a customer. They are so cut off from the fundamental raison d'être of the company that they cannot get their bearings. So we have the "alienation of middle management" that we are hearing about increasingly.

Not that every manager must be committed to the "grand purpose" of an enterprise. Quite the contrary. The functional executive who is criticized for being parochial and overspecialized may be acting more rationally than he is given credit for. He is concentrating on the *results* he is interested in and for which he is probably rewarded. Someone else will have to be responsible for assembling the component results into the desired whole. Organization specialists often speak about the "conflict" between the objectives of middle managers and top managers and sometimes jump to the conclusion that this conflict defies rational resolution. But the problem is not so much one of "conflict" as of "difference." The internal logic in each case may be impeccable, but addressed to different dimensions of accomplishment. We can combine different kinds of accomplishment in a rational mosaic to form a desired totality without having to homogenize the motivations.

Actually there are relatively few people with the talent or the inclination for general management—the "big picture" people, the synthesizers. This is the age of specialists, and most of them are wise not to permit themselves to be promoted out of their specialty. But specialists are motivated by results, too—results in their field of specialization. The results, however, must be real, they must be apparent, and they must be logically related to the larger purposes of the enterprise.

Job descriptions, job instructions, procedural manuals, and many "management by objectives" routines that deal with *how* everything should be done but never get around to saying what should be *accomplished* actively thwart the natural impulse to be productive. They specify activity usually at the expense of productivity.

Such devices are fine for the "willing cog" in the big organizational machine. However, he is just the sort of person who becomes so fascinated by administrative procedures that he forgets that the machine was intended to produce something somebody wants. He is unlikely to make any positive contribution and almost certainly makes life more difficult for results-oriented people. He is the archetypical "Man in the Gray Flannel Suit." It is quite conceivable that he is an endangered species. Let us hope so. Members of the maturing generation resist strenuously all attempts to force them into anybody's bureaucratic mold. They are unlikely to become the "faithful retainer" type and will tend to be very intolerant of the type when they encounter it. This in itself may force a change in management style. The emotional, personal, "humanistic" style of leadership demands loyalty, enthusiastic obedience, and ultimately conformity. Rational management can accommodate a diversity of rationales because it provides a single matrix within which they can be related.

THE ALIENATED PRODUCTION SPECIALIST

Too often management has become so fascinated with its own procedures that it has forgotten that it is supposed to be producing something somebody wants. It has fallen into the existentialist fallacy of elevating process above product. As a consequence the production specialist becomes an outsider in his own organization. The other managers are really not that interested in efforts to produce a product. Communications deteriorate and the ultimate productive element in the enterprise becomes politically isolated and its managers cynical and withdrawn.

The problem is pervasive. "Production people" do not

WHAT IT'S ALL ABOUT

only tend factories. The men and women who "produce" education—the teachers—are similarly demoralized and the discipline of teaching has fallen into disrepair. The distortion of institutional structures, the influx of peripheral functions, and the deluge of auxiliary specialists have made the original intent of introducing new knowledge, concepts, and perceptions to young people seem almost irrelevant. Staff writers and editors on periodical publications complain that the old drive to "get out the book" seems to be gone. Even in a government regulatory agency, the number of actual "regulators" is a tiny percentage of the staff and their immediate boss is likely to be well down in the pecking order. In this case a lot of people might think this is just fine, but the pattern is only too familiar.

If management is to be addressed as an instrument for converting resources into results, then results have to be "writ" back into the equation—and writ large. The last step in creating results is some sort of "production" function. The managers of that function may not continue to be regarded as supernumeraries.

"WE'VE ALWAYS DONE IT THAT WAY"

Many of the seemingly inexplicable practices of managers derive, not so much from a conscious reluctance to proceed logically, as from an uncritical acceptance of habits, traditions, and, particularly, terminologies that have long since escaped their original context. When these conventional misconceptions become embedded in law, the effect is particularly pernicious.

Most managers recognize that "we've always done it that way" is a stillborn excuse for any action. However, if the government seems to insist that you do it "that way," further logical analysis is unlikely.

Less obviously, when such words as "profit," "deprecia-

REDEFINING THE MANAGER'S JOB

tion," "equity," and "reserves" are accepted as literal descriptions rather than conventions that developed in a much simpler time and situation, the result may be formally acceptable but basically unrelated to any objective reality. To the extent that the government, the public, and the securities markets endorse these conventions, the confusion is compounded and the flight from reality is accelerated. Uncovering these semantic distortions is difficult. Rooting them out of management's consciousness may be tougher than getting crabgrass out of the lawn but will be necessary if management is to fulfill its proper productive role rather than merely manipulate symbols.

And remember, it is not only "business" management that has its sacred verbalisms. All kinds of enterprises fall victim to the facile assumption that taxonomy recapitulates cosmography.

Management is the intellectual process by which resources are converted into value. World society, growing rapidly in both size and complexity, is making formidable demands for both material and social values. Resources, we are becoming painfully aware, are limited. There is a critical need to increase the effectiveness of the management process as rapidly as possible if we are to avoid the cataclysmic consequences that current trends portend.

I visited a computer development lab once and was wryly amused by a parts bin filled with a jumble of subcircuitry labeled "Unused Logic." Management has lots of logic it has never used. It will need all the logical power it can muster to deal with the awesome problems of utilizing the resources of the future to supply the needs of the future.

2
MANAGEMENT MYTHOLOGY

If we are going to approach management rationally, we will first have to hack away a mass of conceptual underbrush that has grown up around our perception of human enterprise. Much of it is embedded in our language or in the way we commonly use language. It leads from unwarranted assumptions that are seldom stated to asinine conclusions that are never questioned.

THE PROFIT AND THE NONPROFIT ORGANIZATION

It has already been seen that the dichotomy between "profit-making" and "non-profit-making" ventures is becom-

REDEFINING THE MANAGER'S JOB

ing increasingly ambiguous and is not pertinent to the fundamental process of producing value. This is not to imply that personal gain is not a powerful—and perhaps the most effective—motivating force for individual performance. But the mystical significance accorded the word "profit" and the consequent black-and-white differentiation between the two kinds of ventures leads to some truly absurd folklore. And strangely enough, pretty much the same fairy tales are current in both the pro-profit and anti-profit camps.

"Nonprofit organizations are 'nobler' than profit organizations." Not necessarily. There are productive, frivolous, and even pernicious undertakings of both kinds.

"Profit organizations are better run than nonprofits." Statistically, perhaps, but both sides have their successes and their disasters.

"Nonprofits do not enrich individuals." Now you know that is not true. Many people have done very well with nonprofit organizations. On the other hand, "profit-making" ventures have impoverished a lot of people.

The word profit seems to have a hallucinatory effect. Politicians bellow about "obscene profits" in the oil industry and blindly ignore the compelling fact that the oil companies, one after the other, are diverting capital into other lines of business. Department stores and circuses seem to be particularly offensive acquisitions to Washington. Obviously the men who are most familiar with oil company profit-and-loss statements think there are better ways to make money than to produce petroleum products. The government responds by considering a law to force the companies to expand their oil business, presumably to make more of those "obscene profits."

But wait! Supposedly hard-headed corporate treasurers will blithely consolidate "equity in earnings" from overseas subsidiaries into their reported "profit" just as if it were real money when the possibility of ever laying hands on any of that money may be vanishingly small.

MANAGEMENT MYTHOLOGY

Business managers who consider themselves highly "professional" will often take avoidable actions with the sole purpose of making that magic profit number higher. Of course they then must pay out half the gain to the federal government for the privilege. Profit is truly a "magic" number in the anthropologist's technical sense of the word. It is something to conjure with. The word is invested with an inherent reality, a power of its own, and not seen as a symbol representing some objective reality.

"Everybody knows" the United States is a profit-oriented, profit-propelled society. If you spend much time sitting with the executive committees of large companies, you begin to wonder. The sales manager is trying to talk through a price cut so he can make more sales. The manufacturing vice-president is worrying about how to get more material through the plant. Research has a new product they think is just a dandy. Engineering is trying to promote a new plant with a hot new process. The treasurer is cooking up a new long-term line of credit. Until finally the controller breaks in and says, "Doesn't anyone but me ever think of making a little profit around here?"

He may be more accurate than he intends. In one sense he does make the "profit." He invents it. His profit figure is largely a convention invented by accountants for other accountants. It does not necessarily relate to any physical reality at all. Next year he may "restate" it as a resounding loss. That is one reason why more and more security analysts are looking at net cash flow and ignoring the declared net income figure.

No, if we are going to talk rationally about management, we are going to have to be very careful about words like "profit." The purpose of the enterprise is to produce results. The profit figure may tell you if the enterprise is viable, although it may not even be very reliable for that purpose, as we will discuss in Chapter 11. The reason for building a boat, however, is not to make it float but to provide some transportation.

If it floats, it means the construction didn't fail. It doesn't yet tell us if the venture was a success.

The "profitless" world has its own shibboleths: "liberal education," "quality health care," "meaningful theater," "community service," "public welfare." This is not simply jargon. Jargon words frequently have a technical definition that may be abstruse or even trivial but is there. The really damaging words are those that no one tries to define in any meaningful way, but that are used to justify the commitment of substantial resources to confused activities that produce equivocal results.

MODERN SOCIETY IS RESOURCE-INTENSIVE

We think of countries with predominantly market economies as "capitalistic" and then proceed to the conclusion that "capital formation" is the unique concern of "capitalists," whoever they are. Then "capital" becomes a magic word. We have confrontations between "capital" and "labor." "Capital" is short, or cheap, or expensive. "Capitalist becomes a swearword in the Marxist lexicon. But capital is merely the stored-up supply of resources produced by past efforts and available to be committed to expanded productive enterprise. All industrial countries are "capitalistic" in the sense that they depend for their well-being on the productivity of an accumulated store of resources—in other words, "capital." That is why the Russian leaders literally starved their people for 20 years after the revolution. They had effectively destroyed the capital resources of the country and they had to build them back up.

One of the reasons the "economic miracle" occurred in Germany after World War II was the conscious and concerted government policy to accelerate the replenishment of the store of productive resources by diverting a maximum amount of new value produced away from consumption and into savings, which ultimately meant into new resources. The United Kingdom is in its present sorry state because over a period of many years it did not enlarge, or perhaps even maintain, its resource base. These verities apply whether the polity is based on a market economy, on socialism, or on collectivistic bureaucracy.

It is ironic that "capitalism" is not the most *efficient* system for capital formation—for accumulating resources that can be committed to future productive undertakings. It has been amply demonstrated that a socialistic dictatorship, as in the USSR, China, or even Nazi Germany, can divert a higher percentage of national production to capital formation than can a capitalistic democracy. They simply withhold consumables from the populace. The trouble is that the dictatorships don't produce enough, so that even that higher percentage often doesn't amount to as much as the materialistic democracies have left over after consuming themselves silly.

The social theorists have gotten so passionately involved in arguing over who "owns" the accumulated resources of society that they frequently seem to forget where the resources came from or even what they are for. Ultimately, it is not so important who "owns" the accumulated store of capital resources but rather the mechanism by which they are allocated and the degree to which they can be made productive. In the past, individual "capitalists" supplied the major part of the resources that made productive undertakings possible. In doing so they played a major role in the allocation mechanism. Today that role is insignificant, as we shall discuss in some detail later. So to call the Western economies "capitalistic" is misleading and inaccurate since they are neither more nor less dependent on "capital" than any other economies of comparable development. Moreover, there is no significant class of "capitalists" who play a major role in their affairs.

The term "market economies" is much more definitive and is fortunately coming increasingly into use. However imperfectly, the needs and desires of the ultimate consumers—the markets—are the principal determinant in the allocation of resources in these economies. Some self-appointed arbiters of human values complain that this arrangement leads to materialism, hedonism, lack of social responsibility, and possibly fallen arches. However, it works with relatively little internal friction, does not require an expensive bureaucracy, and in general eventually gets the resources to where they can be most useful.

But "market economy" does not tell the whole story either. You can't allocate resources until you have them. The extent to which you have them depends on how much was produced in the past over and above consumption needs. That in turn depends on how skillfully past resources had been used to produce new value. And that skill, we have said, is the domain of management—which seems to have been the special genius of Western culture. The most precise label for democratic, industrialized countries might be "productionist economies," or even "managerial economies." If that raises echoes of "technoculture," so be it, but "capitalistic" is not the right word.

INFLATING WHAT?

It is because any modern society is resource-intensive that management of those resources is so critical to its economic health. The job of the manager is to make resources productive, but it is the store of resources that makes the manager productive.

The economists may say that theirs is the study of the allocation of limited resources among competing uses, but they don't seem to have got the word across to much of the population. Resources always have been limited and always will be;

therefore, if you commit them one place, you cannot use them somewhere else.

If we want cleaner air and water or safer working conditions, we must commit resources that then cannot be used for another purpose. If we wish to be assured of more comprehensive health care, it will have to be paid for out of the resources of the national economy. If we have to drill deeper for oil or move more tons of ore to get to a ton of iron, that will preempt resources that might otherwise have been used to another end.

If society chooses to commit resources to such acknowledged public benefits as safety, cleanliness, or health, or if it is necessary to expend more work to obtain the materials a society has become accustomed to consuming, then the absolute cost of living will go up, not just the dollar cost. This is not inflation of currency; this is inflation of expectations or, if you will, an ascent to a still higher level of affluence. But "inflation" is a bogeyman word that can be laid on the greedy monopolists or the profligate politicians or the insatiable labor leaders without any attempt at definition.

There are three distinct components to the increasing "cost of living" that is vulgarly called inflation. One is the classical economists' case of too many dollars chasing too few goods. This may be the best-understood definition, but it has yet to be quantified. The second is the increased resource cost incurred when minerals must be obtained from increasingly awkward locations or recalcitrant matrices or when crops are raised on progressively more marginal land. In addition, increasing the price that must be paid to get some people to work at all, or to get others to undertake disagreeable or demeaning jobs, causes the absolute resource cost to rise. This effect is grounded in physical reality and is in no way subject to political manipulation.

The third component arises from escalation in the standard of living, usually euphemized as "quality of life." Society may well be within its rights to demand such amenities as clean air, uncontaminated waters, pristine wilderness, convenient transportation, greater safety at home and at work, and preprepared and possibly exotic foodstuffs. But these things must be paid for either through taxes or in the purchase price. The individual who bears this cost has no volition in the matter and sees it merely as an added economic burden imposed on him by the system. Nonetheless he is "buying" additional value that he did not previously enjoy, and consequently it is not the cost of living but the level of living that has escalated.

Theoretically these surcharges could be reversed, but practically, once the public commitment has been made, only the most dire circumstances could induce a reversion to earlier standards. This kind of inflation is sometimes referred to as "diffusion" of the costs of added services. Some theorists think it is by far the largest component.

Politicians, even economists, can deal loosely with these concepts. The successful resource manager will have to learn to deal with them in discrete reality.

CAPITAL VERSUS LABOR

At least once a year we are informed by the media that one of the national labor unions is going into bargaining sessions with representatives of its industry. This is billed as an adversary proceeding of knock-down-drag-out bargaining— but that too is a myth. There is no reason beyond personal animosity for a collision of interests.

As soon as industrywide bargaining is introduced, "management" loses all incentive to resist the union's demands. It is placed in an oligopolistic position in which it can sustain no competitive disadvantage and from which it is free to pass on any increased costs to the consumer. The industry representatives know that within days of the conclusion of the bargaining sessions—with fraternal handshakes all around—they will release their new price schedules "reflecting increased labor costs."

And everyone accepts this charade of a "contest" between "management" and "labor." Under these circumstances there is no "contest" between the interest of the two sides of the bargaining table. The "contest" is between the unions and the consumers, and the consumers must depend on the company negotiators to defend their interests as a kind of public service. It is not a very reliable representation.

Because of the pervasive economic illiteracy of politicians, they were the last to grasp the true dynamics of these little ceremonies. But in the last couple of decades they have obviously realized that they had nothing to gain either personally or politically from bucking the government-workers unions. So the politicians have given away the store with fine insouciance on the assumption that the taxpayers could be made to cough up the money somehow. That latter assumption becomes increasingly questionable, but a great deal of damage has already been done.

Of course once you enter into this aura of irrational fantasy, all sorts of strange things can happen. We find the coal mine operators reflexively putting up a bitter resistance to the miners' demands for higher wages and better working conditions and at the same time complaining that a growing shortage of miners is thwarting needed expansion of capacity. It is one thing to give a fat settlement to garbage collectors in the presence of an infinite supply of garbage collectors; it is another to impose a "bargain" price on labor if nobody will sell at that price. Coal miners are patently "underpaid" by the simple evidence that in times and places of high unemployment, you can't hire enough of them. If you are going to get on with the business of producing coal, you are going to have to find some way of making the job more attractive—union or no union. In a period of rapidly rising energy prices, there is no question that the consumers will pay for it.

WHAT THEY GET PAID FOR

If we are going to take a rational approach to management, we are going to have to face these kinds of historical fiction straight on. The solutions may not be easy, but they are impossible if we refuse to admit that the problems exist or if we insist that the problems are the same as they were years ago when the scripts were written.

Managers are not the only ones who suffer from losing sight of the interactions between resources and results, but their confusion is the most inexcusable. Their function in society is to direct those interactions and to make them as productive as possible. In the physicist's terms, they are the machine that turns energy into work—resources into results. They are the self-proclaimed experts. Putting it bluntly: That is what they get paid for—handsomely.

Because it deals with the techno-economic function of production, management is constrained to a rational morality. Politics need not be, perhaps should not be, rational. Art may transcend reason. But nonrational management is as inconceivable as nonrational science. Science based on myth is alchemy. Management based on myth is anarchy.

3
WHO MANAGES THE MANAGERS?

Managers are people who are skilled in the productive use of resources. The quality of management is measured by the amount of new value produced from the employment of a given store of resources. But who decides what resources the manager can use? Who decides what he should produce with those resources? Who determines if he is producing enough of it? Who determines the value of what he produces? Rational constructions proceed on the basis of certain premises. Who establishes the premises?

It is impossible to talk about a rational approach to management without stating what the rationale is. Management is good or bad compared to what? When we talk about a "purposeful enterprise," we have to know what the purpose is.

THE OWNERS OF THE RESOURCES

The simplistic answer is, "He who pays the piper calls the tune." Whoever provides the resources the manager uses determines the purpose of the enterprise and evaluates the results against the resource cost. If the manager is an employee, it is the "owners" who make these decisions. If the manager is one of the diminishing tribe of proprietors who back their own ventures, then he pretty much sets the ground rules for himself.

Now you know that's ridiculous. It may have been at least partially true in the nineteenth century; it is patently not true today. In the first place, all sorts of people want a say in determining the value of the output. Leaving aside for the moment the judgment of the marketplace, there are certain products that are officially declared to have a negative value. In most parts of the United States, for instance, you are prohibited from producing sexual services for the public. You may not produce hazardous toys or proscribed drugs. You may not produce a bullfight. Even if the desirability of the product is accepted, someone is likely to question the commitment of the inputs. You may manage to produce coal but not at the cost of destroying the landscape— even if you "own" it. You can produce beef, which almost everybody values highly—but not if you foul up watershed in the process. You can produce transportation, but not at speeds in excess of 55 miles per hour.

Obviously the owners of the resources the manager manages do not have a free hand in determining what values will be produced. But at least they can judge how *efficiently* the resources are being applied—how competent the management is. They provide the resources that are being managed; in the

WHO MANAGES THE MANAGERS?

extreme event they can withhold them if they do not like the way they are being used.

But they can't! For the simple reason that the whole notion of "ownership" of the resources is ambiguous, if not meaningless.

Well, certainly we at least know who owns the tangible and monetary assets that appear on the left-hand side of the balance sheet. In a formal, legalistic sense—perhaps. But in the sense of how they come to be under the stewardship of a particular management—not really.

THE MONEYLENDER DOESN'T CARE

In the first place all kinds of organizations borrow many of their assets either under leasehold or as debt. Depending on how you count it, the average U.S. corporation borrows between one-third and two-thirds of its assets. The immediate source of these assets generally expects only a fixed price for their use, either as rent or interest, and the manager is responsible only to meet these payments. The lenders seem to be very little interested in the skill with which these resources are put to work, as witness the fiasco at Penn Central, or for that matter New York City. The lenders' position is largely a legalistic, contractual one, and the nominal lender or leasor is usually acting only as an agent for the actual owner, who is a depositor or policyholder. These ultimate "owners" have no interaction at all with the people who employ their resources.

What about the "net worth" that is not pledged outside the enterprise? The business corporation, at least, supposedly has some statutory "owners" in the form of equity shareholders.

Their role, however, is more formal than functional. In spite of the rolling pronouncements of the securities industry,

REDEFINING THE MANAGER'S JOB

no thoughtful observer can believe that stockholders, either individual or institutional, actually "own" a publicly held company in any functional sense. Still less can one believe that that benevolent anachronism, the Board of Directors, constitutes the elected representatives of the stockholders. What the stockholder actually owns is the stock certificate, and, in managing his own affairs, he seeks to maximize his after-tax return on the buying, holding, and selling of that property. He is only indirectly interested in the value or the use of the resources that that certificate purports to represent.* This obvious fact is seldom stated publicly, although it is the blood and bone of the stockbrokerage industry.

Except in the case of a new stock issue, the shareholder does not provide assets for a management to manage. When he "invests" in shares, he supplies liquid capital to a previous shareholder. When he wants to liquidate his holding, he sells his shares to another shareholder. There is no way he can retrieve his invested resources from the corporation and thus deny them to the management. And although managers may speak often and ardently about the need to have adequate profits to attract new capital for expansion, what they have their eye on are the lending agencies, and they are thinking in terms of debt coverage. Only rarely do the really big companies ever actually go to the equity markets for new capital resources. In any given year, equity issues seldom provide as much as 10 percent of the new funds absorbed by the corporate community. Usually it is less than 5 percent.

---

*This is true even though, as Peter Drucker has pointed out, in most of the top 1,000 publicly held companies, employee pension funds now hold the majority of the voting stock, and within ten years they will hold more than 50 percent of *all* common equity. In at least one case the majority "ownership" of a company is held by the employee credit union. This anomalous relationship seems to have no perceptible impact on the way the enterprise is managed.

30

WHO MANAGES THE MANAGERS?

The shareholder not only cannot get his "investment" out of the company, he cannot even get his hands on the "profits" the annual report told him he made.* Oh, the management may let him have part of them, but chances are it will "retain" the greater share—typically about 60 percent. If the shareholder objects, he is likely to get the condescending explanation that if the company gave him his profits he would have to pay a lot of tax on them. So the management will "reinvest" them for him without paying additional tax, and that way those profits are really "cheap" money.

Well, they are cheap in another way too. The management doesn't have to pay anything for the use of these funds. It doesn't have to explain to any steely-eyed banker or stock underwriter what it is going to do with them. It just takes them. And sometimes it doesn't use them very well because it doesn't have to think very hard about what it is going to use them for. Nor would it occur to the management that the "owners" might be better off, even after paying taxes, if they invested the funds themselves in high-yielding bonds.

WHO OWNS WHAT?

If "ownership" of the financial resources of a business corporation is a nonfunctional verbalism, then "ownership" of the resources of a nonprofit institution is an insoluble enigma. Who "owns" a university? Not the alumni and other donors who built and endowed it. Not the "members of the corporation," where such exist, although in some respects they may

---

* One CEO at a recent NAM Congress said, "The part [of profits] paid out in dividends is really interest on equity . . . essentially no different from the interest paid on loans." So much for the shareholders' rights of ownership.

stand *in loco proprietoris.* Not the faculty, although they sometimes like to pretend they do. But then who does provide the resources the college management employs?

Who owns the resources of a voluntary hospital, a nonprofit research institute, of a church, of the Ford Foundation?*

What about the resources of the Port of New York Authority, the Army Corps of Engineers, the National Parks? They all must be managed, but who makes the resources available to the managers? The taxpayers paid for them. The political orators say the resources belong to "the public." But the taxpayers—not to mention the amorphous "public"—are even less able to exercise their function of ownership than are the corporate shareholders.

The "public" also makes resources available to nongovernment enterprises, both profit and nonprofit, through the mechanism of tax forgiveness. If we believe there is any economic justification for taxes, then we must contend that any specific exemption from taxation is equivalent to a subvention of public funds. The managers of these favored enterprises enjoy the use of the public moneys thus left at their disposal, but the "public" can only very indirectly influence their utilization.

WHO OWNS INTANGIBLE ASSETS?

To an even greater extent, the source of uncapitalized intangible assets of an enterprise is itself intangible. These assets exist. No one questions that they have value—sometimes very substantial value. They can be used to create more value. They

---

* The case of Stanford University suggests some of the Byzantine situations that can result from this conundrum. It apparently "sold" Stanford Research Institute, which it did not legally own, to the Institute itself as an independent entity.

can be misused and dissipated at great loss to the enterprise. But where did they come from? Who makes them available to the manager? Well, they belong to the company or the institution. Quite so. But these legalistic "persons" cannot supply or withhold resources, much less exact managerial accountability. That needs real flesh and blood.

As a consequence, uncapitalized intangible assets are usually accepted by management with a courteous nod. It is a rare company where consideration is given to how effectively a manager is extracting useful benefit from captive technology, from consumer acceptance, from a smooth-running organization, or from similar resources of very real productive value. Managers of venerable public institutions tend to be more sensitive to these intangible assets but not invariably. More than one college has been taken into disastrous decline, not so much by profligate expenditure of funds as by the irresponsible dissipation of academic reputation and donor goodwill.

The managers of American cities are beginning to observe, even if they do not yet understand, that one of their most valuable civic resources is the intangible willingness of property owners to pay what they perceive to be equitable property taxes. If that resource is not properly managed, the willingness erodes, the tax base deteriorates, and the public value the city is intended to produce inevitably declines. The city's management is undoubtedly at fault in the wasting of this asset, but whence did the asset come? A historical process created the public attitude just as it did the college's high reputation, but you cannot hold the city manager any more than the college president accountable to historical process.

AND HUMAN RESOURCES?

The manager's accountability for the useful application of human resources is even more difficult to localize in any struc-

REDEFINING THE MANAGER'S JOB

tural context. Our Western culture rejects any premise other than that the skills, knowledge, and talent of any individual are the inalienable property of that individual. Ample legal precedent has confirmed this principle—except for professional athletes. The human resources of an enterprise, then, are the property of the individuals in that organization, and the accountability of the manager for the fruitful use of these resources is to those individuals. But how do you institutionalize or proceduralize such accountability? Union contracts deal in wages and coffee breaks and sick leave, but they cannot address the question of whether or not human resources are being used to their fullest potential. A demoralized or poorly directed research department may have a productivity of zero even though all the scientists and engineers are regularly in their laboratories making appropriate motions. But who is to say what could be accomplished by this same staff if it were properly utilized—that is to say, well managed? Even the researchers themselves can only guess. Their professional societies would not even try.

Human resources do have one characteristic to a greater extent than the other categories of resources the manager utilizes: They are relatively easily disinvested. In spite of seniority rights, deferred compensation, and all the other devices that tend to freeze this asset into the organization, the individual still has the ultimate option of withdrawing his participation and seeking a more fruitful situation in which to invest his time and energy. The more potentially valuable his contribution, the more likely he is to exercise this disinvestment option. Particularly in professional service enterprises where human resources are *the* critical resource of management, the result can be disastrous if too many of these mobile assets decide to "vote with their feet."

The fact that human resources may unilaterally deny themselves to management does impose some kind of ultimate accountability for management performance, but it is exercised infrequently. The people of the City of New York are doing it, however.

CONSUMABLE RESOURCES

What people have traditionally called "natural" resources—that is, mineral resources that are transformed or consumed in industrial processes—were in the past thought of in a rather straightforward manner. They were owned either by a government or by private interests. They were sold or used as convenient. Management of such resources was a matter of getting as much of them out of the ground as possible with the least possible effort and of extracting the desired element by the easiest possible means.

Life is no longer so simple. There is a lively debate as to who owns the minerals at the bottom of the sea. The use of petroleum resources for fuel may someday be prohibited to preserve them for chemical feed stocks. The extraction of coal from the ground is subject to ever more stringent constraints. Some forecasts predict that in the future mineral products will be largely recycled so that they will be used but not consumed. The ultimate mechanism of control of the use of these natural resources is not yet apparent, but it is certain that the manager will be accountable to a complex external system, unrelated to conventional ownership and probably tied to a rather rigorous codification of societal values.

WHAT ABOUT PUBLIC RESOURCES?

Finally there are public resources that are at the disposal of the management of any enterprise. We are just becoming explicitly aware that almost any human activity consumes natural—and, it is hoped, renewable—resources of air and water and perhaps of esthetic amenity. We are just beginning to ask to what end and to what effect.

There are man-made public resources that are also critical to effective management: tangible goods—highways, airports, and sewerage systems—and, equally important, the intangible institutions—public education and the system of jurisprudence. User taxes attempt to compensate for the use of some of these resources, but only to an insignificant extent.

There is no question whether or not these public resources— either natural or man-made—should be used. Of course they should be used, although not abused or destroyed. They are intended to be *useful*. The question is: How efficiently, how prudently, are they used? It is the manager's job to get the greatest possible value out of them. The point is: Who is keeping score?

THERE AIN'T ANYBODY THERE

Our rational approach to management is in obvious trouble if we try to pass the buck for determining either the purpose or the effectiveness of the managed enterprise back to the source of the resources the management employs. We get lost in a maze of specious conventions, comfortable mythology, and verbal flimflam. The simple fact is: There ain't anybody there to pass the buck to.

At one time it was believed, and it was even occasionally true, that governing boards, irrespective of how constituted, were the ultimate arbiters of policy and imposed their value system on an organization. It is very difficult to defend that fiction with a straight face today. For all the deference with which they are ceremoniously treated, the awkward fact is that corporate directors and institutional trustees usually function at best as a panel of more or less expert advisers and occasionally as bogeymen to frighten middle management. Most commonly, a board is selected by the management—if the two bodies are not in fact identical—not the other way around as the law decrees and the textbooks claim. When a senior executive is asked to resign, it is almost never by the board's acting as a body but as a result of a power struggle between two or a few individuals. If a "proxy fight" is involved, nobody believes it is a democratic uprising of disgruntled stockholders. It is a contest for control in which board seats are merely markers. This is essentially true whether the enterprise is organized for profit or not for profit.

Perhaps if we abandoned the conceit that directors are the elected representatives of the "owners," we could devise some mechanism for designating a governing body representing various pertinent constituencies that would in fact set directions and judge performance. The demand for union representation, consumer representation, minority representation, and other "public" membership on corporate boards of directors in this country and abroad tends in that direction. Perhaps we could devise such a mechanism, but the performance of similarly constituted boards of trustees for public institutions is not encouraging. Can anyone observing contemporary college campuses seriously contend that the trustees of these institutions are establishing directions and enforcing their judgment of competency? The boards of health care institutions are no more functional, nor are those of most charitable foundations and voluntary associations. Public commissions, variously constituted, which supervise educational, transportation, and other community operations, by and large do not have an outstanding performance record, and quite often have proved downright venal.

The results are not yet all in on the impact of worker par-

REDEFINING THE MANAGER'S JOB

ticipation on the supervisory boards of European companies, or *Mitbestimmung*. In the early days of the experiment in Germany it seemed to merely provide an additional sinecure for a union official. However, there has been a tendency to enlarge the workers' representation, and the system seems destined to extend throughout much of Europe. In theory, at least, this innovation should ensure stricter accountability for the effective use of the human resources of the enterprise. There is little reason to expect, however, that these worker-directors will concern themselves with much beyond the narrow economic interests of the established workforce.

If *Mitbestimmung* does propagate beyond Germany, it will undoutedly bring with it the German system of bilevel boards: a Board of Directors comprising the active management of the enterprise and a Supervisory Board riding herd on the Managing Directors. Ostensibly this system would seem to provide the independent, objective appraisal of management performance that we are looking for. In practice it does not seem to function much differently from the American system of a Board of Directors working through a Management Committee of company officers. Ultimately it still leaves us with the question: "Who watches the watchers?"

If we are resolved to seek some general rationale or set of premises according to which we can logically judge the management of an enterprise, it seems we will have to divide the problem into two parts. The first involves determining the "value" to be created by the enterprise to be managed. The second consists in determining how skillfully the resources have been deployed in the creation of that value.

4
THE BUSINESS OF GOVERNMENT

Business executives are in danger of occupational deafness from being told they must consider other goals than profits in managing their enterprises. In the past few years educational administrators, too, have been getting some gratuitous advice about what their "product" should be. They are being told that, to warrant being entrusted with large quantities of more or less public funds, they should produce something other than self-justifying course credits. The value of the product of health care institutions is being questioned at least relative to the cost of the inputs. Charitable foundations no longer have a completely free hand in choosing their beneficiaries.

REDEFINING THE MANAGER'S JOB

WHOSE SOCIAL AND MORAL RESPONSIBILITIES?

The implication clearly is that the manager should be responsible not only for the productive use of resources but for the social and moral utility of the products of his enterprise. That sounds both reasonable and enlightened, and it thrums resonantly in the pages of the *Harvard Business Review*. Except it won't work.

It might work if there were a self-apparent "right" social ethic or even if there were an articulate consensus on social values. But there is not. The matter remains one of judgmental choice among many possibilities. We cannot expect, we should not even suggest, that management make these judgments if we have any hope of retaining any kind of popular control over the nature of society. When you ask the corporate officer to be "socially responsible," you by implication relieve him of the clear-cut commitment to economic productivity and invite him to consider an unlimited range of activity guided only by his perception of what is "good." If you combine that kind of freedom of decision with his acknowledged power to act, you create a potential for tremendous social confusion.

When the self-appointed saviors and gurus on U.S. campuses in the 1960s set out to rearrange the social fabric closer to their hearts' desire, that fabric remained unrent because of the fortuitous circumstance that the academics were totally incapable of getting anything done. Their initiatives petered out into frustrated temper tantrums and folk sings. If the proponents of social consciousness ever succeed in convincing the business executive that he does in fact have the responsibility for preserving and improving the "quality of life," there will be no such fortunate dampening feedback. The executives will get something done, all right. They will certainly change the quality of life, but what they will change it to is quite impossible to predict.

The rationale of the radical activists demonstrating outside the board meetings of the corporate giants is understandable. The corporate structure has proved itself the most effective device ever invented to "get things done." Frustrated and disillusioned with the slow and largely verbal response of the "public" institutions, the demonstrators seek to influence the "doers" directly.

However, never was there a truer example of the wisdom of the traditional Chinese warning, "The greatest affliction is to attain what you desire." It is hard to conceive of a more frightening and chaotic future than one in which the tremendous resources and proven management ability of the business corporations were consciously but individually committed to bringing about social changes perceived to be desirable by thousands of separate management groups. Common experience gives ample evidence that some corporate officers have pretty weird notions about how society should be arranged. To encourage—much less to give socioeconomic sanction to—their initiatives in the area of "social responsibility" is certainly not a reassuring prospect.

A sense of "social responsibility" is after all what leads to at least some illegal diversion of corporate funds to individual political candidates. Some executive is convinced the country "needs" that particular man in office and his company has a "responsibility" to help get him elected. The Texas businessman who finds some way to use company resources to subsidize far-right, anti-Communist causes unquestionably acts out of a profound sense of social responsibility. A good deal of lobbying, whether legally or illegally funded, is sincerely motivated by a received notion of what the country needs.

RESPONSIBLE *TO* SOCIETY, NOT *FOR* SOCIETY

The question here is not whether the corporation can be held responsible for the negative consequences of its acts. There is no denying that every enterprise—whether for profit or not—is accountable for its degradation of the public resources of air and water. It is becoming increasingly accepted that this liability extends to violence done to visual and auditory amenities, although the subjective nature of these resources makes precise assessment difficult. It is even becoming recognized that private interests may not destroy their own property if there is a likelihood that public institutions will eventually have to repair the damage, as in the case of some strip-mining and lumbering operations. It is generally recognized that an organization has a further obligation not to contribute to racial or other discrimination and not to create hazardous or socially harmful conditions.

Many of these responsibilities and proscriptions are already codified in laws that are daily becoming more explicit. Management is not free to decide whether or not to obey the law, and it is almost equally meaningless to talk about "being a good corporate citizen" as an objective end. It is rather an absolute obligation.

But for a corporation to go beyond acknowledgment of these essentially negative responsibilities and commit resources to the positive production of social advance is wrong in the present structure of our society. It is wrong in the same sense as it would be wrong for a university to set out to put a man on the moon—not necessarily immoral, but inappropriate to the resources available and to the reasons for which the resources were assembled. It is also wrong in a sociological sense, in that it puts the power of initiation in the wrong place.

The law already severely limits what a corporate body—

whether profit or nonprofit—may do to attempt to improve the quality of government. If we want to impose a "social responsibility" on corporations, then, to be consistent, we should legalize political contributions by corporations. We are not likely to do that, and for the very same reasons we should not urge corporations to assume any other social responsibilities. A better case can be made for prohibiting profit-making corporations from usurping responsibility for any broad social goals.

There is a common misapprehension that when a business corporation does "good works," the cost somehow comes out of the pockets of its shareholders. In a corporation of any size, this is almost certainly not true. Whether this cost is "expensed" or taken as an allowable "contribution," it ultimately must be covered by the price paid by the company's customers—and by the government in the form of taxes forgone. Thus, when a corporation decides on its own initiative just what is socially desirable and takes action to achieve that desired end, it is effectively taxing its customers and preempting funds from the public treasury to support that activity. If you happen to agree with that company's assessment of the public good, you might well go along with this process. But what if you don't agree? In any case it is taxation without representation—which at least once in our history has led to riots in the streets.

If a corporation chartered as a creator of economic goods or services diverts any substantial part of its resources to purposes other than "production," it may not only be acting "irresponsibly" toward its stockholders, as Milton Friedman contends, but may be usurping functions for which it has no legal warrant.

THE UNHAPPY PHILOSOPHER-KINGS

The difficulties that arise from trying to locate responsibility for moral judgment as well as accountability for perfor-

REDEFINING THE MANAGER'S JOB

mance in the same site are most dramatically demonstrated in our public institutions. The manager of a not-for-profit enterprise is not granted the easy recourse to simply "make money" as a raison d'être. Furthermore, he has many fewer formal constraints to direct him as to what he should and should not do. And yet, whether he seeks it or not, he commonly finds himself in the position not only of running the institution but of determining the direction and the distance it should run. Few people are comfortable in this dual role. An infinitely smaller proportion can perform it well.

When the academic manager sets out to produce "education"—at least as it was traditionally defined—he can, if he is competent, run a pretty orderly shop. If he chooses to add the production of knowledge to the scope of his institution through a research program, he is still on solid ground. But once the institution itself presumes to determine the value of that education and knowledge and the uses to which it is put, the manager is in trouble. And if the institution attempts to act on its value judgments and impose them on society outside the campus, the result is chaos. The 1960s gave ample demonstration that an "activist" university is unmanageable.

The health care establishment is encountering a particularly dramatic instance of the problems the superposition of roles entails. Technically it is increasingly able to maintain some semblance of life for long periods of time in critically ill patients. The question is: Should it? Quite reasonably, the medical people are saying they do not want to make that judgment.

In the future it is quite conceivable that medical science might be able to sustain life for almost anyone indefinitely—if it can command sufficient resources. If the resources are put at their disposal—as managers of the system, as "producers of health"—they are quite ready to account for the professional and efficient use of those resources. But who decides how

THE BUSINESS OF GOVERNMENT

much of the finite store of national resources will be committed to this end?

If the allocation is disproportionate, and if other values are disparaged in favor of the naked urge to preserve life, is medicine to be indicted for producing a "medicalistic" society? The people who are good at producing "things" seem to bear the onus for a "materialistic" society.

Every good manager can always make more and better goods and services if he gets a chance. And he probably truly believes the world needs more and better of what he is good at producing. This is equally true whether he produces automobiles or education, health or operas. Obviously he is not the right one to decide how much should be made or at what cost in resources.

When society persists in entrusting the productive specialists within the system with the judgment of the proper level of resources to be committed to their area of activity, the consequences are only too abundantly apparent: an educational system in which more—and more expensive—is always better, health care delivery systems that chew up greater and greater chunks of the national income with only marginal improvements in the general health levels police departments that demand ever-increasing budgets with no perceivable effect on crime rates, and the Department of Defense. Only in the case of institutions that are exposed to some modicum of competition—such as the nonprofit research institutes, or even the colleges— do these self-opinionated enterprises tend not to run completely out of control.

It is irrelevant whether we attribute the hyperinflation of certain "public service" activities to misguided professional enthusiasm or to simple greed. The effect is identical. The people responsible for delivering the service must not be charged with determining the absolute value of that service.

COP-OUT TO CHAOS

With this experience in view it is sheer masochism to delegate value judgments to management in addition to its productive responsibilities. We cannot have it both ways. We cannot cry havoc over the frightening concentration of power in a "technostructure" and at the same time insist that the leadership of that structure accept responsibility for making the most profound decisions regarding social goals and priorities.

Furthermore, there is no reason to assume that individuals with outstanding abilities to organize and deploy productive resources have particular skill in making the essential value judgments regarding the optimal goals of society. Do we really want to entrust them with these judgments? Would that not be elitism of the most aggravated kind?

It is unfair, impractical, and ultimately undesirable to expect managers to be accountable for both the value judgment of priorities and the productive employment of resources. This is not to imply that managers as individuals are or should be amoral. Like anyone else, they are entitled to their hopes for mankind and for society. But the function of the management of resources has its own ethic of utility. Someone else must decide, "Utility for what?" If we seem about to resurrect "enlightened self-interest" in a slightly evolved form—relieving the manager of moral responsibility for anything but his own competence—it is because we have no acceptable alternative.

We brag about our pluralistic society. Let it be pluralistic, then. Every individual need not be expected to solve all kinds of problems equally well. The professional manager, if he conceives of his management responsibilities comprehensively, will have plenty to do and will make a substantial contribution to society by ensuring that resources are not wasted but are in fact employed effectively to achieve predetermined ends. You do not expect a 20-game-winning pitcher to seriously concern himself with whether or not the 45,000 people in the grandstand could be better employed doing something else. If we must live with a technostructure, let us attempt to keep that structure in its area of greatest technical competence.

We must seek other mechanisms to determine the relative value of the possible fruits of organized human effort. We must find equitable means to impose an acceptable value system on the managers of organized human enterprises. To fob off onto managers the entire responsibility not only for the efficiency of their management but for the evaluation of the social value of their results is not only a cop-out but an invitation to chaos.

The evaluation of goals and the setting of priorities are of soul-wrenching importance. They must involve many more people than those skilled in management and must proceed through many mechanisms other than the managerial relationship.

USE WHAT WE HAVE

But we have an institution that is intended to perform just this function. The whole elaborate machinery of government was conceived to impose a uniform system of values and priorities on a nation. The philosophy of democracy rests on the intention to make that system approximate the collective judgment of the governed. But government equals control—control in accordance with a system of values. The complex structure of constitutions, laws, regulations, and directives is nothing more than an elaborate attempt to codify a system of values—to declare what is permissible and what is not permissible, what is of predominant significance and what is secondary, what is good and what is bad.

Granting that the functioning of government leaves much to be desired, it does have some tendency to be self-correcting. In any case there is little logic in dismissing it from its elemental function, which is to govern, and attempting to subvert other

REDEFINING THE MANAGER'S JOB

social institutions to a job for which they were never intended.

Government is the only appropriate medium through which society's judgment of the relative values of alternative results of management can be articulated. Government must tell management through carrot and stick what is important, what is praiseworthy, what is inadmissible. This is not government interference with business or education or anything else. This is government doing its job of declaring values so that "business" can go about its job of creating those values with maximum efficiency.

If society wishes to "buy" safer working conditions for its people, only government can arrange that purchase through the imposition of safety standards. The public will pay for it in both taxes and higher prices. But management will automatically see that this new value is created with the minimum expenditure of resources. If society decides to increase the value it places on clean air and water as Americans have in recent years, the management of an individual enterprise can respond independently only at the cost of a severe competitive disadvantage. Government can institutionalize that judgment over broad areas, and then management can translate it into effective action.

Government can and must determine the proper portion of national resources to be allocated for health care, for dams, and for welfare. The machinery of government was conceived and designed to decide what things should be done and to what degree. We should concentrate on improving that machinery so that it does that job better.

There will be errors, of course. Some of the value judgments will be faulty and many will be less than disinterested. However, we are looking for a system that might possibly work, not necessarily a perfect system.

We have suffered overlong from a role confusion that has led us to expect government to "do things." We have only too much evidence that government is not very good at it. When

THE BUSINESS OF GOVERNMENT

President Ford said that if the government made beer, it would cost $50 a six-pack, he may have been exaggerating—but maybe not by very much. The only thing government is uniquely obligated to "do" is make war, and lately the U.S. government hasn't seemed to be very good even at that.

We double our confusion when we ask the operational organizations that are good at "getting things done" to take on the task of sorting out priorities, a job for which they are woefully unequipped. If we hope to improve the effectiveness of our society—and the quality of our management—we will have to let the basic institutions of that society concentrate on those functions they perform best.

Identifying government as the proper instrument for defining relative values does not mean abdicating that responsibility in favor of either a bureaucratic or an intellectual elite—not in a democracy it doesn't. Admittedly we have had ample experience in recent years of stillborn government programs premised on some bureaucrat's notion of what the people "needed." We also have a plentitude of arrogant and articulate members of the intelligentsia telling us what we ought to want. The democratic process may be an imperfect instrument for articulating the value judgments of a society but, as Winston Churchill said, it is so much better than all the rest. It is much more likely that the process will be improved if we understand its essential function. Certainly efforts toward a more participatory democracy would seem to be more promising than flogging the "managers" with the proposal that they should both define and implement the value system.

THE GOVERNMENT OF THE MARKET

The government doesn't have to do it all. A good deal can still be said for the marketplace as an indicator of popular values. As we all learned in freshman economics, money is an

REDEFINING THE MANAGER'S JOB

exquisitely sensitive yardstick of value. The controversy today is over the ability of the modern marketing system to create false values—which is to say, values the neopuritans don't approve of. Anyone who has spent much time around new-product committees has to question that allegation. If it were really possible to "create demand," why waste all that time and money on market research, test marketing, and store auditing? Why did the peerless leaders in Detroit, after they had finally decided in 1974 to go all out for economy-size vehicles, later find themselves in an undignified scramble back into big-car production? Why not just design a reasonably attractive product and go out and "create a demand" for it?

Indeed, Vance Packard's "hidden persuaders" may be so well hidden as to be invisible. Then again, it is not surprising that the Madison Avenue crowd would exert their very best efforts to promote the notion of their own omnipotence. In those efforts they seem to have succeeded even with their most ardent critics. They obviously can sell themselves. Whether they can sell products that people do not want is more questionable. To accuse them of producing a desire for more sweet goods than is good for people, or more speed than is prudent, or more housing than is necessary, or more sex than is "wholesome" is patently ridiculous. Those wants come as standard equipment with every newborn baby. Panderers the marketers may be. But seducers? Questionable.

As a practical matter, every marketer knows that John Wanamaker had the right idea when he said "Give the lady what she wants"—and every textbook and marketing seminar repeats it. No businessman in his right mind is going to take on the cost and uncertainty of trying to create a new perception of value in the minds of his market if he can avoid it. He will try to sell a product on which his target customers already place a high value, if he can figure out what that might be.

So when people buy things, you can be pretty sure they

want them—and want them more than the virtual infinitude of other things they might spend their money for at that particular time. Whether they need what they buy is essentially irrelevant. Whether somebody else thinks they should buy that particular thing is impertinent. The act of the purchase is a thoroughly explicit expression of a value judgment—whether you like it or not. This is equally true if the purchase is of education, of an esthetic experience, or of spiritual consolation.

There is another equally important function that the marketing mechanism performs. It is a virtually frictionless device for distributing social costs— or in the popular jargon, of internalizing external costs. If society wants to improve worker security or clean up the environment, it passes a regulatory law. Industry installs the equipment and the cost is quickly passed along to the buyers of the industrial product—the agonized breast-beating of the industrialists notwithstanding. There is an elegant equity to this system. The economic penalty falls precisely on the beneficiaries of the activity that creates the cost—that is to say, the ultimate users of the product.

Furthermore, the desired effect is achieved with the minimum of government bureaucracy. The people who have to contend with a swarm of regulationists and inspectors may question that statement, but I suggest they envision an alternative situation in which the Environmental Protection Agency, for example, builds and operates all the desired effluent control facilities with public funds—public funds that unhappy politicians would have to raise by exacting higher taxes from screaming taxpayers. The price mechanism is a very unobtrusive tax collector, and it even collects from tax-exempt enterprises. When Colgate University buys a load of lumber, the price includes the cost of cleaning up the woodlot. If the government did the cleanup, the taxpayers would pay for it and the university would get a free ride.

Outside the market we must depend on government to

express the collective value judgment of the governed. No matter how imperfectly it may exercise that function, it has certain inherent advantages in approaching the task. The methodology of government revolves around compromise, and since value systems are inevitably diverse, compromise is essential. Government can deal with subjective, normative considerations. It is not constrained by the rational parameters of productivity and efficiency as is economic activity. Finally, government has institutionalized capabilities for dealing with, if not resolving, conflicting interests—capabilities the other agencies of society do not have.

If we will allocate the responsibility for evaluating the propriety of enterprise to that instrumentality of society best qualified to perform that function, we can proceed to deal with the management of enterprise in its proper dimension of rational economy. If we can agree that the purpose of management is to produce useful results and that the value of those results will be determined by external standards, managers can accept societal restraints with good grace and get on with their job without being subject to unreasonable criticism or distracting self-doubts. It is a marvelously clarifying point of view.

5
THE GOVERNMENT OF BUSINESS

Recently some previously cloistered social observers have noted with great clamor that industrial management is a self-perpetuating hierarchy. To anyone familiar with industrial management, the observations could not have been very exceptional. The viewers-with-alarm have proceeded to infer from their observation that industrial management is inherently irresponsible. This conclusion may be at least misplaced.

The simple fact is that much of human enterprise is managed by self-perpetuating hierarchies, whether in an industrial-capitalistic structure or not. The church, the educational establishment, the institutionalized arts, and large health care organizations conduct massive enterprises within a self-propagating structure. Huge research and technology organizations, "public" foundations, and most of government bureaucracy flourish without a clear focus of accountability. This is not a peculiar, nascent peril of the "postindustrial" society. Human affairs have virtually always been directed by a self-appointed and self-congratulatory leadership. In preindustrial society the levers of power were certainly more highly concentrated and more arbitrarily manipulated than they are today. Perhaps we are merely emerging from a period of transient aberration in which we aspired to an exogenous control of human organizations.

AN AUTONOMIC SYSTEM OF MANAGEMENT ACCOUNTABILITY

If management cannot be trusted to police itself, to pass judgment on its own competence, to guard society against managerial malpractice, what are the alternatives? We have already demonstrated that it is futile to invoke some ectoplasmic "owners" to act as proctors. Should we try a double layer of governing boards in which the upper, supervisory board has no other function than to assess the quality of management, as they do in Germany? Or a "board of visitors" that makes a periodic audit of management performance, as we find in nonprofit enterprises?

These are possibilities and they do address the problem directly. However, the empirical evidence is that they seldom really work. The difficulty is to find members for such boards who are skillful enough to exercise their intended function and who are not otherwise fully occupied, and then to provide those members with sufficient information to enable them to make an informed judgment. In practice these organizational

THE GOVERNMENT OF BUSINESS

devices inherit most of the defects of the traditional governing boards but at one further remove from the action.

The Securities and Exchange Commission, the Federal Trade Commission, and several other regulatory agencies presume some surveillance over corporate managements but can concern themselves only with the grossest malfeasance. The Comptroller of the Currency professes formal responsibility for the "quality of management" of the national banks, and various state insurance commissions have similar statutory charters relative to the insurance industry; but there is certainly no evidence that those industries are more skillfully managed than other kinds of enterprises that do not enjoy such specific attention. The food and pharmaceutical industries now are subject to codes of "good manufacturing practices" that among other things specify the procedures by which top management shall exercise its responsibility for quality of production. The scope is limited, but the code does have teeth in it. However, the prospect of a government agency seriously charged with policing the overall quality of management is horrendous beyond all contemplation.

On the other hand, the law and medical professions have operated self-certifying and self-policing mechanisms for generations. They don't work perfectly. Some people think they don't even work well, but they do function.

On a less exalted level, both in the United States and internationally, there is the tremendous structure of "voluntary standards" organizations exemplified by the American Society for Testing Materials. They produce and monitor detailed specifications for literally hundreds of thousands of items and actions on a completely voluntary basis without either governmental direction or legal power of enforcement. Yet they perform an indispensable function in integrating the affairs of the world. It is inconceivable that this function could be performed by any single, official "Bureau of Standards."

The ultimate fact is: The autonomic system of management quality control that largely prevails today—and that has characterized human enterprise historically—is the only one that has proved to be realistically practicable. We will be best served if we accept that fact and attempt to make that system work better. Admittedly this course exposes us to Professor Galbraith's dreaded, self-motivating, and possibly self-serving "technostructure." It may be a hazardous option, but it is the only one realistically open to us. We know it is not foolproof, but a self-acknowledged and publicly recognized system of management accountability based on a sense of personal responsibility would be preferable to a comfortable, but nonfunctional, myth that some phantasmic "they" will somehow hold the managers to account.

There is no real reason why managers responsible for the production of tangible goods or commercial services should be subject to any different mechanism of accountability than those who provide education or health care or for that matter salvation. Individual industrial organizations have been irresponsible and even vicious. But on occasion churches have run amuck, education has been perverted, and certainly the "public interest" organization of health care has produced a disaster. If management is in fact a generalized function involving the productive use of resources independent of the political-economic source of those resources, then there is no logical basis for sustaining two different systems of management accountability.

A DOUBLE STANDARD

Thoughtful observers, as ideologically dissimilar as Arthur Schlesinger, Jr., and Irving Kristol, have pleaded repeatedly for "business" to "clean up its own house" by denouncing and ostracizing managers caught in illegal activities. From both a

THE GOVERNMENT OF BUSINESS

moral and an image point of view this advice is undoubtedly sound. However, in a broader context it misses the target. There is no fundamental reason why "businessmen" should be uniquely charged with this obligation. Convicted offenders have retained positions of responsibility in unions, in public office, and even in universities. On the other hand, the purchasing agent or traffic manager or public relations executive caught taking kickbacks from suppliers is usually extruded quickly and completely, although he may escape full legal prosecution.

There seems to be a double standard operating here that may be as significant as the illegalities themselves. The illegalities cited against "businessmen" most frequently occur at the interface between private enterprise and government agencies and often involve enterprises that are essentially both creatures and captives of their customers in government. Dr. Schlesinger suggests that it is "business" that has corrupted "government." This argument is about as provable as the one about the chicken and the egg.

Flouting the law is reprehensible wherever it may occur, and we all know it occurs to some extent in every institution of society. However, the courts presumably exist to exact appropriate compensation for legal transgressions. If the laws are not being adequately enforced, this is an indictment of the criminal justice system. They should be enforced. If the courts, as has been charged, are unduly lenient with white-collar criminals, this is improper and should be corrected. But these are problems for the justice system, for the government. To tell "business" or unions or any other group to purge itself of criminality is like telling the people of New York City to clean up the muggers on their streets. They have a police force for that purpose, which is or is not effective.

The larger and more significant issue is whether managers, in business and elsewhere, shall be held responsible for the consequences of their actions—not just the legal consequences, but all the consequences. If their functional fumbles are being overlooked, then maybe it is not surprising that they expect an indulgent attitude toward their legal peccadilloes. Or perhaps the illegal shortcuts are themselves a symptom of basic incompetence. In any case it makes more sense to demand that the management fraternity accept rigorous responsibility for its own competence than to suggest that it engage in a vigilante attempt to preempt the functions of the duly established system of jurisprudence.

PROFESSIONAL MANAGERS

If we build from an insistence on personal responsibility for management decisions, we can begin to take seriously the notion of "professional" managers. This phrase has been hawked around by training promoters and the management fraternity for some time. However, most of the talk has related to technique. Professionalism requires more than a codified body of technique. It is essentially a matter of attitude.

A "professional" incurs a special obligation of competence. He "professes"—announces publicly—his special competence to deal with certain kinds of problems. He claims a special body of skill not commonly held by, and basically not comprehensible to, the general public. The caveat emptor is suspended. The professional's patients or clients—his employers—are presumed to be incompetent to judge the quality of his actions. He and his professional confraternity assume the responsibility for his skill and his effectiveness.

The doctor and the lawyer bear this burden. Presumably the religious does as well, although there is no documented case of a parishioner or his heirs suing for malpractice on the grounds that the client was poorly advised and consequently

THE GOVERNMENT OF BUSINESS

endured eternal damnation.* The "professional" engineer is explicitly differentiated from the general class of engineers by the fact that he may legally certify plans and warrant that they are technically sound.

A professional subscribes to an established code of ethics—a code primarily policed by the profession itself, sometimes buttressed by quasi-judicial bodies. It is interesting to conjecture the possible impact of a corporate officer brought before a professional Board of Ethics for possible censure, suspension, or disqualification because of alleged failure to adequately protect the interests of his institution or for wanton dissipation of resources. Who would have the nerve to hire or retain a defrocked vice-president?

The notion of a collegium of professional managers policing its membership to enforce standards of excellence is a fantasy for the foreseeable future.† On the other hand, the present delusion of accountability to boards of directors or stockholders or other presumed constituencies is almost equally chimerical. It is not working. There just is too much bad management around. Proven techniques are ignored. Resources are squandered or at best lie idle. Enterprise is paralyzed.

However, without fantasizing about Boards of Professional Management Standards, it is still possible to conceive of a system of accountability that would encourage competent management and tend to excise the clods and the clowns. The first principle to be invoked is "bad management begets bad management." The top manager who is not accountable for his

---

* Some clerics are now taking out malpractice coverage to protect themselves against claims of bad advice in more secular matters.

† The British Institute of Management and the Rationalisierungskuratorium der Deutschen Wirtschaft are trying it and the European Council of Management and the World Council of Management are working on it. Progress seems to be slow but at least the precedents are forming.

REDEFINING THE MANAGER'S JOB

own performance can afford to tolerate poor performance in his subordinates. The top manager who is exposed to the consequences of his stewardship will demand competence in his subordinates. This leads to the corollary that if we can apply pressure effectively at one point in an organization, it will propagate itself after a kind of Pascal's law throughout the entire system.

The second principle is that "there is little incentive to good management if there is little hazard in bad management." There must be both a stick and a carrot. The best managers will respond to the carrot, but you need the stick to get rid of the bad ones or they end up filling most of the places.

As the game is now played, most managerial positions are a "heads I win, tails you lose" proposition. The salary, the perquisities, and the prestige that go with senior management positions are most attractive—as well they should be to reward the highly leveraged contributions of an effective performer. But there is not a commensurate risk in the event of failure. Ford Motor Company was assessed one of the largest fines ever imposed on a corporation—$7 million—for gross violation of the Environmental Protection Act, and the top executives' salaries were increased—substantially. The Chairman of Chrysler got a $400,000 bonus while steering the company over a cliff. Even the relatively few executives who are kicked out in disgrace are usually provided a handsome "settlement" to cushion their landing. More commonly the price of "losing" is a transitory embarrassment, the threat of boredom, and lifetime security at a very comfortable level.

No wonder there is so much scrambling to get into the game. If we began to impose professional responsibilities on managers, we would drastically reduce the number of candidates for managerial positions. As it is, the majority of employees effectively opt out of the competition for managerial responsibility fairly early in their careers anyway. They just do not want to run things. However, a substantial number are lured by the tangible and intangible benefits and the relative absence of risk to accept management positions for which they have little or no aptitude. The absolute shortage of real management talent makes these adventures only too easy.

If the responsibilities and risks were made commensurate with the rewards, the majority of these marginal candidates would chicken out and accept roles as administrators or expert specialists. We might also hope that the real "amateurs"—the ones who manage for the "love of the game"—would find a way to get their excitement elsewhere. We could all do very nicely without the executive who feels, "If you know what you're doing, it isn't any fun."

IMPOSED ACCOUNTABILITY

In a fumbling, almost somnambulistic sort of way, society is beginning to impose accountability on those who profess to be managers. One instrumentality seems to be the banks. They have forced out at least one top management—that of Lockheed—for apparent misfeasance. Furthermore, they seem to be well on their way to imposing some rationality, responsibility, and maybe even honesty on local governments. Competence could conceivably follow. This role of bankers as arbiters of managerial effectiveness is probably less familiar in America than in other parts of the world. European and Japanese financial institutions assume it frequently. Less widely known are the many instances in which central bankers in concert with their international colleagues have induced national governments to get their houses in at least the semblance of reasonable order.

The remedies available in existing federal and state laws have not yet been fully explored, but they are being probed.

REDEFINING THE MANAGER'S JOB

Most of the tests so far have been on fairly narrow grounds, as in the Park decision* in which the Supreme Court held a chief executive officer personally accountable for sanitation in one of his company's plants.

The precedent-making principle in this case is that an executive cannot *delegate* responsibility for criminal acts. Executives have always been held liable for their own criminal actions, as in the price-fixing prosecutions in the electrical equipment industry of some years ago. But in that litigation the CEOs escaped attack by proving the crimes were committed without their knowledge. That defense now appears to have been invalidated. If it has, it will eliminate the common practice of withholding sensitive information from top executives or directors in order to protect their innocence. Ignorance is now as much an offense as is complicity.

There are a great many laws—going back to the original Internal Revenue Act of 1862—that provide for individual prosecution of executives for criminal actions taken in the interests of their firms. Recent legislation seems to be more stringent in this regard but in most cases has not yet been fully defined by court decisions. The Senate has even considered legislation that could bar a convicted executive from "holding high-responsibility jobs in the future." No one knows just how such a provision would be enforced, but the sentiment is significant.

New language keeps showing up in legislation. Defining the responsibilities of a fiduciary, the 1974 Employee Retirement Security Act speaks of the "skill . . . that a prudent man acting in a like capacity and *familiar with such matters*" would exercise (emphasis added). That begins to sound like responsibility for competence as well as care and legality, although the phrase has not yet been defined in court.

---

* U.S. v. Park, 421 U.S. (1975).

THE GOVERNMENT OF BUSINESS

The Securities and Exchange Commission, confirmed by the courts, defines "lack of due diligence" as a species of fraud. That may be pretty hard to defend as lexicography, but apparently it stands up in court. Also cropping up is the concept of "reckless default" under which an officer is personally liable for failure to supervise properly employees who violate federal regulations.

In France and Great Britain managers have been fined and/or jailed because their employees have been killed as a result of unsafe working conditions. This kind of accountability will undoubtedly spread to the United States.

In the last ten years courts have held officers and/or directors personally liable for such various acts as improvident investment of corporate funds, improper expenditure of corporate funds in a proxy fight, failure to obtain competitive bids for major purchases, and even failure to exercise "reasonable care" in selecting a depository bank that subsequently failed. There will be others.

The Internal Revenue Service is unofficially encouraging stockholders' suits against responsible executives to recover damages from penalties assessed against a corporation for tax fraud. The money would go to the corporation, but the executives would pay it.

There remains a vast scope of civil actions to exact accountability from professional managers. Some of the regulatory acts do provide penalties for "negligence," but they have been invoked infrequently and then almost exclusively against directors. Very few of these have gone to trial. Most were settled by insurance companies out of court. In the few cases that have been tried, the courts generally required that "willful and reckless" negligence, or some such aggravated oversight, be proved to obtain a conviction. We can expect increasingly broadly based suits charging neither felony nor fraud nor malicious intent but merely incompetence against both directors

REDEFINING THE MANAGER'S JOB

and managers. The growing standing of class-action suits plus the general temper of the times virtually guarantees it. The rising militancy of the regulatory agencies makes it inevitable.

INSURANCE AGAINST WHAT?

The majority of companies, particularly the big ones, carry directors' and officers' liability insurance to cover either the costs to the company of legal expenses or of judgments arising out of such actions or to reimburse the individuals themselves. Supposedly all such policies have exclusions to prevent protecting someone against the consequences of an *illegal* act, but there seems to have been some ambiguity in the interpretation of these provisions in the past. Recently the insurers have become more hard-nosed and are refusing to pay off in the absence of an outright acquittal. A consent decree or nolo contendere isn't good enough.

In the light of some recent awards, the insurance companies are getting tougher about writing any such coverage or in raising limits. Some policies are now being written with so many exclusions that there is considerable question about their usefulness. We may well have another malpractice insurance situation brewing like that in the medical profession.

On the other hand, a good many people in Congress and elsewhere are questioning the propriety of coverage that they claim insulates potential wrongdoers—not necessarily criminals—from personal liability for their transgressions. It seems almost certain that there will be a legal test of the propriety of the companies' payment of the premiums for such policies. Indeed, most states already prohibit a company from indemnifying its officers and directors for judgments if a suit is brought against them by stockholders *on behalf of the company,* so such exposure is already excluded from insurance coverage.

SELF-IMPOSED ACCOUNTABILITY

Ultimately, managers will have to accept responsibility not only for their good intentions and legality but for their qualifications and effectiveness as well. If a manager hazarded not only his next raise or his annual bonus but the possibility of a suit for real and punitive damages if it could be proved that he had failed to be familiar with and to practice management skills at the level of the state of the art, it would improve his concentration immensely.

It is doubtful that any new law will be required to impose such accountability, although new legal ground will unquestionably have to be broken. It is highly likely that more social benefit is to be gained by exploring these possibilities than in prying around for isolated instances of illegal political contributions or in trying to differentiate between legitimate agency commissions and bribes in Arab countries.

A generation ago there were virtually no successful suits for medical malpractice. Now they threaten the entire medical establishment, but the laws are essentially unchanged. Managers facing heightened accountability will probably react much as the physicians have, although without as well financed a lobby. They will claim unreasonable harassment. They will resist taking effective steps to eliminate the demonstrated incompetents who created the situation in the first place. But eventually they will realize, as physicians must, that no one except the culpable individuals will be hurt by such strict accountability.

We can get managers' attention with an occasional legal action, but the solution to better management will lie in the attitude of the managers. Ultimately it is only the management fraternity itself that can enforce management standards. Managers must come to accept and demand full accountability for performance. They must acknowledge the rational relationship between cause and effect and abandon the "let's try it and see

REDEFINING THE MANAGER'S JOB

what happens" approach to their problems. They must realize that they can be judged only on the basis of the results they produce relative to the resources they employ. And they must expect a logical relationship between their rewards and the quality of their stewardship.

Managers must be inculcated, in school but particularly on the job, with the concept that they have been entrusted with the employment of certain resources; that these resources are put at their disposal by some institutional mechanism, the exact nature of which is immaterial, and that their responsibility is to make those resources as productive as possible; and finally, that this is the nature of, in fact the definition of, a managerial job.

But to get this idea across effectively, the whole managerial system has to make sense, has to be reasonable, has to be rational. If rewards are not clearly related to results, if the air is filled with jargony incantations that will not survive rigorous analysis, if a lot of meaningless activity is permitted and even encouraged, and, most of all, if incompetents and supernumeraries are clearly in evidence, credibility will be gone. Managers will be disoriented and diverted into sterile verbalisms, ego-mechanics, and organizational self-defense. And the work of the world will not get done.

This is not an easy prescription for management. In a certain light it may even appear to have the Ayn Randian aspect of a dedicated elite. Certainly there will be only a small minority of individuals who would accept the responsibilities and the risks even for chance of substantial rewards. But then, by choice or circumstance, there is only a small minority who exercise the management function anyhow. It would seem desirable to select that minority or allow it to select itself by criteria that are most pertinent to the function and most likely to produce useful results. A system based on a combination of greed, ego, luck, and an absence of risk does not seem to do that.

Would such vigorous accountability create a shortage of

managers? No, the shortage of managers is caused by genetics or social environment or whatever creates the ability to make productive resource allocation decisions. We might even locate some good managers who are now submerged or subverted by the confused mass of mediocrity in many executive hierarchies. We would undoubtedly find that we need fewer bodies at any decision-making level if responsibility for the decision and for its effects were clearly focused. Certainly the ubiquitous "they" who are evoked to explain so much managerial ineffectiveness would tend to fade from the scene if the individual manager were held responsible for productive results and not merely for his actions.

The effective manager would continue to enjoy considerable latitude for legitimate error in judgment, and he would be relieved of the frustration of having to deal with indolent, ignorant, or simply unqualified colleagues. The social economy would benefit because its affairs would be managed more effectively, its productive resources would be utilized more efficiently, and a great many excoriating inequities would be eliminated. Furthermore, organizations would be able to pay their good managers even better because there would be so many fewer of them.

Society has a tremendous stake in the effectiveness of the management of all its enterprises. We are finally becoming aware of the ultimate limits of our mineral resources. We realize that our environmental resources are finite. We are no longer willing to waste our human resources. We know these resources must be managed—and must be managed productively and well.

MANAGERIAL LAG

The general public is quite right to be incensed when it sees an incompetent manager "manage" an enterprise to the

REDEFINING THE MANAGER'S JOB

verge of collapse—destroying jobs and communities and even an essential national service, as in the case of the railroads—and then sees him "forced" into early retirement on a handsome pension. The man is culpable, but his penalty is luxurious leisure. Similarly, the corporate officer who fouls up a division, misjudges the market, suppresses the aggressive initiatives that would have seized burgeoning opportunities, is too frequently shunted off to a corporate vice-presidency with imperceptible duties to serve out his time until the funded pension plan will take over his salary cost from the company. Of course this offends the rest of the employees at all levels. It doesn't make sense. It isn't rational. If a machine operator produced too many rejects, he would be fired and even the union wouldn't complain.

Much has been made of "cultural lag"—the inability of personal perceptions and communal institutions to evolve rapidly enough to accommodate advances in technology. It is unquestionably a real problem. But paralleling and to some extent overlapping that problem is a managerial lag that is responsible for many of our cultural problems. Within a single career lifetime the size and complexity of human enterprises has increased almost unbelievably, creating a need for levels of management skill that were inconceivable a generation or so ago.

When most of the men who head major corporations today started to work, there were only a handful of billion-dollar corporations in the world. Now there are hundreds of them, and the $100-billion corporation is within sight. University systems with tens of thousands of students and extensive auxiliary programs are managed by men who themselves were educated in colleges with a few thousand or even a few hundred students. Hundreds of politicians and bureaucrats are managing billion-dollar budgets with skills they developed when $100,-000 was a big appropriation. Furthermore, because of the pyramidal nature of management structures, when the size of an

THE GOVERNMENT OF BUSINESS

enterprise doubles, the managerial requirement does not merely double, it is more likely to triple or quadruple.

Is it any wonder that a good many companies are mismanaged—and the world food supply, and the big cities, and a good many national economies as well? It is a very costly deficiency. In an increasingly crowded and complex world it could be a fatal one. It is now generally conceded that the upset in the nuclear power plant at Three Mile Island was the result of poor management practice. Electric power companies generally have been notorious for the poor quality of their management. Society can no longer risk such deficiencies.

Society has a right, and quite possibly an absolute necessity, to demand skillful, productive management of its resources of whatever kind and wherever located. The legal and ethical questions are insignificant. Bad managers can't possibly steal as much as they can waste—not by a thousand times. There is no point in inveighing against the multinational companies. Some enterprises must transcend national boundaries. The multinationals, thus far, seem to be the only institutions that have even relative success in handling such enterprises. We can demand that they be legal; we can demand that they be ethical; but most important, we must demand that they be effective, because we need their results.

Society can create a climate that encourages good management. It can do it through laws. It can do it by demanding accountability through civil court actions. It can do it by merely recognizing that there is such a thing as good management and that "good" in this case means techno-economically efficient. But it is unlikely that any institution other than the management community itself can ensure good management.

If we proceed from the premise that management efficiency *must* be self-controlling, we can undertake to design procedures and conventions that will help us operate the system even though imperfectly. If we assume some outside

REDEFINING THE MANAGER'S JOB

mechanism that we know to be illusory, we can only build structures of bureaucratic filigree with no hope of functionality. Concentrating on the management function as such and separating out the value-forming function may just make the job doable.

PART II

IN WHICH SOME OF
THE PRACTICAL
CONSEQUENCES OF A
RATIONAL APPROACH TO
MANAGEMENT
ARE EXPLORED

6
BY THEIR FRUITS YE SHALL KNOW THEM

The irreducible minimum of what can be expected of any manager is that he know what he is trying to do. A manager with pretensions to professionalism should be able to state his intentions quite explicitly and with a minimum of scope for ex post facto "interpretation." In management jargon, this is called "setting objectives."

"By their fruits ye shall know them"—and it seems reasonable to ask in advance whether we should expect bananas or strawberries. An unambiguous statement of purpose serves several functions. Operationally it permits the manager himself to focus his decisions coherently as he goes along and, in retrospect, to self-judge the effectiveness of his performance. Similarly it provides the only proper standard against which any outside agency may judge him. If the man says he is out to produce cheap transportation, don't complain that he did not produce a work of art. If management is the skill of making resources productive, we must agree upon productive of what: automobiles, education, knowledge of social phenomena, tooth brushes, razor blades, lasers, moon rockets, killing machines, whatever. Without stated objectives, the concept of management becomes meaningless. You will never know if the manager "did it" if he never told you what he was trying to do.

In a broader context, society is entitled to know what any organization proposes to do. Any enterprise is permitted to exist only so long as, and to the extent that, it is useful to society. It is a legal person—not a natural person—and has no "natural" right to existence. This is equally true of Ford Motor Company, the Ford Foundation, or Fordham University.

A PUBLIC DECLARATION OF PURPOSE

It is reasonable to expect any enterprise that enjoys access to public funds— either through direct subsidy or through forgiveness of taxes—to declare its purpose publicly, not in empurpled generalities but in explicit ends to be accomplished. Only then can the "public," as the ultimate source of those funds, have a chance to consider whether it wishes to commit resources to those ends. Admittedly, the public may not exploit this opportunity effectively, but at least the possibility should exist.

There might seem to be less of a prima facie case for insisting that a private enterprise make such a public declaration of purpose. The hesitation to impose such a requirement, however, has its roots in the already discussed confusion about the effective "ownership" of resources in modern society. It can be convincingly argued that a man should be able to do what he likes with his own money subject only to the legal restraints placed upon him by society through its various governmental instrumentalities. But most managers are not dealing with their own money, and furthermore they require the dedication of many other kinds of resources in addition to raw capital.

Actually, the concept of a public declaration of purpose is in no way a new one. Charters intended to serve just this purpose, both for profit and for nonprofit corporations, appear historically at the very beginning of institutionalized enterprise.* However, like so many social institutions, rationally conceived at their introduction, they have atrophied and been to some extent consciously perverted over the years. The language found in such documents today is completely nonfunctional. About all they do is establish a legal address and determine just which set of legal technicalities will apply to some aspects of the enterprise's affairs.

Some sentiment is arising to establish national corporate charters for at least the larger undertakings. There are some good technical reasons to consider such a development. However, if the basic concept of the charter is not revitalized, such a change will be an empty formality. A few nonprofit organizations already have national charters, but there is absolutely no evidence that their special status has any effect at all on the nature or quality of their management.

By the same token the suggestion that multinational corporations operate under international charters has a certain abstract plausibility. In practice, such charters could create a regulatory nightmare. Furthermore, if international charters are comparable in nature to the local franchises now commonly granted, such certifications would give the multinationals flexibility far beyond what they presently enjoy under their national licenses.

---

* The first joint-stock-company charter was issued to Sebastian Cabot by Bloody Queen Mary some 450 years ago, but nonprofit charters go back even further.

REDEFINING THE MANAGER'S JOB

MAGNA CHARTA

However, we are concerned here not with the provenance of the charter but with its content. We must have an unambiguous statement of the purpose of the undertaking by which to judge both its suitability and ultimately the effectiveness of the management in fulfilling that purpose. Since there is no practical likelihood that any conceivable agency could assign the multitude of diverse purposes to which human enterprise might be addressed, it is a practical necessity that these declarations be initiated spontaneously. There is no harm in that. The important thing is that they be recorded. The introduction of national charters may be the most expeditious mechanism by which to institute such a reform—and for that reason alone warrants serious consideration.

Many managers will protest that explicit charters will be unduly restrictive, that they will inhibit the flexibility required for aggressive strategies. Not necessarily. Charters are rather easily amended under present procedures, and there is no reason why those procedures need be made more demanding. The point is to make the intentions public—and, not so incidentally, to force the managers to a conscious decision to change or extend the thrust of the undertaking rather than to just weather-vane from one direction to another.

To actually monitor the quality of management, however, we need more than a global statement of intentions. We need definitive yardsticks of measurement. We need specific objectives. Then the question arises as to just how public these objectives should be. The Securities and Exchange Commission has some strictures on how specific public "forecasts" may be for public companies. Most managements seem perfectly happy to suppress the exact nature of their expectations for the future. They prefer to keep these data in the locked files of the board of directors and the top management group.

BY THEIR FRUITS YE SHALL KNOW THEM

One has to wonder whether the traditional secrecy is merely an anachronistic hangover from the proprietorships of the nineteenth century or whether it sincerely derives from a desire to keep the competition in the dark. Or is it really fear of embarrassment if management's performance should prove inadequate to the task? When a runner goes out on a track, he makes no secret of how far he is going to run or whether he is going over or around the hurdles. He either wins or doesn't. If he trips and falls, he may be embarrassed, but certainly not destroyed—if it happens only once.

Admittedly, there has been a noticeable trend in recent years to record and disseminate the specific objectives of profit-making corporations, at least within the organization. It doesn't seem to do any harm. This trend has paralleled the increasing adoption of formal planning procedures. It is not possible to have any kind of comprehensive planning if people do not know where they are supposed to be going.

In these days of "business analysis departments" and "commercial intelligence groups," competitors are seldom in the dark for long as to where a company is heading. They are almost certain to be the first to figure out what a competing company is up to. The people inside the company and its own stockholders are much more apt to be, like the aggrieved wife, the "last to know." Under these circumstances it is entirely reasonable to require the managers of private enterprises—at least those that are "public" companies—to declare their intentions in advance rather than restricting them in the kind of forecasts they can release, as is currently the case. It sure would change the way the game is played.

A STATEMENT OF OBJECTIVES

Setting forth a rigorous objective structure is not easy, whether it will be subject to public scrutiny or not. It is no acci-

REDEFINING THE MANAGER'S JOB

dent that the adjectives "rational" and "objective" are nearly synonymous. When managers go about "setting objectives," they are engaged in the most rational, the most logical, part of management. If they use the alternative terminology of "goals" or "targets," they may imply a slightly greater intuitive or emotional input; but the difference may be more apparent than real.

If managers approach their responsibilities realistically, they quickly realize that no enterprise can state its complete intentions in a single parameter. There is a lot of talk about organizational responsibilities to a vast array of "stakeholders"—shareholders, consumers, employees, suppliers, the community, society, posterity, and God knows who all—but that is mostly rhetoric and is impossible to translate practically into operational terms. However, there are true cases of multiple objectives: A university may assume an obligation to (1) create new knowledge, (2) inculcate specific skills, (3) contribute to increasing the educational level of the general community, and undertake to pursue these several objectives in parallel.

But even the simplest of operations has complex objectives in another sense. There are immediate results desired and hopes for the future. There are changes to be accomplished and situations to be conserved, growth to be achieved, and stability to be maintained. There is risk to be balanced against potential gain.

Therefore any contemporary enterprise must pursue an array of objectives. Even in the case of a profit-making company, the statement "We are in the business of making money" says nothing that is not apparent from the fact that the enterprise operates under a profit-making charter. It is an arrant tautology. Businesses are to make money. But when? And where? And, most important, how? The institution that says it is in "education" or "health care" is little better off. Its charter also tells us that much. It still has no operational direction, nor does it have any instrument of control.

We need a set of coequal statements of the direction and the degree of progress that is intended in each of the major dimensions of the enterprise. These multiple objectives not only are independent of one another but are usually antagonistic. "We want to grow but not at the cost of reducing our profits below a certain level." "We want to be technological leaders, but we will not borrow money without limit to replace obsolete equipment." Thus there may be no priority among primary objectives in terms of relative importance. They must each have equal force. It is only too easy to increase current earnings at the expense of the long-term welfare of the enterprise. That's almost as easy as bankrupting the company in the present while pursuing pie in the sky in the future.

The relative importance of the multiple objectives is reflected in their magnitude. Those of lesser importance will have modest dimensions. The most important will be extremely demanding. A highly volatile period may require major effort on sales growth to preempt share of market at some cost in earnings growth and even in profitability as new capacity is rushed on stream. A relatively stagnant situation may encourage concentration on product development and diversification with little or no attempt to increase sales in a declining market. Changing demographics could dictate strong performance in research accomplishment and very modest goals in education.

The significance of objective formulation lies in making these dynamic tensions—these tradeoffs—visible and explicit. The objective structure must provide a simple matrix within which to determine whether the several thrusts are compatible in concept and practicable in the real world. The management that acts like the kid in the candy store and wants some of everything may not get much of anything.

REDEFINING THE MANAGER'S JOB

FORMULATION OF STRATEGY

The nature and dimensions of the primary objectives of an enterprise cannot be established by any fixed formula. They will reflect, and they should reveal, the style, the perceptions, and the values of the leaders of the undertaking. The choice of terms will imply a great deal about the attitudes of the managers. Do they feel responsible for the total assets utilized regardless of their source or only for those allocated to the nominal owners? Do they feel a different responsibility to bankers and other holders of fixed obligations than they do for open accounts payable and overdrafts? Do they perhaps grant a special importance to fixed assets? Do they still remember what they paid for things as expressed in gross fixed assets? Do they maintain a sense of time perspective through the use of some form of discounted-cash-flow rate of return? Are they conscious of the continually implied reinvestment responsibility as reflected by the use of market value of assets?

Where they choose to make their measurements is a strong clue to how they conceive their activities. Are they sales-oriented, production-minded, or "bottom-line" conscious? Even the choices between before- or after-tax profits may be significant. Some managements imply that taxes, like death, are beyond their control, and they should not be judged on the effect of taxes. Others are intensely studious of tax effects and feel that tax minimization is a very significant management skill.

Almost every enterprise anticipates some growth. The numerical value of the growth objective is of course the most revealing statement of all. The slope of the growth curve relative to the growth rate of the national economy, the growth of the industry group, the company's own past growth, and other internal or external trends provide a complete index of the state of the organization's ambitions, self-confidence, and morale generally. Some managements will make this relationship explicit by pegging their growth objective directly to some external index.

But growth in what terms? Sales? Dollar earnings? Physical throughput? Earnings per share? Value added by manufacture? The relationships of these objective curves are most revealing. If sales are to grow faster than earnings, the company is following a development strategy. If the reverse is true, it is in a harvesting mode. If earnings per share are planned to grow fastest of all, the balance sheet is being restructured. These planned relationships tell more about the intended strategy of the company than pages of descriptive prose.

Other explicit objective statements can be directly related to competition. Managements may say, "No matter what else we do we will be x percent of such-and-such a specified market," or "We want always to be the technological leaders in our industry," or "We will always have the cheapest model available to the market." These are legitimate objectives and express intentions *in addition to* whatever other goals may be set.

Production objectives, too, may be set in many dimensions: raw-materials conversion efficiency, labor productivity, net sales volume per square foot of selling space, or student/faculty ratios. Sometimes production parameters are related directly to a measure of profit performance, but more often they merely reflect a notion of the *right* way to run the business: the kind of performance that should be possible if you are smart enough. A great many objectives, particularly those relating to financial structure and personnel, reflect the managements' perceptions of the right or prudent way to manage without a direct relationship to any other tangible criteria.

A critical balance to look for within the objective structure is that between current operating performance measurements and accomplishments whose significance will be realized only at some time in the future. This is not the same as

REDEFINING THE MANAGER'S JOB

merely comparing short-term and long-term goals. It is rather a matter of assessing the accomplishments scheduled for the planned-for period that will have an immediate effect on the operating statement as compared with those accomplishments whose major benefits will arise beyond the planning horizon and whose immediate effect is probably to penalize current results. These latter are developmental objectives that involve what is sometimes called "investment spending." It is this balance that most truly reveals the mettle of the policy-level manager.

Company planning documents usually spell out objectives in very specific numbers, but this should not obscure the fact that both the nature and the magnitude of primary objectives reflect highly subjective judgments about the proper direction of the undertaking. Primary objectives specify the dimensions of success accepted by the management and as such reflect personal value judgments. Subsidiary objectives that follow from them or are supportive of them will reflect the perceived logic of the dynamics of the enterprise and as such have a somewhat different quality. But the balance of the thrust of the primary objectives will paint a complete profile of the personality of the organization: its aggressiveness, its self-confidence, its attitude toward risk and novelty, its leadership, its geographical horizons—the whole works.

MAKING THE NUMBERS

Full accountability for management begins with the explicit statement of the primary objectives of the enterprise. These become the specifications of the performances contract the chief executive officer signs with . . . with whom? Interestingly enough it doesn't matter too much whom—or whether with anybody at all. The CEO may take them to his board, but

BY THEIR FRUITS YE SHALL KNOW THEM

the board probably will rubber-stamp them anyhow. If the board, or the senior authority in any relationship, tries to impose specific objectives on the CEO, he has several alternatives. He may accept the objectives with confidence that he can achieve them in the time allotted with the resources at his disposal. He concedes thereby that the board, not he, is calling the shots; but that in itself is not wrong. By becoming a willing and responsible party to the commitment, he still retains control of his own standard of performance.

Alternatively, he may accept the objectives with no intention of fulfilling them unless he gets lucky. In that case he is a palpable fraud, which will become apparent when the results are due. How widely the fraud will be apparent will depend on how widely the objectives were known. But there is one person who will certainly know, and that is the CEO himself. And that alone would have a salubrious effect even if he had written the objectives himself and locked them in his bottom desk drawer.

The third course open in the face of imposed objectives is to reject them. They may be rejected because they are unrealizable with the resources that can be assembled, because they are judged inappropriate, or perhaps because they are not in accord with the CEO's concept of the proper balance of accomplishment for the enterprise. It really doesn't matter why; the result is the same.

There may be a confrontation and somebody resigns. This outcome happens very, very seldom. The much more common consequence is a negotiation. Eventually the CEO agrees to a set of objectives, in which case he is in either of the first two positions described above.

Now it should be apparent that for any of this to work the objectives must be stated in terms of substantive results and there should be little or no room for disagreement on whether or not they have been achieved after the specified time has elapsed. If the language is fuzzy or susceptible to extreme in-

REDEFINING THE MANAGER'S JOB

terpretations, the system won't work. But if the objectives are well conceived and well constructed, the time will come when results can be compared against commitment. Whether the control is self-imposed or is exercised by a superior authority, by public opinion, or by peer judgment, the occasion will arise and accountability will be possible.

With well-stated primary objectives, it becomes possible to play "you make your numbers, and I'll make my numbers." Committed-to results can be parceled out in a widening cascade throughout the organization. Managers can be held accountable for pre-agreed-upon results, results that are interrelated in a rational manner and that can be measured by rational processes. Even though rational management is not necessarily ensured, it is at least possible—that is, rational management within the constraints, rules, and requirements that may be legitimately imposed by external agencies, whether these constraints, rules, and requirements were designed by rational processes or not.

But remember, to function properly, multiple objectives must be structured in such a way as to be completely coequal; they must each be fully achieved independently to qualify the management as "successful." Three out of four won't do. There are no priorities or preferences among objectives structured in this way. The sense of priority is reflected in the relative magnitude of the objective. A high-growth objective along with moderate profit objectives states a priority much more effectively than "We'll do this at all costs and then try to get some of this done, and it would be nice if...." Ambitious research objectives and modest patient care accomplishments tell us very clearly what sort of institution we are dealing with.

But in the words of Elliot Richardson (a good manager no matter what else you may think about him): "We have not really wanted to face the answers that good evaluation [of results] would produce.... We preferred the illusion that we

BY THEIR FRUITS YE SHALL KNOW THEM

were doing something about [a problem] rather than discover we were only going through the motions."

In the future, if managers are to be effective in converting resources into results and if they are to be held accountable to whatever system evolves, they will have to face the objective evaluation of their results. But that evaluation requires that the results are agreed upon in advance in clearly stated, readily determinable objectives. This is the inescapable first step toward any system that would presume to apply an autonomous control to managerial actions.

7
THE HONOR WITHOUT PROFITS

But can you set specific objectives for a nonprofit organization? Of course you can. There are problems, but they are not so difficult as you might expect. In the first place, many "not-for-profit" corporations (note the proper legal nomenclature) are operationally indistinguishable from profit corporations that pay no dividends. It is just that at the end of the year they take any funds left over and transfer them to "surplus" instead of to "net worth." Organizationally these "not-for-profits" are just as interested in investment for growth as the "profits" are, and in most cases will suffer the same dire consequences if they sustain persistent "losses." The distinc-

THE HONOR WITHOUT PROFITS

tion between the two types of enterprises is of interest to accountants and lawyers. It has very little bearing on their management.

Essentially the same may be said for many "public" enterprises. Managing TVA or Petrogorsk Tractor Works is not substantially different from managing Universal Wingnut. The fact that there are no stockholders out there buying and selling fancy engravings really makes very little difference. *Fortune* magazine includes the Steel Authority of India among the "Largest Industrial Corporations Outside the United States." So much for the unique nature of "business."

On the other hand, managing a profit-making but highly regulated company like a public utility or running a captive supplier to the federal aerospace program may have more in common with administering a government bureau than with managing a chain of supermarkets. And the government bureau does indeed have to be managed. For all we have said about the value-codification role of government, when you get down to the operational levels, there is the same old problem of managing resources to produce results.

Apologetic managers of nonprofit enterprises frequently declaim, "It's easy to manage a business. All you have to do is order people around and make a profit!" Well, it's not that easy. In the first place nobody orders anybody around any more—not even in the new Army. Furthermore, "making a profit" is not the precise quantitative measure that all those piles of computer printouts would lead you to believe.

MANAGEMENT IS WHERE YOU FIND IT

Management is a critical dimension in any kind of enterprise: industrial, commercial, social, political, artistic. The judgment of its quality has its own rationale entirely independent

REDEFINING THE MANAGER'S JOB

of the conventions by which operational records are kept or of the legalistic formalities observed.

If we keep the elementary system clearly in mind—management operating on resources to produce results—we can approach the assessment of management in profit and nonprofit enterprises equally well. Not that we can do it with great precision or without considerable subjective inputs, but we do have comparable problems in both cases.

There should be no question that nonprofit enterprises are intended to produce results of some kind. Intangible results, perhaps, but that is equally true of all service industries; often results that are hard to measure in a literal way, but that does not mean they are impossible to evaluate.

In some instances these results are even subject to something akin to the "discipline of the market." This is certainly true of private education and of most membership associations. It is even true, in a sense, of the churches. It would be nice if it were true of health service institutions, but they seem to have organized themselves into an archetypical monopoly situation and are behaving with classical Marxian inevitability.

The managements of nonprofit enterprises are entrusted with the stewardship of certain resources. These resources are finite—some illusions to the contrary notwithstanding. The management's job is to make those resources produce as much of the desired results as possible. Stated that way, the proposition sounds quite simple— even if the execution is not. But the proposition is only too frequently lost.

Certainly we are entitled to ask the manager of a nonprofit enterprise what results he proposes to produce. Even as individual citizens we are paying part of the bill, either directly through taxation in the case of a government organization or indirectly through the diversion of potential tax moneys in the case of a tax-exempt organization. Furthermore, that manager may be around one of these days looking for a contribution.

So if we are to talk in any rational way about the management of a not-for-profit enterprise, we must insist on explicit objectives. They must be as unambiguous as semantic skill can make them. As in the case of industrial enterprise, the objectives will almost certainly be multivariate.

The judgment of the propriety or usefulness of these objectives must be made at another time and place by a different mechanism. Presumably the results of that judgment will influence the amount of resources allocated to the enterprise. Possibly it may even affect the tenure of the manager. However, to the extent that the objectives are accepted, the manager can be held accountable only for the results he set out to accomplish. But he should certainly be held accountable for those results.

INPUTS DO NOT ENSURE RESULTS

One of the results expected from the public school system is education in certain basic skills and concepts. If the schools are not producing these results and we put more resources into the school system and it still does not produce acceptable results, it is not rational to put still more resources into the system. Obviously the resources—including the human resources—now committed to the system are not being employed effectively. Providing more resources to be deployed ineffectively will not change the situation. The problem is neither the quantity nor the quality of the resources. The system is mismanaged—by the simplest prima facie evidence that it does not produce the intended results.

Police forces exist to ensure domestic tranquility. They obviously do not. So we pour more resources into them to be employed in ways that we already know do not work. Not surprisingly, increased police budgets have no perceptible impact on crime rates. The problem is to employ the resources in a way that will achieve results. That is our definition of management, and that is where the failure lies.

REDEFINING THE MANAGER'S JOB

We are told that the metropolitan centers are "unmanageable." Whether that is strictly true or not, it makes no sense to commit large additional resources to "save the cities" in the face of the contention that nobody knows how to use those resources.

Five hundred million people are estimated to be critically undernourished in the world. The specialists in food supply assure us that the resources in land, water, and technology exist to feed these millions and many hundred millions more. Yet the politicians who should be managing these resources prefer to deal in Malthusian alarums to divert attention from their shortcomings. The resources are there. More resources won't solve the problem. Failure of the management function to employ these resources to produce the desired effect creates this human misery.

The function of management—individually and collectively—is to devise systems to make resources productive. It is irrelevant for them to explain that circumstances beyond their control make their job difficult. If they can't cook, then the chef or the kitchen is expendable.

All nonprofit enterprises are chartered by one mechanism or another, to perform a certain function, produce a certain kind of result. If the charter is ambiguous, and it often is, the manager is entitled to, in fact should be mandated to, make his own explicit interpretation of his purposes. Then and only then does it become possible to assess how well he fulfills those purposes. Only then will the value-forming instruments of society be able to judge the worth of those results.

IMMEASURABLE OR IMPERCEPTIBLE

Republican, Democratic, Schlemocratic government activities, no matter where, seem to nurture the proceduralist—

THE HONOR WITHOUT PROFITS

the turn-the-crank-like-it-always-was-turned type, no matter what, if anything, happens. I guess that's what we call a bureaucrat. Although that's not really fair. We, the demos, the citizenry, never told them what they were supposed to accomplish. Read most of the legislation the executive branch is supposed to "execute"—and weep. The statutes never say what they want. They don't say what *results* they will consider satisfactory. They just authorize people to *do* something. Don't be too hard on the typical government slob. He may be merely trying to survive. But even the ones who are trying to do something useful have an almost insurmountable task because their objectives are blurred. It is ironic, however, that countries that have what are often called "managed economies" seem to be the ones that get the least results from their resources—that is, they are the most poorly managed. Talk about "newspeak."

If the nonprofit manager contends that the results of his enterprise are not measurable, we will have to ask him if he means they are imperceptible, in which case we would have to call the entire venture into question. If he merely means the results are intangible or difficult to quantify, the problem should be solvable.

We don't need to calculate an 87 percent management effectiveness rating or a 3.4-point grade. What we want is a qualitative differentiation between good and bad, between improving and deteriorating. If we keep in mind just what we are looking for, that is not impossible. If we have a sufficiently explicit statement of the intended ends, it should be possible—given reasonable goodwill—to agree, at least judgmentally, whether those ends are being achieved to a greater or lesser extent.

Somebody believes it can be done and has made a start at it. In 1974 Congress established an Office of Federal Procurement Policy. The agency recently issued uniform rules for procurement policy throughout the federal government. These

REDEFINING THE MANAGER'S JOB

rules state that no agency may order specific equipment but must *describe the job it wants accomplished by the equipment.* This is a big change, and in a rather surprising place. The detail of government specifications in the past was notorious.

The Air Force spent five years and $140 million *writing the specifications* for the B-1 bomber. And then the cost per plane exceeded the estimate by more than 100 percent because—at least in part—the Air Force tried to control what Lockheed *did* rather than what it *accomplished.*

The Department of Defense alone expects its new results-orientation to save billions of dollars and give it better, more innovative material. That outcome seems quite feasible.

It is meaningless to argue about whether you can or cannot apply "business" management techniques to government or academia or a hospital or a symphony orchestra. There are in fact no such things as "business" management techniques. The business community has been more self-conscious about its management skills. It has studied and developed those skills and to some extent codified them. At one time it paid more for them. But business neither invented management nor does business have a monopoly on it—or even a unique need for it. The universities have contributed to the misunderstanding by offering courses in "business administration" and "industrial management."* Some even have separate schools of "business administration" and "public administration." This is patently ridiculous.

The underlying fact is that the causal relationship of resources and results pertains in any kind of productive enterprise and is not at all peculiar to "business." This is the "economizing mode" that Daniel Bell speaks of so eloquently. It is the mode of management.

---

* Yale appears to have recognized the problem. Its new graduate "business" school is simply "The School of Organization and Management."

92

THE HONOR WITHOUT PROFITS

It is not by any means the only axis along which human activity can be considered, but it is the preeminently rational one. If the function of management is to be approached coherently, it must be in terms of that causal relationship independent of organizational forms. It also must be differentiated from the normative vectors that are the proper concern of other aspects of society.

The manager of a not-for-profit organization may argue with some justification that his administrative problems are compounded by the diversity of his constituencies. He has a less solid posture when he claims his objective structure is necessarily more complex than that of his profit-oriented counterparts. He may be justified in pleading difficulty in legitimizing his objectives in some large socioeconomic context, but ultimately he must accept the responsibility for producing some pre-identified, useful results from the resources at his disposal. He may not be able to do a cost/benefit analysis in dollar-for-dollar terms, but he unquestionably can judge from year to year whether or not he is getting more or less result from an equivalent commitment of resources. He may even be able to compare his performance with that of other similar institutions.

Once he becomes accustomed to the idea, the manager of a not-for-profit organization will have no systematic difficulty in evaluating his own *efficiency*. But before he can do that he will have to abandon the onanistic habit of judging his own righteousness. That judgment must come from some other segment of society. The signs may not be easy to find, but they are undoubtedly there for those who would read them. Those who will not may find that society will withhold resources from enterprises it finds irrelevant—or they may find that they are not as free from the "discipline of the market" as they thought.

8
DO YOU WANT TO LIVE FOREVER?

Objectives are fine, and they are essential to a rational structure of the management function, but one objective that is not permissible is simple survival. People sometimes draw an analogy from biological organisms and say the first law of an organization is to survive. That won't do. A living creature may have a divine right to try to survive; an organization does not. Survival is a policy or a strategy or, most commonly, a reflex—not an objective.

The option of total or partial liquidation of any enterprise always exists, and often is the most responsible disposition of

DO YOU WANT TO LIVE FOREVER?

the resources employed.* A good argument for the economic justification of private enterprise is the very fact that a private company is the only social institution programmed to self-destruct when it no longer produces a desired "good" at an acceptable cost; it goes broke. But in practice, most business managers—not only those at Chrysler—prefer to submerge that characteristic.

CONSERVATION OF ASSETS: A COP-OUT

A slightly watered down version of the intimation of entrepreneurial immortality is the concept of "conservation of assets" that sometimes crops up in corporate plans. It too has no logical basis as a specific objective and provides no guidance in the direction of the enterprise.

When assets are committed to an enterprise of any kind, they are exposed to some risk. Obviously, the purpose of the enterprise is to produce some new additional value through the use of these assets. Equally obviously, the source of the assets expects the venture to be successful, so that either the assets will grow or a return will be made to the investor. If the assets are dissipated, it can only be because the enterprise was not economically justified under the prevailing management and experienced a loss.† Therefore, to say that a primary objec-

---

* Possible exceptions are the francished public utilities, but even they sometimes may have the option of voluntarily selling out to a government agency, as IT&T and American and Foreign Power have proved to their profit in the past. Shenandoah Oil Company liquidated itself for twice the market value of its stock. It happens occasionally but not very often. However, some Wall Street types are beginning to do the arithmetic, and liquidation rumors are becoming more frequent.

† A special exception would be the self-liquidating charitable foundation, which may be both productive of new values and a conduit for dispensing gifts.

REDEFINING THE MANAGER'S JOB

tive is "conservation of assets" is merely to say that the object is to be successful. This is tautology of classic dimensions. It is undoubtedly true, but it doesn't tell us anything.

Managers are entitled to a little human understanding if they tend to evade the possibility of organizational hara-kiri. But acceptance of corporate immortality as an unchallengeable assumption leads to some strange perversions of the management system. It leads to unwarranted retention of earnings and their commitment to ventures that good business judgment would not condone. It leads to "throwing good money after bad." Indirectly it blocks innovative strategic thinking. More subtly it causes spurious arguments about "inventory profits" and "replacement-cost accounting," all of which derive from the unstated assumption that certain expenditures *must* be made "to stay in business."

When a manager states as an unquestioned assumption, "You have to stay in business," or the economist says, "Productive capability must be conserved," it is comparable to saying, "My father was a shoemaker, so I must be a shoemaker." That's a nineteenth-century, even a preindustrial type of thinking. There is no rational compulsion to make that kind of assumption. You know where we would be if all the alligators survived.

If you observe how things are done in the real world, you know there are many exceptions. W. R. Grace changes from a shipping company to a chemicals company. Northwestern Railroad evolves itself out of the railroad business. Less spectacularly but more commonly, companies stay in the same business but change their asset base; they build bigger plants, use a new process, change from electromechanical to electronic technology, or subcontract their production entirely. The world changes. Good managers don't go around in a thoughtless circle grinding the same mill like a blindfolded ox. But that is what the prevailing conventions assume.

DO YOU WANT TO LIVE FOREVER?

INVENTORY PROFITS: ARE THEY REAL?

All the recent learned discussions about "inventory profits" and whether or not they are "real" just won't stand rigorous analysis. They all circle around the central premise that you *must* replace inventories to *stay in business*. But you don't *have* to stay in business. Past profits were generated by the inventory that was sold. New inventory that is bought or produced is a *new* investment in a particular line of business that must justify itself in its own right.

No expenditure *must* be made if it is an unwise commitment of resources. If their prices have gone up, you should buy raw materials only if you think you can make something out of them that you can sell for more than it costs you to make it. What you paid for those same raw materials a year or a month ago is completely irrelevant. If you want to stay in business—fine! It's a more expensive business now. That could have happened through a technological innovation or a new labor contract or lots of other ways, and you wouldn't have thought about changing your books of account.

Claiming that so-called "inventory profits" are not real profits is the most specious kind of reasoning based on the unspoken and completely unsupportable assumption that any specific enterprise has a God-given right to stay in business. You buy some materials at some price. You process them at some cost. You sell the product for a certain amount of money. The difference between what you took in and what you laid out is profit. It is real money. You took it down to the bank and deposited it. That transaction is a business entity unto itself. It is not dependent on any other transaction. If you want to say the profit is realized in dollars that are less valuable than those you spent to set up the business, that is another matter. You are unquestionably right, but that deterioration you accommodate in the return-on-investment hurdle rate or the discounted-

REDEFINING THE MANAGER'S JOB

cash-flow discount rate which you use for investment decisions.

Every day is the first day of the rest of your life, and in no instance is that more true than in inventory purchase. Tomorrow you will buy some new raw materials at some price. If you are at all responsible, you expect to sell the resultant finished product at some price that will yield an acceptable net profit. That is a new transaction. Next week you will buy some more materials possibly under still other cost/price relationships. If you can't make money at it, you shouldn't do it. Fixed costs, business cycles, and noncash items like depreciation complicate and obscure this simple relationship, but the underlying principle remains immutable.

There is never any justification for increasing the price of the goods on the store shelf. That is not passing on a cost to the customer. The cost of those goods did not change. That is extorting from the customer free financing of the additional working capital of the business. And that is exactly how it will show up on the books. It will come in as profit, be taxed as profit, and then be transferred to current assets as inventory.

That, too, is exactly what happens when industrial producers raise prices to cover costs they would have had several months ago, when they made the products they are now selling, if they had had to pay the new current prices for materials and labor. Those extra profits being diverted to their balance sheet are certainly real, yet they, and most of the financial community, would like to claim they are "phony" profits that actually should not be counted in their return on their investment. It's a pretty shoddy argument, but it arises from the uncritical assumption that "we got to stay in business."

REPLACEMENT-COST ACCOUNTING

Replacement-cost accounting for fixed assets is based on this same insupportable assumption. You bought something,

DO YOU WANT TO LIVE FOREVER?

you paid so much for it, and you used it to make something you earned money on. Over some number of years you recover your investment through the depreciation account. You recover your investment; anything above that is profit. Don't tell me the day is coming when you're going to go out blindly and get a new one just like the old one and pay whatever they ask—just to stay in business. No way! When it comes time to buy some new capital equipment, the proposal will go before an appropriations committee and be approved or not on the basis of the estimated future profits that will be generated compared with the initial cost. That will be the procedure if the enterprise is being managed and is not just "surviving." Nobody will care whether the new facility replaces anything. So what's this replacement-cost accounting? It makes sense only if you assume some sort of obligation to keep doing the same thing over and over again ad infinitum. That is not a reasonable attitude. It even *sounds* silly when you say it that way.

The contention that under current accounting practice some companies are unwittingly liquidating themselves because they are not reinvesting enough funds to maintain their position in the business is at least valid—but it is irrelevant. If they cannot attract enough cash resources or cannot initiate enough profitable new projects to support their accustomed level of activity, then that is exactly what they should be doing: withdrawing assets from the business so they can be committed more productively somewhere else—by someone else.

The accounting conventions of equipment depreciation derive from the early days of the Industrial Revolution when prudent businessmen actually put aside a little money each year so they would have funds on hand to buy a new anvil when the old one wore out. There are a few traditionalists around who still refer to "depreciation reserves." But nobody actually accumulates a liquid reserve to build a new plant for cash when the old one gives out. In most quarters, managers who did so would be considered highly irresponsible. How-

REDEFINING THE MANAGER'S JOB

ever, if they did put the cash aside, presumably they would not bury it under the parking lot. They would put it out at compound interest with the result that when the old unit wore out their depreciation reserves would amount to considerably more than they paid for the unit in the first place.

In "normal" times interest rates will equal or exceed the erosion of the value of the currency so that, at any time after the full depreciation schedule is completed, the value of a true depreciation reserve would equal or exceed the current purchase price of the replacement item. Admittedly, inflation rates have on occasion exceeded interest rates, but obviously such a situation cannot persist for long periods or nobody would lend any money. On the other hand, if there were no inflation, the company would end up making money on this scheme. Since major fixed assets are seldom retired at the end of the depreciation period, the compounding interest on such a reserve would continue to accumulate. The company would probably "make money" on it anyway.

This is the classic "reserve for depreciation" concept on which accounting systems and many management and economic theories are based. But it never materializes in the real world. The nineteenth-century accountants who established depreciation conventions didn't understand the time value of money very well. The businessmen today who talk about "underdepreciation" and the ravages of inflation on the replacement of equipment may not understand it very well either.

With the current rate of evolution of markets and technology, a major facility is rarely replaced by identical equipment. If it were, admittedly the cost would be quite different from that of the original unit. But whether or not the depreciation charges plus interest accrued forward to the time the replacement equipment is actually bought would equal the price for that equipment is irrelevant. There is no question that equipment wears out and that this deterioration is a cost of production. But the concept of relating this cost to the problematical purchase of some new equipment at some time in the future cannot be justified either in theory or by the way enterprises are actually managed.

It may be significant that many nonprofit organizations that don't have to concern themselves with tax considerations seldom show depreciation of fixed assets. This often creates a problem when they need a new building and they are widely criticized for their naiveté and irresponsibility; but perhaps they may be only relatively more in error than the complacent corporate controllers.

There is an old saying that "money has no memory." There are no special kinds of dollars in a company's cash flow that are uniquely committed to buying a particular kind of equipment—to replace anything. In present-day lifetimes, at least, it seems that money inevitably loses value, but every dollar loses the same amount. There are no special dollars whose devaluation is specifically tied to the cost of an individual piece of equipment.

CASH IS CASH

When cash flows into a company, there are only three things you can do with it: give it to the shareholders, put it in the bank, or invest it in productive assets. This is true of all kinds of cash flow. In the case of depreciation cash flow, however, people tend to get confused. Partly it is the word "depreciation," which invokes an image of using up or wearing out. The alternative "amortization" is actually more literally descriptive and less likely to mislead but is used only in special cases.

Depreciation cash flow is real money. When it arrives, the management has the usual options. In the rare event that the

REDEFINING THE MANAGER'S JOB

money was passed on to shareholders, everyone, including the tax collector, would recognize a decapitalization of the company. It would be considered a return of capital, a disinvestment by the shareholders. And that is exactly what it would be. It has nothing to do with the wearing out of machinery.

If the management is reluctant to part with all that money but has no good ideas about what to do with it, it can put the money in a bank or other fixed dollar security, but it is unlikely to do this for very long. It would show up under "cash and negotiable securities," and, if that account gets too big, both Washington and the takeover artists get restless.

Actually, when that cash flow comes in, the management almost always commits it as quickly as possible to the most profitable investment available to it at that particular time. If its judgment is at all good, that investment will begin to return substantially more than the prevailing interest rate. As a consequence, funds will grow considerably more rapidly than the inflation rate, and the absolute value will be more than preserved.

If this is what in reality happens, why then persist in the obsolete fiction of a fund for the replacement of assets? Going back to our first option: If passing depreciation cash flow through to shareholders is a disinvestment, why is it not equally a disinvestment if the funds remain in the corporation? Viewed in this light, depreciation cash flow amounts to withdrawing capital from one venture in order to recommit it to another. Whether the rate of withdrawal is or is not related to the physical deterioration of some particular equipment is irrelevant. Eventually all the capital originally committed to a particular piece of equipment will have been reclaimed. The money is taken out of current earnings, which is entirely appropriate since that is the only place it can come from. It is nontaxable—as it should be, since it is a return of capital.

Furthermore, the depreciated book value of the asset now

represents the unrecovered investment in the plant and equipment used in the activity, and that is a real number. The fact that it bears no relationship to the current value of the assets is irrelevant. If ultimately the equipment falls apart or becomes obsolete, either it no longer represents any investment if the cost has been completely reclaimed or the balance must be written off. The decision may then be made on whether or not to invest some *new* money in comparable equipment in anticipation of further attractive profits in the future. But that decision is not foreordained, even though the prevailing conventions assume it is.

The Internal Revenue Service currently determines how rapidly you may retrieve capital invested in a particular kind of fixed asset. However, theoretically you could consider total cash flow as return of capital up until the entire investment has been recovered. If you do that, you have a "payback" calculation that seat-of-the-pants managers have been using for years.

DISCOUNTED CASH FLOW

Maybe these managers are more perceptive than their more sophisticated peers gave them credit for. Because a discounted-cash-flow (DCF) analysis does exactly the same thing—except that it charges you interest on the money you have tied up until you get it all back. A DCF calculation does not differentiate between profit and depreciation cash flow or between capitalized and noncapitalized investments. The money you lay out for development expenses and market buildup is just as much real money as that you lay out for bricks and mortar. And a DCF treats them all alike. It does assume that you disinvest as rapidly as possible. That is one of the reasons it will not correlate with a standard return-on-investment calculation.

REDEFINING THE MANAGER'S JOB

The discounted-cash-flow technique implies that the minute you get your hands on an extra buck you are going to put it to work. You will reinvest it in something—and that something need have nothing to do with the operation that produced the cash. That is exactly what you will do in the real world. You will put the money down on the best bet available at that time. And when the plant wears out or becomes obsolete, you will make up your mind whether to scrap it or fix it up or replace it.

But that is another decision to be made at that time unrelated to anything that has gone before. Or that is what you should do if you are acting rationally if you are not distracted by some archaic accounting concepts, and if you realize you can only manage in the future and avoid becoming a captive of the past. Discounted-cash-flow procedures assumes that every venture is self-liquidating, and it avoids the "we got to stay in business" assumption. Maybe that's why some people are so reluctant to use them.

A disinvestment perspective on "depreciation" really needn't change the way your accounts look. Rather, it induces a change in perception that avoids some irrational assumptions and sharpens managers' decision processes.

Management will use its resources efficiently only if it acknowledges that it is responsible each day for the decisions of that day. The past may be prologue, but the play is on the stage now. Fixed-asset investments are sunk. They are worth now only what they could be sold for now. Every day the responsible manager does not sell them, he effectively reinvests their present sale value and must justify that investment. Fixed assets are never replaced. New fixed investments are made because they promise attractive profit returns. If the new equipment performs the same function as some former facility, it may have enhanced profit potential because of existing distribution capability and market acceptance; but the new plant doesn't "replace" anything.

104

DO YOU WANT TO LIVE FOREVER?

Working capital is essentially recommitted every day. Once that investment can no longer be justified it should be stopped. In the real world such a situation would never arrive as a sudden surprise. The declining profitability of a line of business will be observed well in advance of the time it actually drops below an acceptable level, and a competent management will begin to strategize out of that business, disinvesting working capital in the process.

The assumption that fixed or current assets must ultimately be replaced is not valid in the business world as it actually functions. Managements that act uncritically on that assumption have very poor long-term prospects. Accounting systems and public policies based on this assumption are confusing at best and counterproductive in many instances.

9
WHY NOT?

The corporation's preferential right to life is enshrined in the U.S. tax law in a particularly subtle way. The double taxation of corporate dividends is generally conceded to be a cynical political expedient, but corporate executives don't really seem to be terribly upset about it. For very good reason. The managerial consequences of the practice are studiously ignored.

By perpetuating the pretense that depreciation cash flows are used to "replace" worn-out assets when in fact they are really reallocation of assets to new investments, management gains access to a pool of "free" money for which it need make

WHY NOT?

no justification. But further, it can augment this pool with "retained" earnings. True, it must pay corporate income tax on these earnings, but it is provided with the highly plausible argument that if it paid these funds out in dividends, the "owners" would be liable for personal income tax as well. The managers, by energetically reinvesting these funds, enable the owners to escape double taxation.

This is true. But it is also true that there is a considerable difference between the procedures for committing internal cash flow and negotiating for use of the "real" money you have to get from bankers or new stockholders.

THE COMPULSION TO INVEST

"Managers" not only assume that internally generated cash may be committed with minimum accountability but seem to feel a perverse responsibility to invest it on almost any terms. Managements often feel harried by the salt mill deluge of cash flow that they must dispose of. If they accumulate too much liquidity, Wall Street criticizes them and the raiders drool. If they build a marginal plant that is expected to make only a bank rate of return, there is not a whimper—because nobody knows. The pressure on their judgment is obvious. As a consequence a great many corporate capital allocations could never be justified as freestanding business investments. But to turn the funds over to the nominal "owners" for their use or investment would expose them to further taxation, often at very high rates. It seems almost sinful to give all that nice money away to Uncle Sam.

The result of this psychology is recorded every day in the pages of *The Wall Street Journal*. When stocks sell consistently below book value, either the books are a fiction or the management should be fired. Obviously stockholders think they could do better with the assets than the management is doing and are discounting any funds entrusted to that group of decision makers. Under these circumstances there is certainly no justification for the management's "reinvesting" any of the stockholders' earnings by paying out less than the total profits in dividends. Yet most do not pay out total "earnings," much less total cash flow. Companies that report a return on invested capital well below the yield offered by triple-A bonds are not being managed; they are a happening.

Moreover, it is just these companies whose reported rate of return may be grossly inflated because they are likely to be old companies in which a substantial portion of the fixed assets is carried on the books at values well below liquidation value. There is no way of knowing, often even within the company, what is the effective rate of return on recently committed assets, but it is probably substantially below the reported overall rate. These are the investment decisions the current management has made, and they may be yielding only a few percent before tax on total utilized investment.

The net effect is that established companies with sizable internal cash flows tend inexorably to get larger even if the results of the commitment of their increasing assets are far below industry norms.* These assets are never available to be managed more productively by more competent managers. The opportunity cost to the general social economy is considerable. The cost is incurred because of the often specious assumption that an existing enterprise has a preferential right of access to cheap, pretax money.

Certainly there are cases where corporate earnings are reinvested very productively. However, the evidence overall is less than compelling that corporate managements have earned

---

*In the total business community (excluding financial institutions), two-thirds of new investment typically comes from internally generated funds. In large companies the proportion tends to be greater.

WHY NOT?

preemptive rights to funds through their extraordinarily productive disposition of resources in the past. It would be very difficult for many of them to justify withholding earnings from stockholders who are in a position to reinvest their funds on equal terms. This is particularly likely to be true of small holders who have lower income tax rates and would not be so heavily penalized by the double taxation.

Failing to reconcile the shareholders, the managers would have to go to the hard-nosed banker or the equally skeptical new-share buyer to justify their pet schemes. They would find this to be a lot different from getting their weekend golf buddies on the appropriations committee to approve their capital proposals.

CHANGES IN THE TAX LAW

If the incumbent decision makers are to be cut off from their artesian well of investment funds, the tax law will have to be changed. This can be done in several ways.

Assuming that the policy of double taxation of corporate profits is sustained, then equity demands that a surtax be imposed on retained earnings approximately equal to the average marginal tax rate of the individual shareholders. If this rate were 40 percent, then the small shareholder whose marginal rate was below that level would be better served if the earnings were passed through to him so that he could reinvest them himself. On the other hand, the wealthy shareholder would still escape some tax if the company retained his funds and recycled them. Since the wealthy holder just might have more influence on corporate policy than his less affluent co-owners, this alternative might have the desired effect of encouraging more careful consideration of reinvestment of internal cash flow.

However, the total funds available for investment would

REDEFINING THE MANAGER'S JOB

be reduced, since a substantial part would be bled off in taxes, presumably to be used for purposes other than the creation of productive assets. Since there is an encouraging tendency toward decreasing taxes and a growing awareness that capital formation has lagged in the United States and must be stimulated, this alternative is not attractive either economically or politically. A compensating reduction in the general corporate tax rate could theoretically maintain the total tax take at its current level, but the practical matter of determining the size of that reduction offers prodigious obstacles.

The remaining options involve some sort of tax relief through the elimination of double taxation. Basically there are two alternatives: (1) Reduce taxation at the corporate level by allowing dividends to be paid out of before-tax funds and tax only retained earnings* or (2) allow all dividend income to be tax-free to the payee.

In either case, with an existing payout policy the corporation would have exactly the same number of reinvestment dollars it now has. Only the position of the dividend recipient would change. If dividends were paid before taxes, the gross value of the dividends could almost double. This is great for the "little guy" because he would attract relatively little tax liability on his receipts. It is even greater for the tax-exempt foundation that would get to keep it all. The "fat cat," of course, might have to pay as much as 70 percent of his dividend income as personal tax, but he would still keep twice as much as he can under the current tax law.

If the corporation continued to pay dividends out of after-tax earnings but the dividends were tax-free, the total gross dividend would be the same as it is now. The low-income

---

* Allowing shareholders receiving dividends to credit taxes already paid by the corporation against their individual tax liability would have essentially the same effect.

WHY NOT?

shareholder would save relatively little in taxes; the tax-exempt entity, nothing at all. The high-bracket shareholder, however, would save a bundle. Since the corporation ends up in exactly the same situation under either option and is therefore indifferent to the alternatives, American social tradition will strongly favor tax relief at the corporate level.

If dividends are paid out of pretax earnings, equity financing is placed in parity with debt financing. With higher dividends, stock prices will rise, equity financing will become increasingly attractive, and balance sheets generally will become stronger and less vulnerable to economic difficulties.

THE ROLE OF THE SHAREHOLDER

However, of equal importance, every shareholder whose marginal tax rate is less than the corporate rate now has a real economic incentive to press for dividend payout. Depending on the level of the corporate rate, this could be the majority of the holders. Only if they are fully convinced that the management of the company will do significantly better in investing the earnings than they could do themselves will the shareholders be willing to sustain the additional tax incurred in leaving the funds in the enterprise.

In aggressively growing companies, shareholders might be expected to pay this price gladly for the skillful deployment of their funds. But other managements would find themselves in the unfamiliar position of having to make a strong justification of their investment decisions. Capital gains would be reduced but by no means eliminated.

Superficially such a policy would seem to run counter to the recent tendency to increase internal cash reflux through depreciation concessions and investment credits. However, it is possible to wonder whether these forced infusions do other than encourage investment decisions that could not be justified on "sound business judgment."

Earnings distributed as dividends, after all, do not disappear into an infinite sink. After being taxed, the residue, possibly following several intermediate uses, will find its way into the hands of some individual or institutional investor where it will be available to enhance the pool of funds available to any new venture. Investment decisions would then be dispersed to a large number of shareholders, which should make these decisions more flexible, hopefully more accurate, and certainly more "democratic." There would be a regular infusion of potential new equity investment money that could work to the advantage of the equity-hungry, new and growing firms. Presumably there would be a larger number of equity shares on the market—which some believe is desirable.

NOT ZERO GROWTH

Certainly such a policy would increase the accountability for capital investments and presumably thereby improve the effectiveness with which they are made. It would exert considerable pressure to reduce the autonomic nature of the modern corporation. The current system does not encourage the greatest possible responsibility in the making of investment decisions. "Professional" managers do not feel the same accountability in investing "free" money from internal cash flow as in "buying" the money in the open money marts. And the vast majority of such managers have never had to deal with anything but such automatic capital.

We now have a strong bias in favor of organizational expansion—and consciously so. The question is: Does the silicone injection provided by the automatic cash-feedback loop serve our best socioeconomic interests? Making reinvestment

WHY NOT?

of earnings somewhat less convenient would tend to suppress the geometric growth curves of the large corporations and perhaps relieve them of the necessity to indulge in conglomerate expansion to employ cash flow for which they cannot find gainful employment in their own line of business. There are certainly some who would find this a salutary effect.

If broader distribution of earnings to shareholders would increase the pool of equity capital accessible to smaller, nascent ventures, it would also discourage the entrepreneur who might be tempted to distort the development of his enterprise to exploit the presumed opportunity to roll over partially tax-free income at a high rate in order to pyramid his paper profits through the capital-gains-hungry, new-issues market. Certainly the more extravagant capital gains situations would lose much of their tawdry charm.

The ultimate result would not be a zero-growth situation. Far from it! Channeling the flow of capital to investments that would favor the most highly productive applications would, in fact, enhance the rate of real economic growth.

The practical consequence would not likely be to make any appreciable number of corporations shrink. It would rather be to impose an elastic constraint that, once an organization lost its vital thrust, would tend to constrict it automatically. An organization that was moved to distribute all its earnings under these circumstances would still have its depreciation cash flow to reinvest. Since no one pretends that in the real inflationary world depreciation "reserves" will actually pay for the replacement of physical assets if only depreciation funds are reinvested, the effect would be a gradual contraction in scope.

There is no compelling theoretical reason why this must be bad. Practical evidence does not overwhelmingly support the sanguine effects of growth that common rhetoric implies. The usual analogy between organizational growth and organic growth is only that—an analogy. It has no inherent logic. A

REDEFINING THE MANAGER'S JOB

gemstone must get smaller as it approaches perfection. So what?

THE PUBLIC INTEREST

Society has a vital interest in the skill with which resources are committed—with the way in which capital expenditure decisions are made. Since managers are the professed practitioners of that skill, the preeminent makers of those decisions, they must be reminded of their accountability as expert professionals. Providing those managers with an institutionalized "free ride" on internally generated funds benefits neither society nor the individuals. Subjecting them to the discipline of the money markets can only sharpen their competence. If they want to invest more money, let them ask for it—and not just within the family. If they can justify the project to an outsider, fine. If not, they can go without. If they want to "reinvest" the shareholders' money, let them ask the shareholder what he thinks about it by offering stock purchase rights along with the dividend.* How far would they get with their bankers if they unilaterally informed them that the company was not gong to pay half of the owed interest this year but was going to "reinvest" it for the bank? But that is what they do now to their shareholders.

Economists are pretty well agreed that the rate of capital formation is a key determinant of the continuing economic well-being of a country. Both theory and empirical evidence strongly support that contention. However, for the principle to hold, the capital must be put to productive use. Simple logic would dictate that the more productive the use to which the capital is put, the further it will go. In other words, there is some kind of productivity multiplier involved here. Italy is an unfortunate example of the consequence of locking up too

---

* Or a Dividend Reinvestment Plan.

much of the available capital in low-productivity enterprises.

Economic historians commonly credit much of America's rapid economic development to the existence of an unusually responsive money market. Capital has been relatively free to seek its most profitable employment—not perfectly, but relatively. But that free flow of capital is being increasingly constrained by the combined effects of the preferred status of retained earnings and the locking-in effect of the capital gains tax.

The collateral effect has been to dull management's sense of accountability for the allocation of resources—in this case, capital. It encourages the illusion of the immortality of enterprise by feeding back a continuous supply of life-supporting cash even when economic considerations would suggest that it is time to pull the plug.

10
"... GANG AFT AGLEY"

A great deal has been written about planning during the last fifteen years, some of it rubbish, but most of it pretty sound.

"Planning is the first responsibility of senior management."

" 'Planners' do not plan; they help decision makers to plan."

"The process of planning is more valuable than the plan."

"Planning does not make the future certain. It is a technique for dealing with the uncertainty of the future."

"Planning is not deciding what to do in the future. It is deciding what to do *now* in order to have a future."

"... GANG AFT AGLEY"

"Planning is deciding why you are going to do something before you do it."

The trouble is that few people seem to be paying attention except the other writers on planning, who proceed to try to say the same thing in different words in the desperate hope that somehow the message will get through.

Planning does work for the few people who understand it. It even does some good for a lot of people who don't understand it but who stumble onto some of the principles. It creates a lot of meaningless words and reams of useless computer printouts for those who think it works according to the formula, "Put tab A into slot M and fold on the dotted line." It also scares the hell out of a lot of people who have completed Peter's Progression and are afraid somebody might find out. Planning cannot help but remind you of another great institution of which it was said, "There must be some great good in it or it could not survive in a state of such corruption."

PLAN OR PERISH

Planning will certainly survive. It will become more pervasive. It will become more effective. The learning process may be agonizing—in some cases, fatal. But there is no alternative. As enterprises become very large, the communications problems—both instantaneously across the organization and sequentially along the time dimension— overwhelm less formal mechanisms. Enterprises no longer evolve organically to be assimilated progressively over the lifetime of an individual. The environment changes so rapidly and the personnel relocate so frequently that only a consciously designed system will provide any promise of maintaining coherence of purpose and consistency of progress. Finally, explicit plans provide the only objective basis for measuring the quality of management performance.

REDEFINING THE MANAGER'S JOB

With the rising economic cost of resources, the diminishing tolerance for competitive error, and the growing hazard of regulatory noncompliance, poor management will become a fatal luxury. It is generally acknowledged that most of the companies that have had extraordinary success since World War II have a highly planned management style. In the coming epoch such a style will not provide exceptional competitive advantage; it will be a requisite for survival.

The information-handling capabilities and the logical systems for planned management exist. They will get better. The younger generation of managers is growing up with increasing conditioning to the use of such tools. It will use them. Competitive pressures between individuals and among organizations will propel the evolution at a geometric rate.

The problem with planning is that the concept is too simple. Find out where you are and what is going on around you. Be honest about just what you have to work with. Agree on what you want to accomplish. Decide what is the most promising way to do it. See that something is done about it. Check back to see if your ideas worked out.

With the best will in the world, nobody can write a book about that. Having said it six or seven different ways in the first couple of chapters, you're reduced to larding the book out with a bunch of quotations and descriptions of analytical techniques. Some checklists and sample forms are good to make weight; and if you want to set a high tone, add an appendix with some integral signs in it.

The professors have the same problem. You cannot teach planning in a classroom. After the first week you run out of really significant new things to say. Academic pride, plus the propensity to boredom of most students, won't let you just say the same thing over and over; so you play games with case studies and, chances are, escape to make pretty mathematical patterns on the computer.

The consultant is even worse off. Very few presidents are

"... GANG AFT AGLEY"

going to pay him fancy fees to be told to *think* about the nature of their business, *make up their minds* about what they want to do, and then *see that something is done about it.* It is a lot more reassuring and a great deal less exhausting to buy some resounding phrases on "leadership," a set of fancy forms and formulas, and then go out and hire a high-priced planning "expert" and tell him, "You make us some plans while I go back to running the business." Don't blame the expert if the company does not develop a sense of direction and some positive momentum. Chances are that the expert knows what planning is and has a lot of good analytical skills and techniques. In most cases, he also has a bit of evangelical fervor and will work hard at his mission among the heathen. *But he cannot plan.* He is not running the company, and so he cannot call the shots or police the action.

The reason that planning systems abort is that planning is conceived as a specialized activity like accounting: something a little mysterious and difficult to comprehend that can be best done by some double-domed initiates of the art.

Planning is encompassed in management as the yolk is in an egg and it has the same function. It is the essence of managing. There must be a reason for the existence of any enterprise or else there would be no rationale for management actions. That reason does not come in a black box that you just plug into the organization somewhere. The rationale to tie the operation together cannot be bought by the yard. The manager has to define the reason and design the rationale. It is hard work. The concept may be simple, but its execution can be complex.

WRITE IT DOWN

It all has to be written down. This is one bit of procedure people don't like to do, but if the plan doesn't get written

REDEFINING THE MANAGER'S JOB

down, it won't get done. It doesn't have to be long and complex. It doesn't have to be in a fancy binder. It doesn't have to be great literature—better perhaps if it is not. It does have to say unmistakably: This is how we see the situation, this is what we think is going to happen, this is what we propose to do about it, and this is what we expect the results to be.

There are several reasons why a plan must be in writing. In the first place it is the documentation, the codification, the instrumentality of the logic by which the enterprise will be pursued. It is virtually impossible to check your own logic, much less somebody else's, unless you see it in writing. Furthermore, a written plan is a tremendous communications device. It helps ensure that everybody is playing in the same kind of ball game. If it reflects some good logical thinking, it will reassure people that the boss not only knows what he is doing but knows why he is doing it.

A written plan also gives a fixed point of reference against which a new situation can be measured or an established course of action confirmed. Memories are notoriously fallible, particularly in the hyperstimulation of the executive suite and when personal egos are involved. Do we still believe in the validity of the reasons that led us to start doing what we are doing now? If not, let's stop doing it or find new reasons. Are things turning out the way we wanted them to? If not, why did we think in the first place that they would be different? What was our mistake, not in what we did or did not do, but in taking this course in the first place? Did we underestimate our resources? Depend on the wrong man? Ignore our competitors? Misjudge the market? Expect our organization to move too fast? Maybe we can learn not to make that mistake again. But we can learn from mistakes only if we know we made them and have a chance to determine how and why they were made.

If a written plan is to do its job, it must mean what it says and say what it means. People must understand it and believe

"... GANG AFT AGLEY"

it, and a year hence it must mean the same thing to them as it did when it was written. That is why it will have so many numbers in it—not because the numbers are necessarily so accurate but because they are specific and unambiguous. A plan written in general terms subject to multiple interpretations is like a phony cancer cure. It is worse than nothing because it gives a false sense of security.

There are a dozen good books and a thousand journal articles that deal knowledgeably with the nuts and bolts of planning: how to define corporate purpose, the use of strategic policies, the characteristics of good objective statements, the relationships of objectives and strategies, choosing among alternative strategies, setting up project controls, and on and on. None of them will provide a blueprint to use in a specific organization, but the proven principles are there to be had. If you will hold to the concept of a rational approach to management, you will have little difficulty in assembling a workable planning procedure from the components displayed. But an irrational management will never develop a satisfactory planning procedure, its plans will not be realized, and it is wasting its time in making them.

The essence of planning is the logical structuring of cause and effect, of means and ends. Planned management is rational management—management with and through and against a defined rationale. If a management insists on a rational approach to its responsibilities, the mechanics of planning will come easy. If it tries to graft an essentially rational planning process on a wheeler-dealer, compulsive-gambler, "love-of-the-game" style of management, the organization's innate rejection mechanism will slough off the incompatible tissue.

This is not the place for a detailed discussion of planning techniques, but there is a second major hurdle over which many planning systems stumble. Once the rationale of the enterprise has been thought through and the criteria for success

REDEFINING THE MANAGER'S JOB

have been stated in a set of primary objectives, the process stops. Global objectives, the primary criteria for the success of the enterprise, are all very well but they don't get the corn planted. They are a conceptual device rather than a management tool. They can, however, provide a base on which to build a management structure that provides for a rational allocation of resources and an orderly progression of assignments. The key to planning is successive segmentation of objectives until they are broken down into actionable units.

The trick is not to go out immediately and *do* something. The problem in running any organization is not that people do things wrong—it is that they do the wrong things. If you do the right things wrong, you have a chance to learn your mistake and make a correction. If you do the wrong things right, there is absolutely no way to salvage anything from it. Some companies seem to be doing so many wrong things that one cannot help suspecting that the only explanation for their survival is that they do them so poorly.

You cannot tell from a key objective what is the right thing to do. There is no way to make a direct, logical connection between "8 percent annual growth in volume" and an immediate course of action. If you are going to jump from a pious hope to a foregone conclusion, you may as well forget the whole thing.

DISAGGREGATING OBJECTIVES

Either a structure of connective logic exists between the key objectives and any action commitments or the network will short out. The overall intentions must be broken down into operational subunits if anything is to get done. It is in the construction of this connective logic that the judgmental as opposed to the manipulative skill of management is both displayed and developed.

"... GANG AFT AGLEY"

If we want to achieve Key Objective A—growth in sales volume, say—what are the necessary and sufficient preconditions that must be realized? We must (1) maintain volume in certain products, (2) sustain existing growth rates in others, (3) generate some sales from products we do not presently have, and (4) probably do several other things. Taken together this set of subobjectives constitutes a strategy. Is it the best set—the best strategy—we can conceive? Do we honestly believe that if we accomplish all these subobjectives, we will inevitably achieve the key objective? Do we really need to do all these things to accomplish the key objective? If not, let's prune.

These few statements concerning the key sales objective and its immediate subobjectives represent the essence of our complete perception of our company's marketing posture, but they still do not tell us what to do. "Maintain sales volume in Product Group I." But how? We need another layer of subobjectives. To maintain sales volume we must: (1) reduce costs so that we can afford to sell at a competitive price, (2) retain the Xerox account, (3) improve performance on Model XYZ, (4) arrest deterioration of market position in the northeast region, and on and on. Do we believe it? Is it the best scheme we can devise? All right, we have another objective set that represents another level of strategy.

But reduce costs—how? Cut overheads? Automate the plant? Skimp on materials? Eliminate rejects? Probably several programs in combination. We must be able to see a way, or the strategy at the next higher level falls apart and must be restructured.

CREATING AN OBJECTIVES TREE

The process continues through as many levels as necessary to evolve into specific actions that can be taken *now*. These actions may be set up as programs or projects: sched-

REDEFINING THE MANAGER'S JOB

uled, budgeted, and commenced. Creating this kind of objectives tree has been called an exercise in applied logic. So it is, because if the rational connection between the successive echelons is not valid, the plan will not succeed. It is also the toughest kind of exercise in applied business judgment. The ways the various jobs are segmented will provide a complete schema of the management's judgment of the best way to run the enterprise.

Don't kid yourself. Creating this kind of objectives tree is a lot of work. No one individual or even small group will do it well for even a modest-size enterprise. A lot of people can be and should be involved. But when it is done, it will document the total implications of some of the possibly grandiose ambitions expressed at the beginning. This can be a shocker. It is quite possible that there is just not enough time or money or talent to carry through all of the projects at once.

Well, at least you found out before resources were committed and people rode off in all directions. The hoped-for results could never have been accomplished in any case, but this way you found out in advance. The objectives tree acted as a model, and you can go back through the structure and sort out priorities, decide what you can do without for the present, and lower your sights to a realizable level. You won't have so many nauseating year-end surprises, and everybody will be saved a lot of frustration.

You will have disappointments, however, even if you do work out a fully coherent objectives structure. Some disappointments will come because somebody just did not produce—you need a different man. Others, because something happened outside—a new product, a government action, a price change—that you did not see coming. Better check your intelligence system; maybe the problem could have been anticipated. Some of the "surprises" will come because you did what you said you were going to do and it didn't work— didn't add up to the next-level objective. Well, at least you've learned that your perceptions of the dynamics of your business were less than perfect. You can try another working hypothesis next time around.

Some individual will have the responsibility for each objective on the objectives tree. In accepting this responsibility he also accepts responsibility for structuring the portion of his branch of the tree that extends beyond him. Thus, you have an explicit device for assessing both the operational and the strategic competence of each manager. Any individual can judge his own performance as well as that of his subordinates by this yardstick. The passing grade will probably be nothing like 100 percent, but it had better be well above 50 percent. It should also improve over time as experience reveals the nature of past oversights. An objectives tree is a "heuristic" system, a "learning" system, which inherently provides the basis for improvement.

GOOD MANAGEMENT IS HARD WORK

Imposing this kind of accountability is not going to be easy. Unfortunately, the principal reason for so much bad management is quite simply that bad management is so much easier and so much more fun than good management. Either way, you get the fancy office, the sexy secretary, the carpet on the floor, the generous salary, and maybe even the promotions. The thrill of the high stakes and the tension of responsibility are the same in both cases. But the difference is the same as that between playing roulette and making out your income tax return. If you had a choice, it is pretty clear which you would choose—unless you got paid for it. But managers do get paid for it—usually pretty well—so there is no reason not to expect them to manage well rather than play games.

REDEFINING THE MANAGER'S JOB

Good management is hard work. You have to think and study and get your facts straight and continuously accept that your technique can be improved. It is a whole lot easier to run things by hunch and whim: to wheel and deal and patch up the blowouts as they occur.

Unfortunately, competition or the changing environment ultimately catches up with the seat-of-the-pants boys. But it is fun while it lasts. And if the people who manage managers do not insist on a professional approach to management, they must expect that many of their people will duck the hard work and go for the fun and games.

Some knowledgeable readers are undoubtedly protesting that the concept of a hierarchy of objectives deriving rationally from the purpose of the enterprise through successive layers of ever-increasing detail is a Utopian idea that is completely unrealistic. In the real world, at least in large organizations, initiatives come not from the top but from the bottom—or at least the middle. "Middle management proposes—top management disposes." Ideas originate "down on the firing line," and the "good" ideas are accepted and the "bad" discarded by the upper echelons through some sort of review and approval mechanism. This may be descriptive, but it is not particularly relevant to the argument. The approval mechanism must have recourse to some sort of rationale by which to differentiate the "good" from the "bad." This rationale may be faulty; it may even be disastrous. It may be shortsighted or overly dependent on accounting calculations. But this merely confirms that there are competent managers and incompetent managers. The rationale must be there, and it must be based on some kind of perception of the relationship between causes and effects.

A more cynical perspective will reject this explanation and contend that the supposed "review boards" are essentially rubber stamps, manipulated by the petitioners and denied the essential information to make an informed judgment. Unfortu-

"... GANG AFT AGLEY"

nately to anyone who has spent much time in the supposed corridors of power, this interpretation has a disturbing plausibility. It is possible, as is frequently contended, that the senior executives are basing their decisions on broader and longer-range considerations that are not apparent to the more parochial members of middle management. It is also possible that the senior managers don't know what they are doing.

If the latter case could be proved in any significant number of instances, it would be the most powerful kind of justification for federal action to break up large organizations because of their size alone. If the upper echelons of the executive pyramid are in fact making no contribution to the productive deployment of resources, they are clearly superfluous and an unnecessary tax on the economy as a whole.

On the other hand, if this is the case, then the legal basis for trust-busting and forced divestitures comes into question. It is based on the assumption that these extra layers of hierarchy somehow confer undue economic power that cannot be confronted by normal commercial practices. Reasoning by analogy, the trust-busters infer that because there are economies of scale in production units, there are comparable economies of scale in organizations. This hasn't been proved in the general case. Those extra echelons are awfully expensive. There is a paradox here that will not be resolved for some time.

Some proponents of "management up" take still another position: that the primary role of the top executives is to balance and coordinate the diverse thrusts of the various segments of the organization. This posture of neutral mediator is frequently assumed by college presidents but is by no means unique to academia. It would be fairly easy to respond that under these circumstances the chief executive is no longer fulfilling a management function but is rather serving the political function of arbitrating the balance of power among the conflicting interests of multiple constituencies. This would be cop-

REDEFINING THE MANAGER'S JOB

out by redefinition, a technique that seems to be quite acceptable in many academic circles and may even be valid.

But it leaves unanswered the question, "Who's in charge?" What did happen to the management function? We can draw the analogy to the periods in history when the dukes did take over and the king wasn't in charge. There certainly are cases in industry in which the divisional or group vice-presidents do collectively usurp the power of the throne and battle it out among themselves from the power bases of their respective organizational fiefdoms. These situations are not inevitably catastrophic. The effective result is that of several enterprises of comparable status, although not necessarily of identical power, operating independently.

However, when the several constituencies are different in kind as well as in strength, the central enterprise is not segmented but rather distracted. The essential management function is still required. When a college executive tries to perform simply as a conciliator of faculty, student, alumni, trustee, and other interests, the loss of sense of purpose is only too quickly apparent and the declining utility of the resources employed is perceived at least intuitively. The same thing happens in a business, although the effect may not be so quickly apparent, particularly if the enterprise is large.

PLANNING IN THE REAL WORLD

The mental and emotional discipline required by good planning tasks the powers of all managers, but it has become essential to effective direction of a large modern enterprise. Planning permits quicker reactions to changing situations because it provides a structured context within which to consider alternatives. The delay-making sense of unsureness that arises when no one is really certain he understands the problem is

". . . GANG AFT AGLEY"

eliminated. Decisions are made more crisply and soon enough to exert maximum leverage on the situation, and individual managers have more time to do their jobs. There are fewer interminable and inconclusive committee meetings and fewer heart-thumping crises.

Furthermore, planning provides a framework for approaching all aspects of the management function. The relationships of the successively disaggregated and increasingly specific objectives suggest the optimum organization structure for the enterprise. The dimensions of the various objectives prescribe the nature and the content of the information feedback system that will be necessary to control the undertaking. Individualizing responsibility for specific results provides the incontrovertible measure of personal performance, and the magnitude of those results suggests appropriate compensation. Finally, explicit definition of discrete units of expectations permits precise allocation of resources to individual tasks and the consequent weighing of those resources against the expected results—the ubiquitous cost/benefit analysis.

If managers are to be the instrumentality by which resources are converted into results and are to be held accountable for the effectiveness with which those resources are utilized, they must operate within an explicit scheme of performance, which is to say, a plan.

11

SOME NOTES ON ACCOUNTING

"The Price of Everything and the Value of Nothing"

If management is to be judged by the results it produces from the employment of a given store of resources, we should be able to tell good management from bad management. At least in the capitalistic mode of operation we have a convenient measurement of the excess of the value produced by an enterprise over the cost of the resources consumed. The measurement is called profit. If this figure is compared with the value of the financial resources committed to the enterprise, we have a measure of the efficiency of the undertaking. We call this return on investment. Thus the conventional accounting system provides us with a measure of the effectiveness of a management, at least in terms of monetary values.

SOME NOTES ON ACCOUNTING

RETURN ON EQUITY

Or does it? Ask ten business executives how to calculate return on investment and you will get at least five different answers. One who considers himself a real tough-minded businessman may say, "Divide net after taxes by net worth," because that is after all what the owners make on what they have tied up in the company. But that is arrant nonsense.

Even granting the manager the familiar fiction that the shareholders are functional "owners" of the company, net worth has virtually no relationship to the value of their equity. Net worth is an almost fortuitous algebraic sum of what some founding investors put up, possibly many generations ago, plus undistributed profits and losses realized over a period of time recorded in dollars that have changed in value every year, plus the mathematical reflection of depreciation policies in recent years, plus some more or less arbitrary entries relating to goodwill, accruals, reserves, and other esoterica.

What the shareholders have "put into the company" is the sum of the various prices they have paid for the stock over a span of many years. Theoretically this total could be calculated, but that would require a lot of clerical effort and the total would not mean anything when you got it. What the shareholders actually have *invested* in the company is the market value of the stock today. As long as they hold the security, they are forgoing the use of the amount of money they could realize if they sold it, less any tax they would incur. That is their true current investment. With a listed stock they almost always have the option of liquidating within minutes.

In other cases the procedure may be more cumbersome, but the principle is the same. As long as the shareholders do not sell out, they are effectively reinvesting the funds every day. But because of the unknown and widely varied tax effect involved, the total market value of the shares does not tell us what the shareholders' effective investment is either. It would

REDEFINING THE MANAGER'S JOB

be almost impossible and certainly impractical to determine this true investment figure. One thing is certain: It would bear no relationship to the net worth shown in the company books. Furthermore, this investment figure is constantly changing as the price of the company's stock fluctuates, influenced much more by the neurotic impulses of Wall Street than by any action of the company management. Most corporate executives disclaim any responsibility for the price of their company's stock and will protest that they make their decisions "for the good of the company" without considering their effect on the stock price. The executives who may consider themselves "more progressive" and who do admit to an effort to maintain a favorable stock price "in the interest of the shareholders" are apt to be viewed somewhat askance by their more conventional counterparts. Moreover, if they attempt to influence the stock price too aggressively, they may attract some unwelcome attention from official quarters. It therefore is unfair as well as uninformative to assess managerial effectiveness on the basis of return on the market value of equity, since this will vary substantially with little or no relation to managerial actions.

The return-on-equity discussion is a phony anyhow. The shareholder will never see a good part of the reported net after taxes because it will be "undistributed" and reinvested along with a lot of other cash flow that never showed up as a profit. Net profit seldom is "returned" to anybody. The individual stockholder's "return" is whatever after-tax benefits he can realize from dividends and capital gains as a result of his commitment of funds to a stock purchase. This return will differ literally for each shareholder, depending on what he paid for the stock originally and his tax bracket. The argument that reinvested earnings still *belong* to the stockholder is completely specious. All these earnings do is increase the net worth on the balance sheet. A random comparison of stock prices and book values of shares will demonstrate that there is no direct con-

SOME NOTES ON ACCOUNTING

nection between the two. Hence any attempt by the management to relate its performance to the "owners' " return on the "owners' " investment is obviously futile and delusive.

If net worth has no meaning in terms of owners' investment, it has equally little relationship to any other actual value in the real world. The amount that could be realized on liquidation of the enterprise might be much more or much less than net worth, but it would be surprising if it fell within 20 percent of the balance-sheet value. During the recent years of widespread company acquisitions it has been amply demonstrated that when the chips are down on the negotiating table, the businessman/executive pays little attention to this conventional fiction of the accounting statements. It is a rare firm that is sold for as little as its net worth. When one is, it is considered either a bargain or a cripple and is usually picked up by a raider or, more politely, a "resource manager," who hopes to liquidate all or part of its assets. On the other hand, many companies change hands at many times net worth. Some companies with negative net worth have been sold at substantial prices. Obviously an enterprise as a going concern has a resource value that is nowhere reflected on the balance sheet.

Earnings-per-share criteria are almost as seriously flawed as return on equity. Peter Drucker says flatly that earnings-per-share is "a purely arbitrary figure that has little or nothing to do with economic performance." In the first place, the company makes the earnings, not the shareholder. The shareholder gets what the company management deigns to give him. Furthermore, earnings-per-share figures can be inflated by imprudent debt leveraging or other less savory devices that have no relation to the enterprise's productive activities. Finally, they have the disconcerting characteristic of changing drastically if the financial structure of the company is altered. The new financing may or may not be wise, but it does not change the basic productivity of the company.

REDEFINING THE MANAGER'S JOB

Admittedly, the number of shares outstanding is a real number that can be related to a demonstrable fact in the sensible world. But that number can change without changing the economic performance of the enterprise. Furthermore, the numerator of the indicator, "profit," is itself subject to so many "adjustments" that the earnings-per-share criterion can be a very misleading guide. It is popular because it has a reassuring simplicity for the shareholder. The fact that it is an unreliable index of the vitality of a venture is amply demonstrated by the wide range of price/earnings ratios that exist on the securities exchanges at any one time. If earnings-per-share was a valid indicator of the quality of a venture, these P/Es would tend to cluster around a common mean and rise and fall together with the state of the economy.

RETURN ON ASSETS

Some executives will say that to assess the quality of a management you really must look at return on "total assets utilized," since, after all, it is the total assets, no matter what their source, that the management "managed" in order to produce the indicated profit. The logic is impressive, but the arithmetic is apt to be less than convincing if examined closely.

The advocates of "return on total assets" are usually talking about "book" or balance-sheet values. They usually add interest to profit to calculate return. A still more sophisticated convention is to capitalize leaseholds*—that is, to charge an imputed value of leased property and equipment as part of the investment, in which case rent is also considered part of the return.

---

* Capitalizing leaseholds will become virtually mandatory "accepted" accounting procedure after 1980 under Financial Accounting Standards Board Statement 13 on accounting for leases.

SOME NOTES ON ACCOUNTING

There are other less common conventions for stating "investment." A few companies use "gross assets"—that is, they charge the original, undepreciated cost of fixed assets to investment. This works best in big companies because in a smaller company you get a "step" effect whenever a major facility is scrapped or abandoned. Some managements define investment arbitrarily as "equity (net worth) plus long-term debt." In Europe, particularly, it is common to look at return on fixed assets only, taken either at original cost or at depreciated book value.

The trouble is that all these denominators for the return-on-investment fraction suffer from the same infirmities as net worth. They do not relate to anything in the real world. They do not represent the market value of the assets employed, the liquidation value, or the replacement value. The numbers are a historical accident that reflect nothing more than the way the books have been kept since the company and its acquirees were founded.

If the denominator (the investment component of the ROI expression) is chaotic, the numerator can be sheer fantasy—and still be legal. The most prevalent distortion arises from the universal practice of recording as current expense depreciation or depletion charges that are only vaguely related to the life expectancy or even the cost of the asset involved.

The more the depreciation charge, the lower the figure shown as "indicated" profit.* This in turn has a "sheltering" effect on tax liabilities (for which perhaps we should all be grateful), but it further obscures the true effectiveness of management.

Perhaps the most compelling evidence of the complete artificiality of depreciation schedules is the fact that the politicians have learned to manipulate them arbitrarily to influence

---

*Of course, the rate of depreciation affects the book value of assets, too, but not usually as sharply as it does current earnings.

REDEFINING THE MANAGER'S JOB

the general economy. "Accelerated" depreciation has become an accepted way to give industry a temporary tax break to jazz up the economy with reasonable assurance that the average voter will not understand what it means. Some governments, for political reasons, have allowed depreciation charges of as much as 2½ times the initial cost of the asset, with 100 percent writeoff taken in the first year.* This may be a highly effective way to steer the economy, but it sure makes it tough to find out what is going on in a company from the profit-and-loss statements.†

Discounted-cash-flow techniques are a large step toward reality in analyzing returns from new ventures, but no one has yet come up with a simple comparable technique to evaluate an ongoing business. Cash flow rate of return—that is, profit plus depreciation compared with cash commitment—is indicative and is increasingly used but does not provide a complete answer. A few companies, American and others, that have had to operate in countries with wildly inflating currencies have developed cash accounting systems. These experiments deserve more attention and study. They might teach us something even beyond the distorting effects of inflation.

There are myriad other ambiguities in determining the profit side of the ROI equation. What is the "right" way to look at income expected from equipment leases or the sale of a franchise? When do you charge yourself for a plant you built that will never operate or for the amount you paid for an acquired company above the assessed value of the tangible assets? There are the minor options available in suspense ac-

---

* This is not done in the United States, which, however, gets essentially the same effect with an "investment allowance."

† Some companies do keep two sets of books—legally—showing respectively "depreciation for tax purposes" and their standard depreciation convention. This helps keep them from getting completely confused.

SOME NOTES ON ACCOUNTING

counts, accruals, prepaids, and so forth. There are both legal and conceptual subtleties that blur the meaning of current profits.

Then of course there is "depletion." This is often a matter of charging an expense that you don't pay for using up an asset that was never on your books. Certainly, if you bought the mine from someone, then of course it is on your books and there is no arguing that the property loses value as the minerals are extracted. However, as in the case of depreciation, there is little relationship between depletion allowance and the percentage of the resources used up or between depletion allowance and the purchase price of the deposit, for that matter. And if you discovered the deposit yourself, you never record that good fortune as a windfall capital gain and increase your asset value accordingly. You merely start from zero and effectively write it off from there.

However, there is a still more pervasive factor that in most instances makes it virtually impossible to find out how an enterprise is doing *now*. The tax laws encourage us to expense everything possible against current income. One accounting principle urges, "Identify costs as much as possible with resultant income," but once we get away from the production floor we have strong incentives to ignore the principle. Company divisions skimp on new-product promotion because they are under pressure to show a certain operating income. Executive committees funnel money into ill-conceived research programs because "Uncle Sam will pay for half of it anyway." Expenses of all kinds that cannot possibly have any effect on current operations are charged against current income either because the tax law says they may not be capitalized or because there is a real tax saving realized by not deferring them. Once the practical principle of expensing everything possible is grasped—and even a mediocre manager can usually understand tax savings—the reporting system becomes so confused that it is literally

REDEFINING THE MANAGER'S JOB

impossible to learn exactly what net income is being produced by existing production activities.

Any experienced operating executive can, and frequently does, "adjust" his profit performance by rescheduling expenditures with long-term effects—for example, product promotion, research and development, and personnel training—and by juggling maintenance and equipment charges. If he is in trouble he can always eliminate or defer certain expenditures that cannot have any effect for several years. If he is skillful enough at this he will be promoted into another job by the time the consequences become apparent.

On the other hand, if he is having a fat year, he may "save" some profits for next year by what he may euphemistically call "investment spending" but that might sometimes more accurately be called "prepaid expenses." Then at the end of the year the controller and treasurer come through with the "adjustments" to accelerate or defer indicated profits to smooth out the performance curve. And the public accountants certify it all because it is both legal and within "generally accepted practice." But I defy anyone to find out precisely how much real profit was actually produced by the directly productive activities during that accounting period.

ACCOUNTANTS TALK TO ACCOUNTANTS

The fact is that accountants keep accounts for other accountants, for the tax people, and for the watchdogs of the Securities and Exchange Commission. Like medical Latin, accounting is a language used among a fraternal group and is not intended to inform the patient about what is going on in his innards. The intention, however, is not malicious; it is merely parochial. Most of the reforms now being discussed under the auspices of the Financial Accounting Standards Board (FASB) of the American Institute of Certified Public Accountants are not basically intended to make the language more intelligible to the responsible manager, but rather to prevent certain perversions of the system within the fraternity.

The FASB does have a task force that is attempting to develop a "conceptual framework" for accounting, which, among other things, will attempt to define expressly such critical terms as "earnings," "assets," and "liabilities." It is about time, but the prognosis is not too favorable. Symptomatic of the problem is the statement by Robert K. Mautz, National Partner of the "big eight" accounting firm of Ernst and Ernst, who observed with shock and foreboding that there is some sentiment to change financial reporting "dramatically . . . into a process of asset and liability identification and measurement."* He is obviously under no illusion that that is what it is now.

Typical of the FASB product is their Statement 8, which requires multinational companies to reflect the effect of foreign currency fluctuations on their quarterly earnings statements. This has nothing to do with the cash transaction of transmitting dividends. That has always been straightforward. It rather involves complex formulas for converting foreign assets and liabilities into dollar figures on the U.S. books. These are strictly accounting adjustments and have little if anything to do with earnings performance of the overseas subsidiaries— or with anything else in the sensate world. All they do is make reported earnings yo-yo up and down with the currency markets or, alternatively, lead financial officers to indulge in costly currency hedging operations to avoid wild fluctuation in the earnings figures and the consequent lengthy explanations.

They got into this mess years ago when there was a rush to

---

* "Inflation Accounting: Which Method Is Best?" *Harvard Business Review*, November 1977, p. 11.

"consolidate" the books of overseas subsidiaries with those of the parent companies. This didn't have any effect on the economic performance of the foreign companies either, but it did make those magic numbers in the U.S. annual report bigger. Of course some of those assets that got consolidated proved ephemeral or at least inaccessible, and a lot of those "earnings" incorporated as "equity in earnings" have never found their way to North America. But never mind; the proper forms were observed and there was an appearance of greater productive activity.

It might reasonably be said that, at best, standard accounts tell you "the price of everything and the value of nothing." The accounts do not help decide what to do but merely provide a history of what has happened; but very few realize that even the history is written in a garbled language. Under current practice we cannot look to the books of account to help us in trying to judge management on the basis of the value it has produced relative to the value of the resources it used. Return on investment in any of its forms is a fiction, since we do not believe the "return" figure and cannot relate the "investment" to anything in the real world.

12

HOW WE CAN KEEP SCORE

If tradition and legality have so distorted accounting records that the cliché measurements of managerial effectiveness are uninformative, what can we do about it? We can without unreasonable effort quite simply design an information system expressly to tell us how well a manager is using resources to produce new value. It won't replace the conventional accounting system for legal and record-keeping purposes; it won't be so neat or so explicit; but it will give us some idea of the quality of the current management decisions and of their implementation. After all, in the words of Sandy Burton, former chief accountant for the SEC: "If financial statements are irrelevant, it doesn't matter how understandable or neutral they are."

REDEFINING THE MANAGER'S JOB

If a manager is to be responsible for the productivity of resources, it follows that he must be explicitly informed of the extent of the resources he deploys. At the very least he should know the value of those resources that can be measured in dollar terms. Yet it is shocking how many organizations fail to attempt to provide even minimal investment information to senior executives. Even the executive who naively accepts the balance-sheet evaluations of corporate assets is, as we have seen, most likely deluding himself. Perhaps this is one reason why we have so few competent managers.

How many medium-size companies have come to grief because they forgot that they needed to make an investment in working capital as well as in fixed assets as their company grew? How many retailers use the same markup on two items, one of which turns over twice a day and the other twice a month, and think the items are equally profitable? How many manufacturers think they have a highly profitable division in a fully depreciated plant when the plant site alone is worth 20 times the original cost at which it is carried on the books? How many college presidents have any idea of the value of their campus?

The frequent objection is that it is too difficult to divvy up investment in multipurpose equipment, that it is too costly to assign inventory and receivables and payables to product lines. Yet those same objectors may have complicated and somewhat arbitrary systems for allocating overhead charges and elaborate labor-hour-record paraphernalia. Of course it is important to know if there is any net left after completion of a certain job or operation. But there is a balance sheet that pertains to every operating statement. Let us give at least some time and effort to some *management* information. The business of management as well as the management of business involves the productivity of resources. That's what the balance sheet is all about. Let's not forget it.

HOW WE CAN KEEP SCORE

ALTERNATE USE VALUE OF ASSETS

Once the tangible resources committed to a given activity are identified, there is no mystery about their proper value. It is not a number to be found in the formal accounts. It is the number of dollars we cannot get our hands on because they are tied up in that activity. It is the net market value adjusted for tax effects or, in some cases, the value of the asset if it were used in a different activity. It is the *alternate use value*. If someone would buy a product line for $1 million, that is the present investment in that line. If the plant site could be sold for $5 million, you had better see a return on more than $5 million before you build a new facility on that site. Never mind what the accounts say.

By the same token, if you made a mistake and built a plant that is obsolete before it is finished or one that just will not run, it is worth only its scrap value unless you can think of something else to do with it. Anything else you might do with it need only yield more return than you could get on the proceeds of scrapping the works, because that is all it is worth to you now. The difference between its cost and its current value has already been lost. Sunk costs are really sunk.

This is equally true for expense money already spent. Past research-and-development, advertising, and training money is gone. The great, the most insupportable fallacy is, "We have so much money in it now, we can't afford to quit." If you have spent $80,000 on an R&D project or on mounting a Broadway show, it is ridiculous to say, "Boy, we've got to spend the other 20 on the chance of getting the 80 back." That $80,000 is gone. You're never going to get it back. What you have to figure out now is your chances of getting a return on the $20,000 you haven't spent yet. If it pays off at five to one—great! But that's the game. The $80,000 doesn't enter into it.

Don't get hung up on history. We cannot manage the

REDEFINING THE MANAGER'S JOB

past. What should we do next? What benefits can we generate from this time into the future?

In effect, a manager reinvests his resources every day. If he does not withdraw them from an activity, he in fact recommits them and at a constantly changing cost. Practically, he cannot rethink all his decisions daily, but he can take stock of his position at least annually. To do this will undoubtedly be instructive in assessing what he has accomplished in the past year, particularly in comparison with what he set out to do. But his most critical analysis will be of what he is about to do next with the resources at his disposal. To do this, he must have a meaningful appraisal of those resources. And to be meaningful, such an appraisal must be related to *current* reality.

Thus, alternate use value of assets must be reestimated at least annually. This will take some doing, granted, but that is much better than massaging a mass of meaningless numbers just because they happen to be readily available. A few companies already reappraise their assets annually, at least in part. Others apply alternate use value when committing assets to new ventures. It really is not so difficult once you get the hang of it.

There is a related philosophy behind *zero-base budgeting*, which demands that every expense budget item be justified in terms of anticipated results from the next dollar to be spent without reference to previous levels of expenditure. The point in both cases is to escape capture by the past for either habitual or legalistic reasons and to approach management decisions entirely in terms of the present and future, which is the only time in which they can have any impact.

THE CURRENT MANAGER'S COMPETENCE

It is in the nature of most corporations today that most of the assets entrusted to any individual manager were put in play

HOW WE CAN KEEP SCORE

by a predecessor. The current manager is committing assets that will eventually be managed by his successor. It is ironic, but probably coincidental, that the lead time for most major capital projects is now roughly equal to the period between managerial promotions.

All the current manager can do with precommitted assets is decide to sell them off, reassign them to some new use, or operate them. That is the only investment decision he can be held responsible for. If he chooses to operate the assets, then the only significant performance criterion is how much product he gets out of them; further, how many sales dollars are realized; and ultimately, how much cash flow is generated. The investment is the money that is not available because the assets are tied up in this operation. The return is the cash flow that occurs as a result of this operation and that would not have occurred otherwise. This is all you can hold the current manager responsible for. It is irrelevant to haggle over whether the assets are valued at original cost (gross book), net book value, replacement cost, or on any other basis, because the current manager has no relationship to those values. They should not enter into the judgment of his competence. Let the accounting boards and the tax economists worry about them. They have real problems, but these are different from the problems of assessing management competence.

If we are going to evaluate a manager realistically, we have to know not only the real value of the resources at his disposal but also what he is actually spending to produce the current results. We have to distinguish the expenditures that relate directly to the new values being produced currently from those made in expectation of a productive result at some time in the future. We have to be able to find out what a given asset under the direction of a specific manager is producing for us *now*. And we have to do this also without reference to what the tax people think we should do.

Actually, once we get over being uptight about the tax accountants, it is not really such a big job. There are major categories of expenditures that are clearly not expected to contribute to the current year's results: research and development, engineering design work, and product development up through test marketing, for example. Those should not be charged against current operations. Introductory marketing costs are expected to yield a return over the anticipated life of the product according to some sort of sales development curve. Only a small part of that return is expected in the introductory year, and only a proportionately small part of the expenditure should be charged against that year. Certain kinds of maintenance expenditures are on a multiple-year cycle and should be spread out over their useful life. Recruiting and training expenditures should be spread over the expected tenure of the trainee, but most administrative overhead charges would be counted currently. The principle is pretty straightforward, and the implementation should not give a cost allocation accountant any technical trouble.

So we will charge current operations with only the expenditure on materials, labor, supplies, marketing and distribution, and services required both directly and indirectly for current operations. The difference between these charges and the net income from sales is the cash flow generated by the management of the operation. This comes close to what some companies call "operating income" but is more rigorously and logically defined. What is done with this cash flow is another whole set of decisions.

Until we have a set of accounts like this, we will not really know for sure what is going on. A company reports that its return on sales has improved 1 percent this year, but in fact it has reduced its level of research-and-development expenditure from 4 percent of sales to 3 percent. The improvement in margin is a phony. The division general manager reaches his "contribution" target, but he had to drop $200,000 worth of planned

HOW WE CAN KEEP SCORE

marketing programs to do it. He is kidding somebody, maybe even himself.

But what about those deleted expenditures from which we expect delayed benefits? Are we just going to forget them? Are we merely talking about amortizing long-term-effect expenses over several years—carrying them as deferred charges? Not at all; that would merely muddy up the system again. We are trying to find out how well the managers are managing; we are not making up a nice neat procedure for the bookkeepers with all the figures conveniently balanced across the bottom. The manager cannot unspend what has already gone out for research or advertising or training in past years. He cannot even liquidate it at salvage, as he could a fixed investment. Whether he himself authorized the past expenditure or not, he can make decisions not only to exploit the situation in being. We want to be able to tell how well he makes those decisions.

POST FACTUM ANALYSIS

We will do our best to relate the long-term expenditures to the actual benefits they produce. We are finally going to honor the venerable accounting principle of comparing an expenditure as closely as possible with its resultant income, but we are going to do it across time. We are going to keep track of expenditures made for a given product or process or other strategy over the years, and we are going to compound at a negative discount rate until the resultant cash inflow pays the expenditures back with interest and begins to give us a positive return. In other words, we are going to treat so-called "investment" spending like an investment.

Specific investment ventures—whether involving a new plant or new products—we will track over time to see if they worked out as they were supposed to. And we will remember who initiated the particular venture and see that he gets appro-

REDEFINING THE MANAGER'S JOB

priate credit (more about this in Chapter Fifteen). Ongoing activities, such as an operating division or a product line, will be tracked in a continuing account. Each year we will charge that account with the marginal cost of money times the unrecovered investment in that activity as of year end. That unrecovered investment is the sum of all long-term expenditures—whether capitalized or not—charged against that activity since the account was opened, less any credits for return of capital. If the after-tax cash flow generated by that activity exceeds the cost-of-money charge, the balance will be credited to the account as a return of capital. If the current net cash flow does not cover the cost of money, then the shortfall has to be added to the investment.

It will quickly become apparent that the unrecovered investment in some accounts continues to rise every year, possibly at an accelerating rate. That business segment is in strategic trouble, but the profit-and-loss statement might never show it. The economically productive units will ultimately liquidate themselves, at which point they will begin to show an absolute return. You will be surprised how long it takes even a good business to reach that true breakeven point.

We can follow the performance of an individual manager by treating him as a "new venture" the day he takes on a new responsibility. We will do it on a "dollars-in, dollars-out" basis without regard to preexisting expenditures and without differentiating between expenses and investment. Thus, at any point, we can calculate a discounted-cash-flow rate of return to date; or, on the other hand, if we wish to apply a standard discount rate, we can determine whether or not we have yet got our money back "with interest" and just how the "enterprise" is making out.*

---

*To do these calculations, we will charge the alternate use value of any assets committed at the beginning and credit a liquidation value of the enterprise at the end.

HOW WE CAN KEEP SCORE

You will notice that we are doing these post factum analyses of "ventures" by a discounted-cash-flow (DCF) technique. This is most likely the way they were justified when they were initiated—at least when the capital appropriation was made. One of the most ironic characteristics of the management literature is the frequency with which it observes that it is impossible to correlate a DCF rate of return with an accountant's return on investment. Having made this obvious pronouncement, it stops. Quite clearly, to determine whether the project worked out as expected, the actual cash flows must be compared against those that were predicted to see if they match. If both sets of figures are done in constant dollars for the year the project was initiated, it is even quite simple to net out the effects of inflation. You don't even need a computer. But almost nobody does it. Maybe it is just too embarrassing.

Now you may complain that we are counting the same profits twice—once as the product of operational skill and again as the result of strategic decisions. You would be right, but we are not going to add them together. Before we finish our complete management information system, we are going to have several other indices of management performance that obviously cannot be handled additively. We will accept these two measurements as parallel indicators of strategic and operational competence, respectively.

The objection that these two indices are mutually dependent is more substantive. There is no question that the most perceptive strategic decision can be nullified by poor operational performance. It is equally true that the most elegant operational skill can seldom salvage a strategic situation that is inherently disastrous. On the other hand, this is no excuse for muddling the two kinds of figures together so that there is no hope of finding out just what is going on. By differentiating the two facets of management performance, we will improve the chances of identifying both problem areas and occasions for kudos.

REDEFINING THE MANAGER'S JOB

It is also clear that different managers will require different balances of operational and strategic skills. Very senior managers will make most of their contributions strategically. So will certain functional executives: for example, in research and development and in market development. Other responsibilities are almost purely operational: in manufacturing, perhaps, or in sales when differentiated from marketing.

When you use this scheme for functional units, you will get tangled up in the old transfer pricing controversy, but it won't be any worse than it is in a conventional accounting system. The cleanest and most meaningful way to handle it is to transfer at market price less marketing costs. The primary reason this procedure is not followed more commonly now is that other formulas often have tax advantages—another example of tax considerations obscuring the control of the management function.

How do you square a management accounting system with your statutory records? That is a technical matter to be worked out between the accountants and the lawyers. Certain legal requirements must be met. There are more and less advantageous ways to record certain transactions for tax purposes. When the government, for political reasons, suggests and legalizes intentional distortions in corporate records to permit tax deferral or avoidance, obviously it would be negligent not to take advantage of them. Just do not mistake these "generally accepted" legal records for an indication of the effectiveness of the management. Depend on the legal/accounting technicians to protect the company's best interest relative to the established authorities, and keep management's attention on the utilization of resources. There is nothing illegal about keeping two sets of books if they are not used to defraud anyone.

The basic fact is that you don't and you can't reconcile these two kinds of accounting procedures. True, there is no

HOW WE CAN KEEP SCORE

known direct correlation between a DCF rate of return and a conventional accountant's return on investment. However, if resources are consistently productive, both in the short and the long term, there is no way this performance cannot ultimately show up favorably in the published annual report.

ACCOUNTING FOR THE UNCOUNTABLE

What about the awkward question of accounting for the utilization of resources that are not easily evaluated in dollar terms? There is little precedent or current practice to guide us on this road. Intangible properties that conservative accounting methods accord nominal or no recognition on the balance sheet may in fact have a "market" value. Some patents and trademarks can be sold or licensed for a price that can be estimated. If they are not so exploited, then the income forgone becomes part of the investment in their exclusive use.

These are easy ones, but what about legitimate goodwill, brand franchises, customer acceptance, know-how, and industry reputation? These may actually be hazarded in a particular management strategy and certainly will be instrumental in the productive outcome of most activities. Perhaps we should revert to an earlier convention and attempt to put an estimated dollar value on these intangibles and charge appropriate aliquots as part of the resource investment in individual undertakings. However, except for cases in which it is likely that the resource will be consumed or lost, such a charge would violate the principle we have accepted of freeing the present from responsibility for expenditures made in the past. We must view these resources as the product of sunk costs of the past which have no present meaning except as they are exploited through continually renewed initiatives. If they cannot be sold or realloted to some other productive use *in the present*, then you are

REDEFINING THE MANAGER'S JOB

not forgoing access to any value by virtue of their current commitment.

Even if we do not assign these nonmonetary assets any present value, we can still gain some useful insights into the quality of their utilization. What is the current return from a certain brand franchise compared with the historical record? How well are we exploiting our exceptional access to the printing market these days? Are we realizing all the benefits possible from our technological leadership in widget design? We have a unique distribution system. Is the cash flow to which it contributes growing as fast as its operating costs, or is it rapidly becoming an expensive but nonproductive tradition?

The product manager who shows increasing cash flow performance but at the cost of a declining share of the market is obviously liquidating a corporate resource and bringing it over into current income. This may be exactly the right thing to do, but it should not pass unnoticed.

The individual analyses may take a little imagination, but once the principle is accepted that these intangibles are real and valuable assets to be productively employed to maximum effect, a relative basis for judging the skill with which they are employed is not too hard to devise. The primary trick is to disaggregate activities in order to isolate the area in which a particular intangible asset is being employed. This can be done by segmenting markets, defining sharply specific areas of technology, and examining individual organizational subunits.

The second necessity is to avoid a hang-up about double counting. Although you may end up with figures denominated in dollars, their significance is as indices. You are going to use them to compare magnitudes with other figures of the same kind, to compare last year's performance with this year's, the new manager with the old one. For those purposes the figures do not have to have any absolute significance.

HOW WE CAN KEEP SCORE

THE PROPER STUDY OF MANKIND

Let us admit at the beginning that evaluating how effectively human resources are utilized is a subjective enterprise at best. No reasonable man will claim he can determine precisely the constructive potential of an individual. Therefore, nobody can say with certainty how much of the human potential has been utilized. Furthermore, we must again accept that we will use a different index for determining effectiveness in utilizing people than for measuring the productivity of other resources. There is no known common denominator that will put on a single scale the skill with which a manager works his cash account and the degree of productive effort he extracts from his design engineer.

It is helpful to keep in mind, however, that individual capability is an asset that is rented by the hour, the day, or the year much like a building or a piece of equipment. It is not a consumable raw material that can be held in inventory if it is not used. As in the case of a building, whether we use it at all or use it well or poorly, the rent—in the case of the employee, the wage or salary—goes on inexorably at the agreed-upon rate.

Imperfect as they may be, there are relative and derivative techniques for gauging human resources management, and the subject is much too critical to abandon for lack of perfect precision. Employee turnover and morale generally may indicate how well the individuals themselves feel their potential is being utilized. There are many reasons why this self-evaluation may be subject to a general bias, but it can be ignored only at great peril. Human resources accounting developed by Rensis Likert at the University of Michigan provides a procedure by which certain expenses relating to personnel are capitalized, thus relieving current operating statements of recruiting and training expenses not related to current results but imposing severe penalties for excessive turnover in the form of writeoffs

REDEFINING THE MANAGER'S JOB

against the operating results of the superior. The system does not provide a direct index of human resources management, but it very directly reminds the manager of his responsibilities in this regard.

Various forms of manpower budgeting are being used. No matter how subjective and how approximate, the exercise itself is highly instructive. These efforts will be intensified.

If we make the simplifying—and perhaps simple-minded—assumption that payroll expense is roughly related to the human resources applied, we can often make some edifying observations. Volume of physical production or dollars of gross margin produced per dollar of manufacturing payroll is a fairly common operating indicator of productivity. But what of the nonproduction people—including the management personnel? Should 50 percent of the middle management payroll really be concentrated in the eastern division? If 15 percent of the head-office salaries are in the public relations department, does that really reflect a proper balance of resource allocation? When there are apparent discrepancies between the manpower cost involved and the relative importance of the results achieved, it suggests that either the salary schedules are haywire or there is a misallocation of human resources. Either these guys are paid too much or there are too many of them.

It is not unusual to discover that the hot new division that is expected to make the future of the company enjoys the services of only 2 percent of the support-staff payroll. Can you really expect it to come through with the results you hope for with only that allocation of specialized skills? Is the manager managing human resources effectively?

Of course you could "capitalize" human resources, as some sophisticated managements do other expensive equipment they borrow to use. A common factor used for capital equipment is "three times annual gross rental." For real estate it is apt to be seven or eight times rental. Since there is no hope of

HOW WE CAN KEEP SCORE

being elegant about this calculation, let's say that the resource value of personnel is five times their annual payroll cost. If wage or salary costs are analogous to rent, maintenance, and operating costs of the asset, return from management must be over and above that. If you recalculate your operating statements with these assets added to your total utilized asset figure, how well is the management performing?

Actually, five times annual salary is probably much less than the sums spent by parents, taxpayers, and previous employers to produce the human resources you employ. From the point of view of the social economy as a whole, you really should have to realize a much higher productive output from those resources. If the Thirteenth Amendment had never been ratified, think of what you would have to pay today for a skilled slave. Manpower, Inc., might be in the business of raising and training employees for American enterprises. What would you expect to pay for a qualified maintenance engineer, accountant, copywriter, lathe operator, file clerk? Manpower, Inc., remember, has been supporting him for some 20 years, maybe sent him to college, and has discounted its investment forward at 10 percent a year. Remember, too, that you are still going to have to feed him, clothe him, furnish him recreation, and provide for him in his old age—in other words, effectively pay his salary. If you put that imaginary purchase price onto the asset side of your balance sheet, how would your return on investment look? No wonder slavery never was a popular institution in the industrial states!

Actually the classical dichotomy of "capital-intensive" and "labor-intensive" enterprises is fundamentally misleading. People represent a tremendous amount of capital investment—particularly in our modern society. It is just that the people investment never shows up on a balance sheet because it is made by society at large, not by the organization that employs the people. If you think in terms of that kind of "social

REDEFINING THE MANAGER'S JOB

capital," you wonder how much added value society should expect from the talent committed to something like the space effort or other talent-consuming government programs.

If we are going to judge managers by the effectiveness with which they utilize resources, we need some kind of accounting that will allow us to view manpower as a resource rather than merely as an expense. We need a way to focus the manager's attention directly on the problem of getting the maximum contribution at the highest possible level of competence from each of the people he deploys. This will not be done by imposing a certain schedule of personnel development courses, by enforcing regular review routines, or even by demanding trouble-free hierarchical succession. We need to avoid looking at the "book value" of people as codified in their conventional organizational relationships and to accept responsibility for a return on their maximum use value.

When personnel costs are perceived to be "too high," it is frequently because manpower resources are not being effectively deployed—which simply means they are not producing enough value to justify their commitment. The fault may be that the value is just not there or that the system constrains the productivity of the people. In either case it is the function of management to see that this resource is positioned so that it does make an optimal contribution. Reasonably good managers will seldom commit new capital to a marginal enterprise. They will frequently try to salvage a sick project by "putting more men on it." If they look at their people as a resource rather than as an expendable, they will not make this error so frequently.

THE LABORER IS WORTHY OF HIS HIRE

In spite of some envious sniping from other departments, there is usually little institutional resistance to paying salesmen

HOW WE CAN KEEP SCORE

well. This is not because selling talents are particularly scarce or because the salesmen's contribution is uniquely more important than that of other functions. It is because the relationship of salesmen's productivity to their income is so clearly apparent. To the extent that the salesman is on commission, every time he makes another dime the company makes another dime. As a consequence, rather than resent his rising income the company will spend money on sales literature and technical support and advertising to increase his take-home pay—and his sales. The company very much wants to increase his productivity.

The same rationale should apply equally to all other positions in the company. It is just that the relationship is not so self-apparent and its calculation is complex at best. Clearly, if you could double the output of a milling-machine operator *without committing other additional resources,* you would gladly double his wage rate because you would have also doubled his contribution to profit. Most commonly, such productivity gains do require other resources—specifically capital—but the allocation of the benefits between the two kinds of resources is really not that difficult, since the return required on the money investment can be calculated precisely. Unions that resist increasing productivity are perversely insensitive to this basic fact, in that they impose an artificial ceiling on the value of their members as productive resources. But managements should also be acutely aware of the tremendous advantage of deploying their human resources in such a way as to enable them to make the maximum possible productive contribution.

Supporting personnel are much harder to evaluate than production people, but, in principle at least, if you have a $30,000-a-year engineer who is worth having at all, presumably he produces value somewhat in excess of $30,000. Wouldn't it be nice if you could make him twice as valuable to the enterprise, pay him $60,000 and at the same time double that marginal contribution? You might be able to do that without additional

REDEFINING THE MANAGER'S JOB

capital investment because the productivity of professional people is notoriously volatile under changing circumstances.

Certainly it would be satisfying if we could devise a convenient index reflecting turnover, assignments completed, skills developed, and maybe a brainwave reading that would tell us how well human resources are being used. It's been tried with singular lack of success. We will have to rely on indirect measures and subjective evaluations.

Emphasis on results will certainly help. If the results are not forthcoming, there is a human deficiency somewhere: faulty judgment, inappropriate assignment, inadequate training, improper organization. Open communications help, too. Suggestion-box bonus systems work pretty well for some companies, but have you ever heard of one being used to suggest a reorganization or reassignment? You might get a comparable effect from an ombudsman.

There is one very simple, logical thing that can be done. If you want managers to get the best out of people—pay for it! A cash bonus related to salary, for each subordinate promoted, is the most obvious way to call this desire to people's attention. It may produce a little unhealthy flesh peddling, but that will be more than compensated by the reduction in talent hoarding.

The other simple thing that can be done is to hold managers responsible for the success of the personnel assignments they make. The prevailing system that blames a failure on the assigned person is backward. It is like blaming the unsuccessful capital venture on the quality of the money that went into it. The really good "judges of people" are the ones who spend a lot of effort understanding people. If the scoring system makes it explicit that such consideration is required because the results will be evaluated, there is a much higher probability that it will get done.

The most significant step, however, is to make a specific provision to rate every manager on his success in enhancing the contributions of his people to the enterprise. This is not the same as encouraging "management development" that tends to deal with raising potential and can degenerate into a sterile routine of seminars and workshops. Potential is great if you ever cash it in, but we are talking about the productivity of human resources now.

The manager must be impressed with the realization that he and he alone can create the opportunity for people to be productive. At the very least he has to enable his people to produce, enough beyond what they would have if he weren't there, to cover his salary and expenses. This is a very important part of his job. In fact, in some respects it is the essence of a managerial job. Managers should understand that they will be judged on it.

"FREE" RESOURCES

Managers of all kinds of enterprises do employ public resources and are being reminded of it with increasing force and frequency. Some of these public resources, such as air and water, were once used in economics courses as classical examples of commodities that have value but no price because they are infinitely available. We realize now that this was a poor example, because they increasingly do have a price, either in effluent charges or treatment costs.

Airports, harbor facilities, highways, and navigable waterways are traditionally built with public funds. So are waterworks and sewer systems. These resources are provided on the assumption that they will serve some useful purpose. To the extent that the facilities are enjoyed by institutional users, the managers of those enterprises are accountable for the value produced through their use. Enterprises are effectively subsidized through access to these free capital assets and sometimes to services as well.

How may we judge the quality of management's steward-

REDEFINING THE MANAGER'S JOB

ship of these public resources? We can at least begin to set some boundaries. We can demand that managers not be profligate in their use of these resources, that they not squander them wantonly or thoughtlessly, whether or not legally constrained.

We can pretty much assume that in the future the sociopolitical system will forbid any manager from completely consuming or destroying a nonrenewable public resource. We must accept, too, that the cost/benefit analysis of the use of even a renewable resource like air or water or social amenity will be imposed by institutions outside the managerial context. This to some extent relieves the manager and his evaluators of the necessity to determine how many cents of cost saving per ton of steel produced is a reasonable return on a 10 percent degradation in the quality of the atmosphere. "Society" will sometimes express its cost/benefit judgments in the form of user charges or taxes, as in the case of highways and harbors, municipal services, and even effluent penalties. Sometimes only the absolute limit of the judgment is codified as a legal proscription.

Mostly society is ambiguous, vacillatory, and in disagreement about the value of public resources and of the benefit that would be an acceptable recompense for their use. The responsibility of the manager, then, can only be to attempt to estimate where the median of the public evaluation lies and to employ the public resources at his disposal to try to realize a benefit commensurate with that judgment. This is an uncomfortable position because almost no one will agree with his specific balancing of use against benefit. It also is expedient and wishy-washy and smacks of "getting away with what you can." However, it is the only reasonable solution. The alternatives are, on the one hand, to deny any responsibility for the use and conservation of public resources or, on the other, for each manager to assume access to revealed truth and impose his personal evaluation of just how much good for General Motors is in fact good for the country.

In our management appraisal system, we can require that every manager periodically file, not an environmental impact statement, but an "environmental interaction statement." He should specifically acknowledge any tax forgiveness his enterprise enjoys, any tariff protection afforded, any public facilities he employs. He should document his interactions with public agencies, both the regulatory and the helpful ones. He should acknowledge any particular burdens he imposes on any public facilities for waste disposal, or transportation, for instance, any nuisances he creates in the form of noise, smells, ugliness, and any changes that have occurred in these impositions since the last statement. And then he should relate these consequences to specific productive results.

An idle gesture? No, not entirely. If we acknowledge that control of professional managers must ultimately be self-control, we have to start educating them to accept that responsibility; and we have no choice but to assume that for the most part they are capable of carrying that burden. The first step is to make them aware of the complete scope of their responsibility.

Over and above that, and perhaps of more immediate significance, these statements as part of a management information system will provide a valuable record of the interactions between the enterprise and the public environment. No matter how perfunctorily prepared, the statements will provide an opportunity to detect and monitor bad or deteriorating situations. And they will provide an opportunity to assess how well and responsibly an individual manager is dealing with his obligations to avoid abuse of these public resources. In the evolving social climate in which senior managers are likely to be held legally responsible for actions of their subordinates that are adjudged to be inimical to the public interest, this is of no small value.

RETURN ON RESOURCES (ROR)

What we are developing is a multidimensional feedback system that gives us several parallel indicators of how well the enterprise is progressing—how well it is being managed. The common central concept is "return on resources."

First we have the dollar-denominated resources that we will look at in two ways: strategic and operational. Although the calculations will be different and therefore the numbers will come out differently, the rationale is a refinement of the conventional return-on-investment calculation. We shall call it "ROI_1."

Our second factor is the return on the organizational, commercial, and technological resources of the enterprise that normally do not appear on the balance sheet but that are real nonetheless and can be identified quite explicitly. We may call this index "return on intangibles"—"ROI_2."

Then we have the measure of how well the human resources are being utilized—how much value is being produced per time/quality unit of manpower committed. We will call that "return on individuals"—"ROI_3."

Finally we have the underlying resources of social institutions, public facilities, and the natural environment that must be available if the enterprise is to function at all. A valuable output must result from the consumption or utilization of these resources or their use will eventually be denied to the managers. We can view these prerequisite resources as "infraresources" and conceptualize a "return on infraresources"—"ROI_4"—even while acknowledging that assessment of this return must be largely subjective.

Thus we have a management information system that gives us a measure of the efficiency of the enterprise as a utilizer of resources according to the formulation

$$ROR = f(ROI_1, ROI_2, ROI_3, ROI_4)$$

HOW WE CAN KEEP SCORE

As a refinement we can profile individual positions in an enterprise by weighting the parameters within this formulation. We have already commented that different kinds and levels of responsibility will change the relative significance of the two components of ROI_1. Both components of ROI_1 bear particularly heavily on a manufacturing executive responsible for massive physical facilities or a financial officer disposing of large sums of money. A marketing manager or a patent counsel might find the great bulk of his accountability in ROI_2. The director of research or the sales manager would be heavily biased toward ROI_3. The general counsel or director of public communications would justify his performance largely in ROI_4.

But the key rationale is that management employs resources to produce results.

13
WHAT HAPPENED TO PRODUCTION MANAGEMENT?

What has become of the hero of the 1940s—the production expert in the slouch hat and dirty khakis, shouting and stomping about in the dirt and the noise, keeping the wheels turning and the product coming out by a combination of scab-knuckled know-how and personal determination? Is he dead or in hiding? Did the system force him out or has he been bred out of the race?

He concentrated on results, at least in the sense of physical output. He had a hands-on awareness of the physical resources he employed. And a good one had a high regard for the people who worked for him.

WHAT HAPPENED TO PRODUCTION MANAGEMENT?

DECLINE AND FALL OF THE PRODUCTION MANAGER

Production managers should be the first to grasp the concept of management as the agency by which resources become results. But they are not. Production management is the critical soft spot in the U.S. management system. The much vaunted American production savvy, long taken for granted, is slipping through our fingers. Foreign-made products are outclassing their American competition in price, performance, and delivery all over the world—including the United States. Faulty merchandise has become a public scandal. Missed delivery dates and cost overruns are accepted as a commonplace. Plant personnel frequently blame the problem on the deteriorating quality of production labor, and the front-office types shake their heads ruefully and go on to write impassioned after-dinner speeches in which they point out that the world is going to hell.

The simple fact is that the production managers have been faked out of position. They no longer are managing production. They seldom are consulted about the design of the production facilities. They often have little control over the quality of their raw materials. The union and the industrial relations department carry on a continuing dialogue that usually excludes the production managers. Safety, quality control, and environmental experts are constantly second-guessing them. While the production managers were not looking, somebody stole their lunch.

As a consequence, production managers have become alienated from the rest of management. They do not view their responsibilities broadly because they feel they are not permitted to. They become preoccupied with technical matters: unit efficiencies and fancy instrumentation schemes. They are "too busy" to participate in general management committee meet-

REDEFINING THE MANAGER'S JOB

ings because no one is interested in "their" problems. And the meetings go on quite cheerfully without them because their dour silence when they are present contributes little to the general management agenda. The sense of isolation feeds on itself.

When there is a production foul-up comes the ultimate put-down. The chief executive officer doesn't call in the production manager and boot his tail, much less fire him. The CEO knows that if he doesn't get a completely demoralized "these things happen" kind of response, he will hear, "I told them this would happen," or "The damn plant never was designed right," or "How do you expect us to process this crap they are giving us for feed stock?" There are always a lot of "theys" to take the blame. Call this garden-variety buck-passing if you like, but the potential is so great that it is virtually irresistible.

Rather than go through this routine, the CEO is much more likely to order a revision of interdepartmental procedures, direct the personnel department to arrange some short courses in interpersonal skills, and, almost always, set up a top-level "operations committee" to meet weekly. This committee will bring together those who have been making the critical decisions but who will point out that they have no "operating control" over the production manager, who has nominal operating control but denies responsibility for results. The CEO presides. Faced with this zoo, he frequently ends up trying to run the production department himself through the committee, even though he may have no manufacturing experience. The results are seldom satisfactory.

"YE MUST BE BORN AGAIN"

The solution is obviously to put the production people back in charge of production. That means changing a lot of

WHAT HAPPENED TO PRODUCTION MANAGEMENT?

prevailing attitudes in many parts of the organization. That is not easy; but if you keep the principle clearly before you, it has the credibility of a certain compelling logic. Production managers must be broken out of their largely self-imposed isolation. They have to be reintroduced as fully participating members of the management team. They must exploit the potential for innovative contribution from members of the production organization rather than let them function as a two-legged accessory of the manufacturing machinery.

Support services must be made supportive, not dictatorial. The relationship between production and engineering—now often approaching trench warfare—must be depolarized. Of transcendent importance, the responsibility for results must be specified and localized. The only reasonable place to locate it is with the production manager.

The production people have custody of the major part of the enterprise's fixed tangible assets. They must be impressed with the principle that they have a direct, personal responsibility for managing those assets—making them productive. They are the only ones who can "get their hands on them," turn them on and off, move them from here to there, make them work. The other officers are at least one or two organizational steps removed from these assets. The other departments have other resources they must manipulate profitably. But the production people are the ones to get the maximum value out of the production resources.

It helps to do the arithmetic for them. Whether it is a unit manager, a plant manager, or the vice-president of manufacturing, he must know the alternate use value of the fixed assets and any inventory under his control. He must understand the company's goal for overall return on assets employed, and be made to realize that the company must depend on him to make his portion of the assets at least that productive.

Almost certainly the production people, with false mod-

REDEFINING THE MANAGER'S JOB

esty, will demur and say, "Many people must contribute to the profits of the company." This is undoubtedly so, but they have been entrusted with the primary stewardship of all this value and they must accept primary responsibility for its utilization in a moral sense. Don't let them get bogged down in accounting sophistries.

When they begin to absorb that notion, they are ready for the fact that many of the resources they control do not appear on the balance sheet. For example, there is the established production know-how of the company, whether or not patented. If anyone is going to enhance the benefits derived from that know-how, it has to be the production people, because no one else is really working on the problem. They should be judged and compensated for their skill in exploiting these resources.

There is more. They have many dozens or even hundreds of workers in their plants, probably the largest number of personnel in the corporation. These people have skills, intelligence, potential for enthusiasm and innovation. They also constitute a resource over which the production managers have the most direct control. These managers therefore have the responsibility to see that this resource is utilized with the greatest possible productive results—not as slave drivers, certainly, and not necessarily out of humanistic sentiment, but as responsible resources managers. This concept will probably be a great shock to them.

Finally, they must accept their responsibility for managing the public resources they employ—air, water, and social amenity—but this concept will be the hardest of all to absorb and the process may require considerable persistence.

How do production people react to such a charter? With shock, bafflement, and inevitably the plaint, "We cannot accept such overall responsibility. 'They' have to cooperate. We have to depend on 'them' to supply us with supporting services." The proper response is that this may very well be so, but the organization really has to depend on production manage-

WHAT HAPPENED TO PRODUCTION MANAGEMENT?

ment to make the production resources productive and as a consequence must also depend on production management to obtain whatever advice and expert services it needs to manage production.

Once production people are convinced that these are really the rules of the game, the effect, once the fright reaction wears off, can be quite electrifying. The top production management group in one company, presented with this definition of its responsibilities, almost literally ran out of the conference room at the end of the session to begin doing things it had previously thought were impossible or not in its province. The measurable results in the next few months were worth hundreds of thousands of dollars.

LINE AND STAFF

To make the system continue to work, of course, you have to be consistent in the way you manage your managers. If you tell a production man that you are paying him for maximizing the productivity of the resources placed at his disposition, you must in fact reward him on that basis and not for good intentions. You must point out to him that if he finds himself in the position of taking over an ill-conceived and clumsily executed new facility, no one will suffer more than he. *He* will sustain the excessive down time, the bad morale, and the high scrap rates that will directly affect the productive performance on which *he* will be judged.

Obviously he will not be permitted to reject the "baby" after it is deposited on his doorstep. It will do no good to complain after the fact that those eggheads in engineering or on the site selection committee "goofed again. If they had only asked me!" It becomes clearly his responsibility *and* in his self-interest to ensure that he contributes his special insights before the fact—before the plant is put in the wrong place, designed for

REDEFINING THE MANAGER'S JOB

unattainable uniformity of raw material, laid out so that service personnel cannot get at the machines for maintenance, dependent on unreasonable standards of operator attention.

If he thinks he knows a way to do it better or faster or cheaper, it must be on *his* initiative that somebody hears about it and listens. *He* has a direct concern in working out a testing routine with quality control to keep his reject rate down. *He* should be begging the industrial relations people for advice on how to handle a sticky personnel problem. *He* becomes a "buyer," a demander of staff services; and it should be abundantly clear that *he* is expected to get the services he needs and get the best ones he can lay hands on.

There can be no ambiguity about the fact that the production manager is primarily responsible to see that the company has the kind and quantity of manufacturing capacity it needs—no other and no more—and that the available resources are used with maximum profit effectiveness. He does whatever is necessary to fulfill that responsibility. His superiors in turn must exploit every device they can conceive to relate his monetary and organizational rewards to his resource effectiveness.

If production executives are put in this position, they automatically become part of the comprehensive management of the enterprise—part of the business. They can no longer withdraw into the plant and simply turn the crank on the manufacturing machine. They must be concerned; they must inform themselves about all aspects of the undertaking. You begin to break down the "two cultures" into which so many production people like to dichotomize the world—the "makers" and the "paper shufflers." You avoid the typical gripe: "Keep those head-office guys out of *my* plant!" Or later, when things fall apart: "Don't bother me with all that crap now! Can't you see I've got enough problems?"

Of course you have to tell the same story to the staff service departments. They too have corporate resources for which

WHAT HAPPENED TO PRODUCTION MANAGEMENT?

they are responsible; but they cannot—and should not try to—control the production processes of the company, because that is another area of responsibility. Their responsibility definitely extends to the maintenance and development of certain areas of expert competence required to meet the recurrent needs of operations, but you don't expect them to shove it down anybody's throat. On the other hand, as a "seller" of professional services, they are surely going to go out of business if nobody buys.

Similarly, even as a "buyer," the production manager cannot *command* performance from his "suppliers." He cannot do it even if he contracts for services outside the organization. However, that is part of his education. He has to find a way to obtain the help he needs on the priorities he deems to be appropriate—because he will be accountable for the results and will not be permitted to alibi that "they" fell down on the job. If this makes the production manager more of a "politician," so be it. That is part of management too, and at least it will get him around talking to people.

Will this procedure invariably work? Not 100 percent. It will help because it is logically sound, but a deep accretion of bad habits and attitudes will have to be worked off, and that will not be easy. However, if the resources/results concept of management is not established in the production function, it will not take root anywhere.

It is symptomatic that the image of the get-the-job-done production man is so badly tarnished. The whole concept of actually producing something of utilitarian value has become obscured if not actually spurned. The prestige engineering schools are producing "engineering scientists" almost exclusively. The cream of the crop from the other schools goes into research or design, if not into sales or planning or something even more "white collar." Production engineering just has no appeal.

The production management departments in the MBA

REDEFINING THE MANAGER'S JOB

programs are starving for lack of students—even the students with undergraduate engineering degrees usually elect other options. One big college of business not only has eliminated the option but doesn't even have a single course in production management. In recent years the literature of "management science" has been nearly devoid of significant contributions in production management. When was the last time you saw an article on "production" in the *Harvard Business Review?*

"THE TIMES THEY ARE A'CHANGING"

With few first-quality novices in the field, with a dearth of innovative ideas, and with a pervasive lack of recognition and prestige for the senior practitioners, the field is sick unto death, all right, and it reflects a pervasive social attitude. But the situation may be ripe for a swing. The social attitude may be changing. Young people in increasing numbers say they want to do something "real"—usually meaning something tangible, something with their hands. Well, plants are where "real" physical things happen—not just at a potter's wheel. Plants are where pollution happens too, and can be made not to happen. The production man with his hands figuratively on the levers of control is ultimately the major determiner of the degree of environmental insult. Maybe the "new culture" will induce some would-be stockbrokers and copywriters to come into the works and get their hands dirty and make things happen.

The "works"—the "satanic mills"—have a bad image. They dirty the environment. They exploit and degrade the workers. They produce a lot of trashy nonessentials. But these are superficial attributes. They can be changed. In fact they have changed a great deal since the stereotypes propagated by the liberal establishment were created several generations ago, and they are changing more rapidly today than ever before.

WHAT HAPPENED TO PRODUCTION MANAGEMENT?

A factory creates something tangible and of value out of gross materials. It need not be dirty, depressing, or wasteful; nor are many of the products trivial. There is a real social value in making a useful product better, cheaper, more efficiently. An old tradition of pride in this kind of accomplishment seems to be almost completely suppressed. Perhaps this kind of satisfaction could be made to appeal to a "now" generation, stridently critical of empty formalities.

But to attract recruits to this kind of function requires that it be given some substance. It must truly entail responsibility for making things happen. Production people must be given back their manhood. Industry really has no choice. Exogenous factors are forcing innovation. Automation, the escalating capital intensiveness of virtually every industry, changes in the workweek, shifts in the sources of energy and materials, the demands for environmental protection, and the burgeoning production efficiencies of foreign competitors—all demand new responses from those responsible for the manufacturing function.

Industry must put some really able young people into production responsibilities and then must repeatedly retrain the higher echelons of production managers to make them conceive of themselves as managers, not just as exalted operators. Industry leaders must reestablish the traditional balance between money, marketing, and manufacturing. They may even have to restore a little bit of the pride that inspired people to say, "We are steelmakers," "We are railroaders," or "We are bakers," before it became fashionable to say, "We are in materials of construction," "We are in the transportation industry," or "We are in the business of satisfying consumer needs."

The responsibility for utilizing the production resources optimally must be placed squarely on the shoulders of the production managers. Some will buckle under the load, but many will respond with enthusiasm, initiative, and responsibility.

REDEFINING THE MANAGER'S JOB

Somebody has got to be in charge or, as is only too apparent, the stuff doesn't get made, it gets made wrong, or it costs too much.

With materials running short, energy costs skyrocketing, competition becoming brutal, costs of fixed investments climbing, and pollution-free operations mandatory, production management has got to be the key to successful enterprise in the remainder of the twentieth century. We cannot permit the "makers" to persist in a role of second-class managers. Nor can we afford the luxury of second-rate operation of our productive facilities.

14
BEGIN AT THE END

There is nothing wrong with organization charts. They act as sort of a road map to tell you where to find people, how they are grouped together, who is responsible to whom. They are a kind of notation to record the relationships of the people involved in a group activity. Like a musical notation, they record which combination comes after which and where the solos and the ensemble work come in. But they don't play a song.

There is nothing wrong with job descriptions. They are in effect footnotes to the organization chart. They tell you—if they are well written—what goes on in all those little boxes and

REDEFINING THE MANAGER'S JOB

what those solid and dotted lines mean. They may even clue you as to what the titles mean.

What neither the organization chart nor the job descriptions tell you is how things get done. They are concerned with what people do and how they are supposed to work together. Neither says anything about what is supposed to get accomplished or why. Nor do they tell you what the people can use to get their jobs done. It is not surprising, therefore, that juggling the boxes or changing the titles seems to have very little effect in getting things done.

This is not to say you don't have to organize people to get things done. If everybody is trying to do everything, you have nothing but a conscientious mob. But it does seem perverse that almost all organization structure is designed around the kinds of activities that people are supposed to engage in. If the purpose of an organization is to employ certain resources to produce certain results, why not structure it around the results? The first consideration should be the specific ends that have to be achieved. The relationships of people should be structured accordingly, and the routine continuing tasks distributed for maximum convenience. Current practice is first to make sure all the routine bases are covered and then to fob off the important jobs on ad hoc task forces that people are supposed to serve on in addition to their "regular responsibilities." It is convenient, but it doesn't make sense.*

It is particularly convenient because the routine tasks don't change very much. The boxes on the chart pretty much stay put, and the good loyal employee can progress regularly up through the levels until he reaches Peter's Pinnacle, and nobody has to think very much about it.

---

* It has been suggested with considerable plausibility that formal organizations should perform only the routine tasks. All important work is always accomplished by spontaneous, unofficial "huddles." See V. Dallas Merrell, *Huddling: The Informal Way to Management Success*, AMACOM (1979).

BEGIN AT THE END

Unfortunately, the objectives that are important to an enterprise keep changing. The threat or the opportunity that arises unexpectedly outside the organization requires a quick, concentrated response, or the situation will pass beyond control. But that means continually redeploying resources, both human and other, to concentrate them on the important jobs. Yes, it does, and that in turn requires a lot of thinking and evaluating, and that is a lot of work. But the alternative is to shuffle along in the comfortable old shoe organization that, at best, reflects what was important some time in the past.

THE OBJECTIVES TREE

"Designing an organization structure is not the first step but the last," Peter Drucker said. Alfred D. Chandler put it more succinctly: "Structure follows strategy." You must know what has to be done before you can design an optimal organization structure. That is why a complete objectives tree (see Chapter 10) is the best key to an effective organization. Visualize the entire tree on one huge chart. In practice it will probably be in a book or a file.

The four or five Key Objectives are arrayed in a column on the left and the long list of individual project objectives in a column on the far right. The chart is then further divided into columns, each column representing a level in the organizational hierarchy from left to right: chief executive officer, group vice-presidents, functional vice-presidents, staff department heads, product managers, section heads, project supervisors—or some such sequence. All the intermediate objectives are then arranged in the columns corresponding to the organizational position of the person responsible for attaining the objective. The CEO is responsible for the key objectives on the left, since he is the only one who has the scope of authority to control sales growth, profitability, and other global intentions.

REDEFINING THE MANAGER'S JOB

The project supervisors obviously must complete the project assignments on the right. The middle managers are in the appropriate columns in the middle, with the intermediate subobjectives for which they are directly responsible arrayed below them. The relevant objectives are connected to give a sort of family-tree effect.

Just charting the objectives tree in this way is likely to reveal the problem. If it looks like a plate of spaghetti with lines criss-crossing and twisting all over the sheet, only one conclusion is possible: People are not arranged in a way that makes it easy to get the important jobs done.

Are divisional department heads frequently responsible for subobjectives in support of staff department heads' objectives? Does the divisional sales vice-president have to scrounge all over the organization to achieve the subobjectives necessary and sufficient to fulfill his objective responsibility? Does the corporate financial officer have to look in a couple dozen places for the performance that will ensure achievement of his cash flow objective? Some criss-crossing and level jumping are inevitable; but if there is a great deal of it, that would strongly suggest that your formal organization is working against the work flow. There is a structural dislocation in the organization that is incompatible with the declared objectives of the enterprise. Better change the organization to fit the job than try to redivide the responsibilities to fit the organization.

It makes a lot more sense to group people together who have to work together toward common goals than to keep them together in boxes labeled with the kind of college degrees they have or the kind of equipment they use. It will shorten the lines of communication, decrease paperwork, and greatly enhance the likelihood of achieving those results that are critical to the enterprise. When the objective structure changes, the people will have to be shuffled. So be it! Institutions reorganize now more often than they like to admit, be-

BEGIN AT THE END

cause none of the classical systems of organization really work.*

Packaging up units of results to create a hierarchy of objectives rather than a hierarchy of individuals affords an automatic insight into the true human dynamics of the enterprise. The distribution of the assignment of objective responsibility at any level makes it immediately clear where the work of the enterprise is really expected to be done. Are there individuals in supposedly responsible positions whose names just do not appear at all? If so, just what are they supposed to be accomplishing? Are they just there to keep the machinery running smoothly? You don't pay an oiler what you pay the operating engineer, even though there may be a whale of a bang if the oiling is not done.

Is the same individual shown on the chart as responsible for a dozen or more significant objectives? That looks like a bottleneck. Whether it's because the guy is competent, a sucker, an empire builder, or whatever, George seems to be doing it all. George had better get some relief. Even if he could get it all done on time, which is questionable, the stress on him will be terrific, and the organization would be in an awful bind if he were to get hit by a truck or a job offer. Spread it around a little bit.

TASK FORCE ORGANIZATION

Call this "task force organization" if you like; the principle is to group people by what they have to get done, not by the

---

* The U.S. Department of Health, Education and Welfare averaged almost one "final" reorganization a year during its 25 years of existence. Now, of course, it has been completely bifurcated.

REDEFINING THE MANAGER'S JOB

kind of activities they engage in. You could call it "zero-base organization," too.

The conventional objection to this procedure is that it makes people feel insecure—they have no organizational "home"; there is no center line of continuity in their activities. There is less to this objection than meets the eye. In the first place it is based on the long-outmoded assumption of lifetime tenure in a single organization. The fact is that the middle managers and the specialists who are most likely to be involved in multiple reassignments are notoriously job-mobile. If they are not reassigned fairly frequently, they are quite likely to reassign themselves unilaterally to a new team in another organization. Task force organization is much more compatible with the increasingly individualistic lifestyles than is the traditional line-and-staff structure.

It is contended, with considerable plausibility, that people "enjoy being with their own kind." Granted, but the mathematician who works with a biologist on a research team does not feel particularly alienated. The oboeist who sits next to the horn player does not necessarily pine in loneliness. They recognize a fraternal community with other mathematicians and other oboeists, respectively, and they exercise that sense of community outside their working structure. Accountants will talk to accountants and salesmen will seek out other salesmen no matter what. There are many ways in which these collegial associations may be facilitated. It is not necessary to commit the formal organization structure to this purpose.

Quite the contrary. Grouping similarly oriented people in conventional "functional" departments can be quite literally dysfunctional. It leads to nothing so much as empire building. The individuals, by the act of their choice of specialty, imply that they think their chosen expertise is particularly important to the enterprise. It follows quite naturally in their opinion that the enterprise would benefit by having more people like them.

BEGIN AT THE END

The consequence is an inexorable pressure to enlarge their departments.*

The task force leader, on the other hand, except perhaps for some semipermanent teams as in plant production—has little incentive to build an empire since he anticipates eventual reassignment for himself and for the members of his task force. Furthermore, if he is to be judged not only by the results to be achieved but by the magnitude of the resources employed to achieve those results, he has a positive incentive to keep his team lean and active.

It can and will happen that one individual may end up assigned to fulfilling objectives that link him to more than one superior. This produces that bête noire of organizational orthodoxy, the person with more than one boss. But this arbitrary bogeyman is becoming rapidly deflated. Matrix-type organizations, becoming increasingly common, quite simply ignore it. Any independent contractor lives with it continually and accommodates it or does not survive. The fear of two bosses is a holdover from the days of dictatorial and often whimsical managers. In the presence of a "do as I say and don't ask questions" style of management, double accountability can be a real nutcracker.

On the other hand, if objective results are clearly defined and freely negotiated, accountability to more than one individual is not necessarily a problem. There is no system that can overcome the debilitating effects of divided responsibility, but divided accountability is easily tolerated if the total management system is suitably designed. But the design principle must be that of performance, not that of authority.

The least substantial objection to task force management

---

*C. Northcote Parkinson, creator of Parkinson's law, presents plausible documentation that in the conventional organization, administrative staff will increase 5 to 6 percent per year regardless of the workload.

REDEFINING THE MANAGER'S JOB

is that it is difficult to administer. Frankly, it is impossible to administer if you insist on a strict hierarchical, continuous supervision of everybody's activities. However, with results-based accountability such supervision is not only unnecessary but undesirable.

It does present some problems in assigning and scheduling people, but actually these problems are somewhat autotherapeutic. There will be individuals who will be chronically under- or unemployed—that is, who are seldom involved in a task force. The conclusion is pretty obvious. Either (1) they are simply redundant, (2) they are incompetent and no task force leader will put up with them, or (3) they may be useful and competent but are just too expensive. If the task force leaders are somehow held accountable for the resources they employ, including the salary budget, they will let you know very quickly if somebody's salary has gotten out of line. In any of these cases a separation would seem to be indicated.

With the best of planning, however, there will be some slack in the system; some individuals at any given time will be less than fully employed on priority projects. But keep in mind that the organizational system did not create the slack. The marginal excess of staff would have occurred under any system. It is just that in a rigid conventional organization it is almost impossible to identify temporary overcapacity in personnel. It may be somewhat discomfiting to have such frictional idleness shoved under your nose, but it does at least provide an opportunity to assign these people to low-urgency projects or to employ them in speculative explorations.

Of course somebody has to assign office space, explain the new profit-sharing plan, interface with the payroll department, and so forth. Remember your old homeroom teacher in high school; that's the sort of thing she used to do. It wasn't a full-time job, and she did it for about 25 kids. Yes, you always have to retain some kind of permanent, formal organization structure, but it has minimal importance and is not the overriding consideration in getting the work done.

And what about keeping the order-processing department running, or supervising the library or the personnel records, and doing all the other things that have to be done to keep the shop going? Well, you could sort of deal these around the management group wherever they seem to fit conveniently. However, you may be better advised to entrust these routines to less talented people—administrators rather than managers—perhaps some of those you have discovered you are not willing to make responsible for important objectives. The trick is to keep the organizational power where the leverage is and not squander it on the merely necessary.

Actually, after a shakedown period, the lines of responsibility in the hierarchy of objectives will tend to stabilize into something that looks pretty much like a conventional organization chart. But don't let it ossify. The job determines the organization; the organization doesn't dictate the job. However, in certain ongoing activities—notably sales and production—the nature of the objectives will not change much over time and the organizational relationships will therefore tend to be relatively permanent.

LINE AND STAFF

What happens to the classical dichotomy of "line" and "staff" under this kind of organization? Well, in the first place, we will have to acknowledge that those categories are pretty well muddied up already.

Once upon a time—and maybe it is a fairy tale—staff people were the expert advisers, and line people had the power of decision and ultimate responsibility for results. This is seldom clearly the case now. "Line" and "staff" no longer have

REDEFINING THE MANAGER'S JOB

any explicit meaning. In extreme instances, the staff people set the procedures, make the schedules, do the planning, buy the raw materials, hire the personnel; about the only thing the so-called "line manager" can decide is when to paint the building. Now who is responsible for what results?

The opposite case is at least as familiar. The "operations" people say in effect, "Keep those feather-merchants from headquarters out of our hair! Let them shuffle their papers while we get on with the business!" But when things go sour it is because engineering designed a lousy plant, or the lab did not come through with new products, or industrial relations did not prevent a strike. This is the "heads I win, tails you lose" situation. The "line" takes credit for successes and has an official scapegoat for the problems. No wonder staff people get irritable. If we start by assigning clear-cut responsibility for results, however, the buck stops passing at the very beginning.

The task force leader could very well be a "staff" specialist or a "line" operator. In either case, whoever has the objective responsibility has the concomitant responsibility to cajole, coerce, negotiate, or otherwise contrive to obtain the special services needed to solve the problem. If a task force manager is too stupid or too inflexible or too irascible to obtain the expert help he needs, he will not achieve the results expected from the resources at his disposal. Then he is in hot water, and there is no question of where the fault lies.

He may bring a specialist into his task force as a full-time member for an extended period of time. If the performance requirements are persistent, the association may become essentially permanent. To the extent that this occurs, some staff departments will tend to disperse throughout the organization. Some may actually disappear. This is entirely consistent with the principle of putting the resources where the job that has to be done is.

However, there will be tasks that require special competencies to a limited degree or for a short time. In those cases the responsible manager will effectively negotiate to obtain those services from a central group of specialists. If for any reason he does not think he can get adequate assistance in house, he is free to contract the service from outside.

HELP FROM OUTSIDE

If too many managers go to the outside, there is obviously something wrong with the professional competence, the willingness, or the cost-efficiency of the in-house group. Presumably there is a staff manager explicitly responsible for recruiting and training specialized personnel to provide certain services. He has to deliver those services when needed and at an acceptable cost. If he does not, there is no question of who is at fault. The staff did not achieve the results that would justify their existence.

This is a buyer-seller relationship, and it is the only one that will ultimately eliminate the traditional frustrating, resource-wasting, line-staff frictions. One party is responsible for ultimate results and the other for professional competence. This kind of interaction has been carried on successfully for thousands of years. It is involved in hundreds of thousands of transactions every day, and no one worries very much about the personal interactions. Yes, there are unhappy buyers and inept sellers. But the problem tends to be self-correcting. Nobody worries too much about how the general contractor gets performance out of his subcontractors. There is no question of where the responsibility lies, and the prime contractor is very unlikely to get any relief under his contract on the basis that "they"—the subs—didn't perform as required. If the prime contractor takes a beating a couple of times, he finds some way to obtain the special services he requires—or he is going out of business.

There is nothing ungentlemanly or junglelike about this

REDEFINING THE MANAGER'S JOB

relationship. If it were so brutal or unnatural or unpleasant, there could not be so many people who persist in operating their own businesses.

Now it may very well be that there is a temperamental difference between the kind of people who enjoy conducting their own businesses and the kind attracted to organization management. But if that difference is solely in the willingness to accept personal responsibility, then we are in bad trouble indeed.

There are very few corporate services you cannot now buy from truly independent commercial organizations: engineering, research, advertising, maintenance, accounting, distribution—right down the list. The only reason for maintaining in-house capability is cost, convenience, and quality—in other words, superior economic performance. By operating the specialized services on a project/results basis, you can keep the issue of who does what, when, and for whom on a completely rational basis. It is the best possible insurance against empire building.

There are certain central staff groups that should not be dispersed through the objective-oriented organization. They are the control services (as differentiated from the support services): safety, quality control, sanitation, the controller's office itself. However, these groups too are intended to produce some kind of results. They work for somebody. That somebody—the president or the board of directors, perhaps—should know what results are needed and will negotiate a commitment to get them.

The big advantage of concentrating on results instead of actions, of course, is that such a policy is likely to produce results rather than excuses. There is a big secondary benefit, however. The organization can be "flatter." If you will package your objectives and resources and delegate them as integral units to be related to results and not activities, you will be able to en-

BEGIN AT THE END

sure direction and guidance with much less direct supervision. By concentrating on accomplishments instead of on what people are doing, you can eliminate a lot of the conscientious babysitters ensconced in the middle of the hierarchy, busily watching how somebody else does his job.

SIMPLE ARITHMETIC

A fairly widely accepted rule of thumb is that the organizational "span of control" is about six. But what if you could increase that to ten? The Roman legions did. In an organization with 1,000 people at the working level and with a subordinate-superior ratio of six, you might have a chief executive, 4 vice-presidents, 26 department heads, and 167 supervisors. If you could raise the average ratio to ten, you would eliminate 67 supervisors and 20 middle managers. Think of what that would do to overhead salaries. And you would eliminate the vice-presidential level entirely. Think of what that would do to the volume of memoranda and the efficiency of communications.

If, as you subdivided your results responsibilities, you parceled out the subobjectives to ten subordinates, you could provide them with a good deal of direction, counsel, and control—if you keep your mind on results and keep your hands out of their operations. The fact that they may be responsible to you only for the results and may not work for you in the "traditional" sense will improve your concentration.

Consider this possible scenario, idealized perhaps but not entirely impractical. You would schedule one whole day to spend with each of your constituent managers each month—not an hour but a whole uninterrupted day. You would train that manager to arrive with his information in good order and up to date, and you would follow a fixed agenda. First you

187

REDEFINING THE MANAGER'S JOB

would review progress toward the agreed-upon objectives for which he is responsible to you and you would evaluate variances. Then you would review the assumptions on which the original objectives were set and see whether they are still valid or whether the objectives should be reconsidered. Then you would invite any new observations or proposals he might want to introduce. If there was any time left, you would listen to any operational problems or current crises on which he chose to request your advice or assistance.

If he wished to invite colleagues from his team or from parallel groups to participate for any part of the day, that would be his privilege. It should be his session, except that the order of the agenda with results first and operations last would be mandatory.

These sessions would take about 120 days a year; and if we assume that you spent a day a month with your boss, that uses up a little over half of your working time. That leaves you the remainder for seeing major customers, negotiating with outsiders or other in-company groups, going to trade association meetings, and arguing with government representatives. But what about committee meetings? If responsibility for results is clearly an individual matter, there will not be occasion for too many meetings. Such meetings will have only two functions: the first as a communications device to advise people of new information that for some reason is best transmitted face to face; the other to make decisions in broad policy areas or about matters that clearly fall outside any individual's delegated result area. All other matters would be handled in bilateral or occasionally multilateral negotiating sessions.

Would it work? Not perfectly, but consider what you might accomplish if you really blocked out a large enough chunk of time to thoroughly examine a single set of problems. You may not have a lot of choice much longer. If, as is being predicted increasingly, changing attitudes and lifestyles are destined to change large companies into "confederations of entrepreneurs," negotiations based on results will be the only way to deal with fellow workers; there won't be any subordinates any more. After all, that's the way you deal with your plumber. (See Appendix B.)

15
PAVLOV WAS RIGHT

It is all very well to speak of motivation, psychic income, and sense of accomplishment. In certain kinds of management responsibilities, these values may in fact be the predominant considerations for performance. However, even a manager of a not-for-profit enterprise has to eat, and in most of our material world, money is in fact a way of keeping score.* Men will make their self-evaluation and infer their value to the organization by the size of their financial return. Herb Buetow, president of

---

* This may not be generally true in Japan, but even there remuneration for top executives is tied to performance.

PAVLOV WAS RIGHT

3M in its most meteoric days, once said he didn't understand why people were so surprised that he had so many highly aggressive and effective young executives. He thought that problem had been solved several thousand years ago when they invented money. He may have been just slightly oversimplifying, but he was on the right track.

Money won't solve all problems, of course, but it is convenient, it is easy to measure, and, let's face it, it is the strongest single motivator for the vast majority of people. It is ridiculous to pretend this is not so and thus fail to use it in a conscious and coherent way to encourage productive behavior.

The correlation coefficient for the compensation of the chief executives of the 50 largest industrial corporations in the United States in 1977 as compared with their return on invested capital was a flat 0.0—in other words, completely random. The correlation coefficient for the compensation and the batting averages of the 14 highest-paid baseball players (excluding pitchers) was 0.8, or problably about as close as you can humanly expect. Something is wrong here. Management compensation is not being related to management performance.

Sure, managers like psychological strokes as much as the next guy; but if they are smart enough to belong in management, they are smart enough to know they can't cash the strokes in at the supermarket. A manager you can con with inspirational rhetoric and psychological sweet talk is bad news; you had better get rid of him because other people can play him for a sucker too. Sooner or later he's going to cost you money.

WHATEVER TURNS YOU ON

We all know that different people react differently to different incentives. But we proceed to forget that when we set up

REDEFINING THE MANAGER'S JOB

"incentive" programs. Standardized fringe benefits have almost no motivating force. A few people have begun to realize this in regard to annual bonus schemes and have moved from across-the-board "profit sharing" to more highly leveraged formulas. But almost nobody even tries to get maximum impact out of other costly programs.

Almost every organization these days has quite a smorgasbord of goodies to offer: vacation, fancy office, private secretary, insurance, pension, more travel, less travel, opportunities for education, conventions, professional activities, job security, changing assignments—and, of course, money now and the opportunity to make more money in the future. Some are more attractive to any given individual than others. How do you find out who relates to which? Why not ask?

Make this part of the discussion during the periodical performance review. Why should everybody get a fourth week's vacation after ten years? The guy who sometimes doesn't take all his vacation now is not going to be impressed. Someone else would really like to have six weeks. And don't say you do it for his own good. Let him decide what's good for him.

Why should every department head have a two-window office with a credenza and a sofa? To some people it's very important; others couldn't care less. Some people like familiar jobs; others get stale doing the same thing. Why not ask and find out so you can keep the short-attention-span type turned on with new assignments? The guy who is really hipped on job security—why not give him some kind of guaranteed tenure? (Make sure he understands that he is paying the price for it, however.)

Would this be a monster to administer? Not really. In the first place it would force the superior conducting an annual review to consider "what turns this guy on." That's already a gain. In the second place, even in this hedonistic age, it isn't necessary always to provide instant gratification. If you know the kind of rewards a person really would appreciate, you can look for opportunities to provide them. Ultimately most of the potential fringes can be equated on a dollar yardstick. An extra two weeks of vacation is equivalent to about a 5 percent raise, for instance. Those that can't be equated in this fashion may actually not cost anything at all beyond a little thought. And you will get a lot more bang for your incentive buck.

Of course, not everybody will be treated alike. Exactly; and you want to be absolutely sure everyone knows that. If Joe has a bigger office than I have, it doesn't necessarily mean the company considers him more important than me—*he* wanted a bigger office. If Jane gets two weeks of vacation and Joan gets four, all it means is that Joan has more things to do on her vacation. This eliminates a lot of petty squabbling over who gets what.

When you try to treat everybody the same, you inevitably end up edging toward giving everybody as much of everything as the most demanding one would like. Of course you can never give enough vacation to the guy who really wants a parttime job, or enough money to the one who is constitutionally incapable of living within his income; so you don't satisfy them. And you end up wasting benefits on other people who have different values and would like different forms of compensation. Actually all conditions of work can be negotiable, including when, how long, and how often. The ultimate implications of this possibility are explored in Appendix B.

THE UNSPEAKABLE

For some inexplicable reason many senior managers don't seem to like to think about the remuneration of their subordinates. Perhaps that explains the popularity of the various salary administration systems that give the illusion of a nearly automatic formula for salary determination. Actually some of the good systems are better, more equitable, and more closely related to individual contribution than are the whimsical nonsystems combining favoritism and habit that they often replace. However, these systems, as well as the personalized intuitive practice, seem to shy away from anything approaching a vigorous "value received" rationale.

The systems—and I suppose this is why we think of them as systems—place tremendous importance on neatness and order. Remuneration should not change too drastically at any one time. If the formula seems to call for too large an increase this year, then hold some back so "we will have something to give him next year." Of course this cheats the recipient of some money he should have gotten this year and he will never make it up, but nobody seems to talk about that. Individuals at roughly equivalent levels on the organization chart are supposed to get salaries and benefits within a certain range. Now this is backwards. If compensation is rationally determined, then people who get salaries and benefits within a certain range should be placed at a certain level on the organization chart. The cause and effect relationship is consistently reversed.

The older, less "scientific" approach to salary administration invariably comes under the accusation that the scheme is to pay the guy as little as possible and still keep him from quitting. This accusation is not always completely just; but to the extent that it is, it has a certain Scrooge-like reasonableness. In the case of more "modern," more "human" organizations, however, the reluctance to relate remuneration to contribution is more difficult to fathom.

Granted that in many modern organizations of substantial scope, individual contributions tend to be interrelated in a complex network and are sometimes difficult to evaluate quantitatively in terms of contribution to the main mission of the enterprise. But this is not an acceptable excuse for not trying to develop a compensation logic based on the principle that every employee is employed because he is expected to accomplish something and what he is expected to accomplish is more or less important to the enterprise. If you know what the man is trying to accomplish, then somebody at least subjectively can decide how much to pay for it. If no one can tell how well a man is accomplishing his job, we may be permitted a certain skepticism as to the value of the job. If the job is so highly specialized that it "takes one to know one," you'd better get an outside opinion. It is much more likely, however, that the job has just not been defined well and should be sharpened up or eliminated.

The logical and therefore surefire thing to do is to tell a man what he's getting paid for, tell him how much you're willing to pay for it, and, if he produces, pay him for it. This is management by results or management by objectives, but carried to its logical conclusion. It is one of society's major mysteries how the so-called personnel experts can tell us with a straight face that we must separate performance reviews and salary discussions. We all started playing marbles "for keeps" when we were eight years old. What are we doing now? Playing hopscotch?

If you have asked a man to do really useful things, by definition those things are valuable to the organization. They must be worth more to the organization than you expect to pay the man for them. Don't begrudge him his cut of the pie. You can't lose if he produces. If you have asked him to do trivial things, whatever reward you give him will be too much, and you can't afford it. But if you try to use behavioral gimmicks as a cheap substitute for valid motivation, you deserve the shoddy management you will probably get.

FOR YOU OR AGAINST YOU

There is really no effective alternative to trying to develop a compensation system that relates to the accomplishment of

REDEFINING THE MANAGER'S JOB

constructive results. Because money is such a strong personal motivator, either in substance or as a symbol, there is no such thing as a neutral or random compensation structure. Even if the practice is completely whimsical and chaotic, the recipients will impute a rationale to it; and, whether it's real or imagined, any logic that's not clearly based on productive results will work against the enterprise. If the prime consideration appears to be "not upsetting the boss," then every time a conflict arises between an optimal decision and the chief executive's digestion, the outcome is likely to be a contented chief executive and not the most productive decision. If the system pivots on maintaining a "happy shop," on freedom from errors of judgment, on length of service, or on any criterion other than coordinated accomplishment, you will inevitably get management decisions that maximize the assumed desideratum instead of enhancing the progress of the enterprise.

In a very literal sense, you "get what you pay for." A compensation system can work either for you or against you. But it will not be neutral. I know of one case in which an executive resigned after many years with a company immediately after he received the largest annual bonus of his career. He had been caught in an organizational squeeze play that made it impossible for him to function, with the result that his contributions that year had been negligible. He reasoned that "any company that is so stupid as to pay extra compensation for that performance—I don't want to work for." An extreme reaction, perhaps, but not a unique one.

Even supposed performance bonuses can be misleading and consequently harmful. We all know the stories about the Soviet experience with production quotas: If they set the quotas in terms of tonnage, they got nothing but railroad spikes; and if they set them in terms of units, they got nothing but carpet tacks. We laughed at them. Yet we continue to base salesmen's commissions on a percentage of sales volume and

PAVLOV WAS RIGHT

then wonder why we always seem to do well on large-order, commodity-type products but have trouble getting new products introduced, have bad credit loss experience, and are constantly contending with salesmen who are relentlessly propagandizing for price cuts. If it's profits we want, or growth, let's tell them and pay them accordingly, not try to patch up a structurally unsound system with brownie points in special incentive campaigns. One marketing executive says most salesmen's compensation systems are "like putting a plant on piecework rates and firing the quality control department." He is only too right.

YOU WANT IT—PAY FOR IT

We brag about our production technology and then tell the engineer he didn't get the promotion because he "didn't have any general management experience." We take a division general manager and tell him he is responsible for the *future* development of his division and then explain to him that he will be eligible for an incentive bonus based on the performance of that division in the *current* year. Either from his own age or from the history of the company, he knows he is likely to be in his present position from three to five years. If he is any good, he also knows there is very little he can do that will have major impact on the division in much less than three to five years. The best things he can do in the short range are all negative. He can screw down on some operating costs—make people turn off lights and salvage tools—but there is not too much he can do there. He may be able to eliminate a couple of ineffectual staff departments that somehow have persisted on inertia. Maybe he can eliminate a few no-profit product lines. But if his predecessor was reasonably competent, there is little he can *initiate* immediately that will effect the current year's

REDEFINING THE MANAGER'S JOB

operating statement, unless he is both bright and unscrupulous—or dumb and conscientious. Then he can cut a great many expenditures that are conventionally recorded as expenses but are in fact investments in the future. He can cut advertising, cut public relations, cut research, cut new-product development, cut market research, cut maintenance—the opportunities are tremendous. If his strategy works out, he will make such an impressive showing in current operations that he will be promoted out of the job long before the division begins to cave in from having mortgaged its future. If the guy is particularly glib, he may even succeed in convincing people that the division went to hell after he left it because no one could run it as well as he could.

Senior executives make their most important contributions in decisions affecting the long-term directions of growth and development in the organizations for which they are responsible. Why not pay them for that contribution rather than for something else? It should not be inconceivable to tell our new general manager that he is eligible for an incentive bonus, but that it will be based on the profitability of the division five years in the future. If he chooses, he may take an estimated bonus in the current year in the form of an interest-free loan due in five years. He will furthermore have a continuing although decreasing financial interest in the maintenance of improved divisional performance, which will be arranged as a form of deferred compensation. Provisions would be made for reorganizations and other extraordinary displacements. Why not base retirement pensions for senior executives on the long-range profit performance of the activities for which they set the policies and chose the long-range strategies? It would make them very thoughtful about recommending their successors.

It would seem reasonable to adjust the lead time on the calculation according to the level of responsibility. For some corporate presidents, it should perhaps be as much as ten years.

PAVLOV WAS RIGHT

For upper-middle managers, five years, for other middle managers, it might be as little as a year or two. The foremen, the lower-middle managers, and certain staff people are the ones who can be effective in improving short-term performance, and they should be compensated accordingly. Do you want senior managers to think big, plan, create the future, be innovative? Pay them for it.

In an ongoing situation, this system would ultimately result in people's being paid currently on the basis of what they did in the past. Actually that's not much different from what we are mostly doing now, except that this system would make it explicit.

By focusing senior executives' attention on the kind of contribution they have always supposedly been paid for, we would also concentrate attention on short-range results in a place where they can be best controlled. The lower levels of management down through the foremen would be clearly on notice that they are responsible for short-term results, and there would be a big fat carrot out in front to emphasize the point. The "big bosses" would be much less disposed to inject themselves into current operations since their bread is buttered on the long-range side. The managers who are living with the operations, who are closest to the operating information, who can make a decision and get it implemented directly, would have maximum responsibility and incentive to do something about current productivity—*now*. This is indeed similar to the practice in Japan except in Japan it is not tied into the compensation system.

Policy-level executives would be compensated, not indirectly for the smart things they did years ago that got them up on mahogany row, but directly for the quality of the management decisions they alone can make in the present. Operations-level executives would be able to take operational actions quickly and get a direct feedback into their paycheck if they were right. Both ends of the managerial hierarchy would be responsible to the familiar question, "What have you done for me lately?"

DON'T KID YOURSELF

If a manager can't or won't produce the kind of results required, get him out of there. If useful results are not being produced, you are better off with the position vacant. If somebody has to countersign the vouchers, put in an "acting" manager, but never anyone you would consider for the permanent assignment. An "acting" manager can be God's saddest creature, particularly if the implication is that he is only there until "they" find somebody "really qualified." If a new incumbent does ultimately arrive, what happens to the "temporary" after his brief taste of command? If, after an awkwardly prolonged interregnum, the "acting" is confirmed with the full title, both he and the organization are degraded: he because he was not thought of highly enough to get the job in the first place, and the organization because it obviously couldn't attract anyone better.

And don't kid yourself that you are trying out the acting manager to see "if he can handle the job." That's simple cowardice. Every time you make an appointment, you are trying somebody out to see "if he can handle it." If you equivocate with an "acting" appointment, you will probably never find out. The ambiguity of the appointment will undercut the manager's authority, encourage protective political maneuvering in his organization, and undermine his self-confidence. Put somebody on the job and tell him he has so much time to achieve such and such results. If he doesn't make it, he will be reassigned at the end of the set period. Tell him so—and mean it. It's the only thing that makes sense. If you don't get the results you need, you have to go back to square one anyway.

PAVLOV WAS RIGHT

Finding people to do the job that has to be done is difficult. Not impossible, but always difficult. Every time you hire or promote someone, it is like picking a wife. The temptations to self-delusion are overwhelming. We always hope for a paragon—someone who will solve all our problems. We seldom get one. This eternal hope is a pervasive human weakness. It is too bad. It is also rather nice. It is also inescapable.

Operationally, the problem is what to do the morning after. One option is to insist on your ability "to pick men." If *you* hired him, obviously he is the right man for the job. This option will probably eventually dent your ego and foul up the organization; it may even eventually destroy the man.

The next available course is to assume you can "develop" him. This might be called the "sow's ear syndrome." It really doesn't matter whether you're sincerely trying to make him "realize his potential" or whether you're merely trying to justify your own judgment. If he ain't got it, you're really only wasting your time, his time, and the organization's money when you try to equip him to do a job that's wrong for him. It's an easy trap to fall into because it's so morally reassuring. You're trying to help a fellow human being better himself. Or are you really trying to prove that you are capable of "making something" out of anyone?

If you've read enough "management" literature, you may decide the problem is one of "motivation." This means the guy doesn't want to do what you want him to do, but if you play the right behaviorist trick on him, you can confuse him into forgetting it. More unkindly, but more honestly, this is called manipulation. Why not do it the easy way? Why not spend your energies looking for the guy who wants to do what you want done and then put him to work doing it? Or more precisely, and more realistically, find out what the guy wants to do, and if it's compatible with what you want done, use him. This means being sure you understand the man you're putting on the job. "Cut and try" is not a good technique for this purpose.

REDEFINING THE MANAGER'S JOB

Trying to get your money's worth out of people need not be the same as cynically "using" people. The engineer who "uses" titanium for one design and aluminum for another makes no moral judgment. If he tries the wrong material for the wrong configuration and finds it doesn't work, he scraps it and tries something else. He feels no sense of guilt or incompetence. He's a professional. However, he doesn't modify his design specifications. He doesn't feel he must build his machine out of the materials readily at hand or in the stockroom. Although he doesn't try to jam round pegs into square holes, he doesn't round out the hole to fit the pegs either. If the engineer insists on using aluminum at high temperatures, the metal gets burned up and he doesn't get the performance he needs. He also probably doesn't get another design job. The manager who insists on cramming inappropriate talents into a job design is no less unprofessional and no less incompetent.

SOMETHING OF VALUE

The vast majority of enterprises—both profit and non-profit—are presumably trying to produce something of value for society, and maybe make a little money, too. Keeping this principle in mind is not so easy as it may seem. It requires a lot of hard, uncomfortable decisions and actions that it is very tempting to avoid. It means above all that the individual or the organization structure that does not contribute to the intended goals must, in good conscience, be removed. Tradition—or habit—is not an excuse for inaction.

Neither is humanitarianism. Most supposed managerial humanitarianism is just sheer cowardice. The reason you will not be unkind to "good old Joe," who has been with the organization yea these many years, is because you know Joe and you don't know the many other people who are undeveloped,

PAVLOV WAS RIGHT

thwarted, even subverted because he is where he is. He is the embolism—the bloody clot—in the circulatory system of the organization that prevents others from doing their jobs to their own satisfaction and denies them the opportunity of assuming greater responsibilities. They will either leave the organization or atrophy where they sit. In either case they will be hurt so that *you* can enjoy your magnanimity toward Joe.

If Joe isn't quite that old, you may well be doing him a disservice as well. Chances are that if he's reasonably bright, he knows he's not "doing the job." He's therefore unsatisfied, maybe frightened. If you can put him on a job he can do—not necessarily an inferior one—you both win. If you cannot, at least give him the opportunity—maybe by kicking him out—of finding that job somewhere else.

The point is to decide what has to be done and then look for the man to do it. You will have to do some marginal adjusting of the "job to the man" because you can never find a perfect fit, but, to start with, the defeatist notion of accepting whatever results a person can contribute is self-destructive and, furthermore, dishonest. You will not accept him as he is—"for better or worse"—but will inevitably treat him as a piece of material to be cut to the requirements of your particular pattern. By the same token, if you make a mistake—and that will happen from time to time—concentrate on the results expected from the position and take whatever steps are necessary to see that they are accomplished. Then worry about what to do with the man.

This sequence is not inhumane. It will always result in the greatest benefit to all the individuals involved in the enterprise and, in a surprising number of cases, will be advantageous to the individual relieved of the job he cannot handle.

The simple fact is that there are people suitable to do certain jobs and realize personal satisfaction from them and there are people who are not. No amount of motivational manipula-

REDEFINING THE MANAGER'S JOB

tion or management development is going to change that. You can accept that fact and manage, or you can try to buck the system, but it will be much easier if you acknowledge the facts as they are.

The value of this realization is increasing all the time. It is exceedingly difficult to convince members of the "coming" generation that they want something they are not really interested in. Blame it on education, sophistication, or social ambience; they are awfully hard to con. This doesn't mean there are not plenty of them who want to be productive—who understand the basic economic fact that you have to put in more than you take out. This doesn't mean you have to do it their way. But it does mean they will not put out to achieve a result they don't recognize as important, no matter who tells them to. There is no reason to believe they will not work in an organization—an "establishment"—to achieve results they think are significant. But they will be very difficult to mobilize for what they would call "Mickey Mouse" tasks, no matter how many behavioral psychologists you turn loose on them.

Constructive motivation—the desire to accomplish—is a real and powerful force. If you can harness it into an organizational thrust, it can contribute tremendous forward impetus. If you attempt to divert or manipulate it, it will inevitably suffer some attenuation and may resurface in very awkward directions.

Motivation for security is also real and can be quite powerful. However, it is in essence static and therefore not constructive. You ignore it at your peril, but you cannot build anything on it.

The way to maximize the productivity of human resources is to get the right ones in the first place and put them in positions of appropriate responsibility. Organizational theories or behavioral techniques can support this principle but not replace it. A man will do well what he is good at and what he wants to do. Most personnel problems arise from a failure to remember this self-evident truth.

To use the principle, however, it is necessary to know what you want done so that you can in fact match individual skills and motivations with tasks. Motivations, particularly, relate to something to be accomplished. Barren descriptions of activities and organizational networks describing the relationships of activities cannot mobilize individual motivations because they exist in an entirely different dimension.

The unavoidable fact is that work, as such, is always objective and impersonal. The structure and design of a job must be task-focused. But equally true, the job itself is always done by a person. Now that person, we are increasingly told, wants "to do his own thing."

Paradoxically, the only possible way for him to satisfy that desire in an enterprise of any size is by being given explicit instructions concerning the results desired. If he then accepts that those results are within the scope of his capabilities and interest, there is minimum additional need for him to subordinate himself to the larger goals of the organization or to gear his activities to the needs and demands of others. Vague responsibilities or procedural directives inherently require the submersion of personal satisfaction in favor of organizational uniformity.

Remember that some of the greatest masterpieces in fine art were produced under commission. A pietà or an oratorio was specified. Its execution and the satisfaction in having executed it well remained with the artist.

A MEDIUM AND A MESSAGE

The vast majority of organization leaders complain that their communications are not good. But what seems to have

REDEFINING THE MANAGER'S JOB

gotten lost in the development of most management systems is the recognition that, except in Professor McLuhan's philosophy, communication consists of two parts: a medium and a message. The secret of communication, either personal or organizational, is having something to say. If you tell a man, "I've got two and I need two more; I'd like you to make them for me," you're apt to end up with four. But if you go to the head of your technical development group and say, "What we need is more innovation around here," or "We need a technological breakthrough," he hasn't got the foggiest notion of how much of what kind you want and you're not very likely to get it. He doesn't even know what you mean by technology. And he surely doesn't know how to whomp up a breakthrough.

So what happens? He can't understand your words so he has to read your personality. He decides you're a dumb bookkeeper who can't understand engineering, and you decide he's a stiff-backed engineer whom you can't talk to and who won't take a realistic attitude toward business. If you knew what you wanted, he wouldn't care whether you understood engineering or not. And if he produced what you needed, you wouldn't care whether he was an engineer or an alchemist—or whether you enjoyed talking to him or not. The person who initiates the exchange has got to be able to say what he wants in a way that has some substance, and that means he has to know what kind of results he wants.

People are more at ease if they "know what is going on." If they can understand why things are happening—understand the relationship of cause and effect—they tend to be relatively relaxed even if they don't entirely approve of what in fact is happening. But, they get particularly critical or noncommunicative and very uneasy if they feel they don't understand what is the likely cause of what they observe—particularly in matters that affect them personally, such as salaries, bonuses, and promotions.

206

PAVLOV WAS RIGHT

This was of course the theory behind the great flurry of "communications" activity in management a few years back. The trouble with that movement was that it became completely preoccupied with the channels of communication. It forgot that you must have something meaningful to communicate. Most formal corporate communications today—whether in coordination committees or house organs or informational memoranda—communicate nothing but a bunch of noise, if in fact they aren't outright cynical crap. Communications with stockholders are usually a particularly aggravated form of this perversion.

It is far from a coincidence that when a president tells you he has internal communications problems, the first evidence he cites for his conclusion is the prevalence of interpersonal friction in the organization. There is line and staff polarization. There is lack of cooperation between divisions.

Of course there is polarization and lack of cooperation. It isn't that the communications channels are faulty; there is nothing to feed into the channels. There is no rational conceptual structure on which there can be cooperation. Of course there are interpersonal frictions. If there is no dimension of rational substance on which the individuals can interact, they will interact on a gut level. And if, as is highly likely under the circumstances, they are feeling personally frustrated and insecure because they are not sure whether they are doing the right thing and they are quite sure they are not being fully productive, their gut is going to be pretty sensitive. The reaction is apt to be unpleasant. A person doesn't come to the office to be "loved." He is more interested in working with compatible temperaments than in being liked, although the two are obviously related. What he does want is assurance that he is doing a good job, that it is recognized, and that he will be appropriately rewarded for it.

Communications with well-thought-out, substantive con-

REDEFINING THE MANAGER'S JOB

tent that invite a rational response eliminate many of the sources of superior-subordinate friction, and save a lot of time as well. Where it doesn't eliminate the friction, it still has the advantage of bringing it into the open early enough so that an appropriate adjustment can be made before, rather than after, the half-hearted or confused effort has been made and the failure to achieve results has been detected. Even more important, disagreements can be explored on a factual basis rather than emotionally: "My old man can lick your old man." Rational communications also eliminate many of the interpersonal problems that occur among nominal peers, simply by eliminating the artificial and dysfunctional confusion over who has the right to do what, with what, and to whom. The question of "rights" becomes moot. The atmosphere becomes more that of negotiations between the classical willing buyer and willing seller.

The common formulation inverts the function. It says that if people get along well with one another, they will work well together. That is true but trivial. It is much more significant that if people can work productively together, they will tend to get on well with each other; the question of whether they "like" each other then becomes tangential.

Watch the members of a basketball team after winning the big game hugging and slapping each other on the back. Affection is slopping all over the court—because they won the game. It is the members of a losing team who are at each others' throats. Athletic managers often explain a losing season by saying there is dissension among the players, but they probably have the cause and effect reversed. Significantly, the manager is usually the one who's replaced if the situation is bad enough.

You don't clear up a communications problem by setting up a lot of committees. In the absence of a rational set of objectives, this is only an expensive way of bringing together a

PAVLOV WAS RIGHT

number of people to share their confusions. You don't do it with house organs or memoranda or a more sophisticated management information system. In fact, if there is confusion of purpose, reaming out these conduits will serve only to inform more people more thoroughly of the extent of the confusion. The last, best course under these circumstances is "If you don't have anything to say, at least have sense enough to shut up!"

BUT YOU CAN'T SHUT UP

Except that doesn't really work either. In any hierarchical situation, people are avid for signals from their superiors. Child psychologists tell us that, despite all appearances, children desperately seek clues to what their parents would like them to do. Anthropologists record the frequently grotesque efforts of primitive peoples to interpret natural phenomena as some sort of instruction from divine powers. In any kind of productive enterprise people will aggressively seek cues to desirable performance from the actions of their superiors. If the formal communications are garbled, if the words are unintelligible, they will seek those cues from other media.

"Actions speak louder than words." What a cliché! But clichés become clichés because they are self-evident. When the sales manager rises at the annual sales meeting and gives his patented, purple, inevitable spiel about the primary importance of quality and responsibility and responsiveness to the customer's needs, but the promotions always go to the guys who move the goods with no questions asked about how they did it, the sales force gets the message. And this may be exactly the message the sales manager intended to transmit. The formal speech may be just ritual.

But that same evening, when the president addresses the meeting and soberly importunes the group on the need to im-

REDEFINING THE MANAGER'S JOB

prove profits, cut costs, and concentrate on new products that "contain the seeds of the future of the company," after which he declares annual bonus awards directly related to gross sales volume, the message gets reinforced. But the president may not realize it and he thinks the salesmen are irresponsible, "cannot see the broader picture." He tells them and tells them and tells them, and still cannot develop any profit consciousness in them. It's because he tells them and tells them and tells them even louder with his actions that he can't see beyond sales figures to underlying profitability either.

The "modern" manager who spends an annual performance review session discussing personal development, soliciting personal aspirations, and extolling the value of personal initiatives in furthering the interests of the enterprise, and then at the end of the session says, "John, when you get that new conveyor-belt layout worked out, bring it in and I'll check it before you go any further," has done his communicating in the last 30 seconds and not in the first hour.

The air is full of words such as delegation, responsibilities, authority, initiative, target, forecast, and plan. But the messages coming through may read, "Don't stick your neck out." "Don't rock the boat." "Don't get buddy-buddy with Cartwright; I don't like him." "We need a good man in that spot—but with a name like Lieberwitch?" "Don't worry about profits; all the old man wants to talk about is engineering." "Don't worry about deadlines; no one ever pays any attention to them." And on and on. Murphy's law says, "If anything can possibly go wrong, it will." Kastens' law says, "If anyone can possibly misunderstand you, he will." If you're not exactly sure about what you're trying to say anyhow, he certainly will not beat his brains out trying to understand your words but will read your actions instead. And if there is any hint of contradiction between your words and your actions, he will believe the actions every time.

Much of what is labeled irrational human behavior is really a matter of communication. You tell them to do one

PAVLOV WAS RIGHT

thing and they go off and do something else. But is that necessarily irrational—or even perverse? Maybe they didn't understand what you wanted. Maybe they heard you all right, but they got another message louder and clearer through another channel. Maybe they figured you would forget what you told them, and if you didn't, they could always talk you out of it. Maybe they just thought the "something else" was more important. The odds are overwhelming that their response was indeed rational. You just didn't see the logic—because it wasn't your logic. It is awfully easy to write a thing off as "irrational" when you don't understand it.

No, the communications systems in most organizations work pretty well. Notice how they wind into action when someone notices the finance vice-president's car parked outside his secretary's apartment building all night. But the lines may be carrying the wrong messages, at least from the management's point of view. If the formal verbal network is not bringing in any meaningful messages, new circuits will quickly be created to bypass the sclerotic conduits and maintain the supply of information. The workers will get information—right or wrong, constructive or not—but it will be information they believe and will act on.

So the manager really has little choice. He will "direct" the course of the effort for which he is responsible, be he ever so humble—or deaf, or mute. The only question is whether his communications support the purposes of the enterprise or not. If he is a good manager, he will tell his people unambiguously and specifically just what it is he wants done. The easiest and surest way to do that is to state his requirements in terms of the results to be achieved and not the actions to be taken. But that means the manager has to know what results are significant. He has to understand the rational relationships among a myriad of component accomplishments that will combine to create the total enterprise.

Motivation as such is not the problem. Most people are

REDEFINING THE MANAGER'S JOB

motivated largely by self-interest. The trick is to make that self-interest coincide as closely as possible with the needs of the enterprise. When simple observation reveals that rewards, financial and other, are passed around for some other reason than the production of useful results, people will be strongly *motivated* to concentrate on the activity that's likely to be rewarded. It is just that simple. There is no lack of motivation. The stimulus is being applied in the wrong direction. The dog won't ring the bell if the food pellet comes out when he presses a lever.

People are rational—at least part of the time. Most of them would like to be rational more of the tiime. If you put them in a rational system and give them some understandable signals, you can take advantage of that characteristic. It's a shame to waste it.

16
THE FEAST OF REASON

Herman Kahn, the futurist gnome of Croton-on-Hudson, always prefaces his optimistic scenarios with some such stipulation as "barring bad management." Perhaps this is why so many people dismiss his predictions as being hopelessly ingenuous. On the record the prospect for good management would seem tenuous at best.

And yet, do we have a choice? A long bookshelf of widely read jeremiads describes in great detail the alternative consequences of mismanagement in the future. The world cannot afford bad management. It probably cannot survive bad management. We must therefore assume that the management function will become increasingly effective and address ourselves to the problem of how that improvement may be brought about most expeditiously.

RESULTS, RESULTS, RESULTS

The first step is to achieve an explicit appreciation that management is the process by which resources are converted into value—nothing more, nothing less. Whenever resources, of whatever kind, are committed to a purposeful end, there must be management—good, bad, or indifferent. We must excise the notion that the management function is somehow coterminous with profit-making enterprise. That construction becomes less and less tenable every day. Common experience denies it. Too much of the work of the world today involves interactions between "managers" of private enterprises and representatives of government or public organizations who have completely comparable responsibilities. In international operations this kind of interaction is increasingly dominant. To differentiate these individuals by politico-economic categories not only is irrelevant but ultimately leads to grossly distorted perceptions. Because the health care establishment has a humane rather than an economic purpose, it is assumed that the resources committed to that system do not have to be managed. Only in recent years has that assumption been challenged seriously, but it will have to go. The educational system is in a comparable transition to a self-appreciation of its managerial requirements.

The candidate for public office who promises to bring "business management" into government operations makes a serious tactical error. He may think that he is using a shorthand convention to imply efficiency, economy, and accountability; but he brings along in the baggage the assumption that public affairs can somehow be "managed" by a different technique than are business enterprises. The university that maintains both a Graduate School of Business Administration and a graduate School of Public Administration on the same campus suffers from and perpetuates the same confusing fallacy.

As society becomes increasingly aware that resources of all kinds are finite, it will become increasingly sensitive to the skill with which those resources are utilized. And as a higher and higher percentage of those resources are committed to social rather than economic ends, we will have to acknowledge that management is a unique function of surpassing importance; but it is not the special province of any one kind of human activity. Accurately defining management as the process by which resources are converted into value makes explicit the critical relationship between management and resources. Profligacy with resources is synonymous with bad management. We can no longer afford to be profligate with resources.

The optimum mode for organizing the affairs of a nation will undoubtedly be a subject of lively and even bloody controversy for many years into the future. It may be that good management is more likely to flourish in a system motivated by personal gain. But even that hypothesis does not dictate a "profit-making" mode, and in any case that argument arises in an entirely different dimension. It is essential to differentiate the results from the mechanisms. If human needs are to be met from the limited resources available, they will be met only by results, not by organization structures. If people go hungry because the land is not fully productive, changing the ownership of the land will not fill their bellies. If the land is poorly managed, who owns it is incidental. Change must be made in the way the land is managed by whatever process is appropriate. Millions of people have starved in this century alone in the face of "reforms" addressed to irrelevancies that ignored the basic issue of the productivity of resources.

If the trend toward a rational appreciation of the process of management sometimes seems imperceptibly slow, there are other trends that are much more readily apparent. Government agencies, particularly in the United States, are intensifying their activities as the instrument by which society's values are codified and imposed upon the operational units of that society. Call it regulation or call it interference, but it is here. And it is here to stay. No one seriously doubts that there will be more of it in the future, although there are hopes that it may become somewhat more realistic and cost conscious.

REGULATION FROM WITHOUT AND FROM WITHIN

Interestingly enough, as the regulators gain experience, they are learning something. One thing they are learning is just how powerful and potentially brutal the regulatory weapon is. A certain amount of humility is creeping up on some of the more perceptive bureaucrats, and they are becoming more thoughtful about the ways in which they deploy that weapon. It is this growing perception that fosters the hope for more sophisticated regulatory processes in the future.

Something else they are learning is that, as regulations become more complex, only the large organizations can cope with them effectively. Bureaucracies relate to bureaucracies, and only the large companies have adequate bureaucracies. Thus the regulatory agencies need the large companies. There has been much comment to the effect that the large companies subvert the regulatory bodies. More subtle observers predict that the interests of the private bureaucracies and the governmental bureaucracies will tend to merge and form a kind of a hybrid that is neither governmental nor corporate. This is not necessarily a bad thing.

THE FEAST OF REASON

And it leads to the most significant revelation of all. The regulators are learning that they, in and of themselves, cannot regulate. As the Internal Revenue Service has long since learned, government agencies are acknowledging that the essence of regulation is voluntary compliance. To enforce in detail any one of the recent regulatory acts—say, for example, the occupational safety legislation administered by OSHA—would require such an army of agents and such offensive intrusion onto private premises as to be economically ridiculous and politically impossible. Do you think the Federal Trade Commission enforces antitrust regulation? No so! During a recent 12-month period (June 30, 1977, to June 30, 1978), of 1,977 antitrust cases brought to court, the federal government was the plaintiff in only 32. The rest were private cases.

So we do have a self-policing system. There is no use agonizing over the imminent hazard of an "autonomous technostructure." We have one already. It is in place because it is the only system that has any chance of working. Ultimately, we will have to acknowledge this fact and take positive steps to make the system work better.

One nongovernment policing mechanism that is certain to evolve will arise from the changing role of the corporate board of directors, and perhaps other governing boards as well. Certainly the time of the completely "inside" board is over. Probably the days of any inside board members other than the CEO are numbered, and the CEO may ultimately be denied the chairmanship. If, as becomes increasingly likely, board members are to be held liable not only for their own judgment and probity but for their knowledge of the activities of the organization, the position of director will become much more demanding. It may not become a full-time job, but it probably will be incompatible with other heavy executive responsibility. The professional director, who already appears with increasing frequency, will become a commonplace.

REDEFINING THE MANAGER'S JOB

But these professional directors will increasingly represent specific constituencies. We already see de facto representatives of consumers, minorities, and "society" on the boards of many major companies. Either social pressure or regulatory decree will ultimately enforce this practice. It is also unlikely that U.S. corporations can escape indefinitely the wave of demand for labor representation on the board that now seems to be sweeping Europe. At some point in this evolution, confidentiality of board proceedings will surely disappear. What you will have is a quasi-public body, a kind of board of overseers. The analogy with the congressional oversight committees that supposedly monitor the executive departments of the federal government comes immediately to mind. The comparison is not entirely felicitous, but it is the best one we have.

The myth of the election by stockholders of representatives to the board will finally be laid to rest, and the ritual itself may ultimately disappear. Presumably appointments will be made on the basis of recommendations of a nominating committee very much as they are today. All that will change is that the Postal Service will be relieved of the burden of carrying all those proxy cards back and forth. Will this kind of representation provide better supervision of management than the present incestuous system? Probably not in a direct fashion. There is bound to be a certain adversary relationship, and the information flow is bound to be constricted.

On the other hand, the processes of management will be opened up to broader scrutiny, and accountability will inevitably be enhanced. The manager who willfully withholds unfavorable or derogatory information from his board would be subject to legal action. Certainly he would have to share with them his intentions, at least in general terms, and would eventually have to report to them the extent to which those intentions were realized. The prospect may not be entirely pleasing to those most likely to be involved, and the total consequences of this mode of governance are far from clear at this point, but the direction of change is abundantly apparent to those who will see. Most of the current discussion of the proper role of directors is addressed to fighting a war that is already over.

MULTIPLEXUS

The same kind of wishful rhetoric characterizes most of the commentary on multinational companies. There were "multinational" commercial enterprises before there were nations—or at least before there were nation-states—and there may be multinational corporations after the nation-state has withered away. The simple fact is that the modern multinational company is the only instrument we have that shows any competence for dealing with the complex relationships of an increasingly interrelated world. If it did not exist, we would have to invent it. These organizations are sometimes pejoratively called "supranational," with the implication that they are above and beyond national governments. Just so! That is exactly why they work and why they are necessary. They have the unique capability for organizing resources wherever they may occur and deploying them to a useful effect. They are relatively free of parochial concerns and ultimately respond to the transcendent rationale of getting some useful work done, usually in the most economic way possible, subject to the distortion imposed by local governments.

Admittedly, multinationals have on occasion been rapacious, venal, greedy. But so have a great many governments. Except for occasional ineffectual potshots from anarchists, no one has attempted to outlaw or incapacitate governments as institutional realities. In fact, in recent years there has been a global tendency to positively encourage their proliferation. It is possible to question whether the world needs 165 national

REDEFINING THE MANAGER'S JOB

governments, some of them in circumstances that make it virtually impossible for them to provide significant useful services to their citizens. In the world of complex resource networks, sophisticated communications, and growing but uneven population densities, it is not possible to survive without some enterprises that can transcend national boundaries—and occasionally even national interests—to bring together the physical and intellectual resources necessary to create a humane existence for the greatest number of people. Perhaps that is why the declamations of some politicians become so vitriolic as they contemplate the activities of the multinationals. They recognize their personal vulnerability—their expendability—and are frustrated by the knowledge that the targets of their attacks are capable of enriching the lives of their constituents.

No, the multinationals are here and here to stay—as long as the world continues in something like its current socioeconomic condition. Everyone, rich and poor, in and out of the multinational organizations, will be better served if the real situation is acknowledged and efforts are concentrated on developing mechanisms to enhance the accountability of the multinationals and increase their opportunities to do the thing they have the greatest capability for: producing the greatest amount of value from the minimum commitment or consumption of resources. Efforts to wish them away or incapacitate them will be wasted at best. If those efforts should be successful, the consequences for humanity would be most unfortunate.

One thing almost all the true multinationals have in common is that despite their large size, they are far from monolithic. They comprise a bewildering array of relationships including commercial joint ventures, joint ventures with governments, management contracts, public corporations, subsidiaries, licensing agreements, minority equity positions, long-term supply contracts, agency agreements, and relationships that defy categorization. And yet they preserve the sense of a single enterprise. Both commercial considerations and local government mandates have forced them to learn or to invent organizational flexibility. They are still learning and inventing.

Pervasive trends are under way in the United States and to some extent in Europe that will force even domestic companies to acquire some of that flexibility. Governmental thrusts against "bigness" as such may have some impact, but the more potent influences will come from changing lifestyles. It is clear that we are destined for a more dispersed society. Demographic data in the United States have documented, first the migration to the suburbs, somewhat later the preferential growth of the small cities, and still more recently the resurgence of the "rural" counties. Rapid improvements in communications capabilities make this diaspora more feasible. Increasing costs of transportation and the possible exploitation of diffuse energy sources from the sun or from earth heat will make relocation economically attractive.*

However, these migrations of themselves would probably not affect the managerial relationship. Two other phenomena almost certainly will. One is the increasing importance of "knowledge" workers in all enterprises. The other is the shift in management styles away from close supervision and toward strict accountability. The knowledge worker is notoriously mobile. Not only can he work almost anywhere with little fixed equipment, but he tends to change his job to wherever his talents can make the greatest contribution. The prophets of the communications era tell us he will work at home and interface with an array of communications devices. Perhaps so. In any case, if he is to make a specific personal contribution, be judged on its competence, and compensated accordingly, why should he be embedded in an organizational matrix?

Actually the outflow of knowledge workers from large

---

* European futurists expect resource economics alone to force such a dispersion of activities. See Peter Hall, *Europe 2000,* Duckworth, London (1977).

corporate organizations is long since under way. Already the bulk of engineering, market research, and advertising is probably done by independent contractors. Almost any kind of staff service can be obtained under contract. There is some evidence that the independent sales force—the "distributor"—is staging a comeback. In international trade the "trading companies" seem to be enjoying a renaissance. Domestically, in the food industry at least, there is a movement away from direct sales forces back to food brokers. Even in production there may be an increase in contract manufacturing and "tolling."

A strong centrifugal force is acting on the large organizations. It is compounded of techno-economic factors, the solipsist orientation of the "me generation," and the need for flexibility in a rapidly changing environment. The trends in management style will intensify it. If the tax laws are ever reformed to eliminate the preferential status of reinvested earnings, the force will become even more persuasive.

The social observers who are concerned about the inexorability of organizational growth are very likely to lose their issue. Small may indeed prove to be beautiful, but not for the reasons Dr. Schumacher posited.*

ACCOUNTABILITY

The crux of the development of management in the future comes down to explicit accountability in terms of results produced from the resources employed. The good managers want it, and they are the ones we want to encourage. The spirit of the times encourages it because it is the only system that provides the freedom of action and the opportunity for self-motivation that are the goals of the increasingly well educated,

---

* E. F. Schumacher, *Small Is Beautiful* (New York: Harper & Row, 1973).

somewhat introspective, and slightly cynical workforce. An economy of limited resources demands it because it goes directly to the matter of obtaining maximum value from those resources.

The question of "accountability to whom?" remains unresolved. Perhaps it must ultimately be resolved in a typically messy democratic fashion. The first step is obvious. Strict accountability must be required within the hierarchy or there is no way the organization as a whole can be held accountable. The management system must be designed in all its particulars—including appropriate rewards and penalties—so that when there is a commitment to certain results, there is full expectation that those results will be forthcoming. No matter whether such commitments are more or less hierarchical, there must ultimately be one individual who is responsible for the entire enterprise.* Who will hold him to his commitments?

At present, and for the immediate future, the only candidate we have is the much-maligned board of directors. No matter how the body is constituted, it seems likely that its members will continue to attract increasing responsibility for both the propriety and the efficacy of the enterprise they serve. However, even given an independent staff, which boards now have in some companies and will have in all large corporations in the future, there is no way that board members can be conversant with all the operating details of a sizable enterprise. As the nature of the representation broadens, the average board member will be less and less competent to evaluate such information if it were presented.

But a reasonably competent board collectively could with conceivable effort monitor certain critical dimensions of per-

---

* Even in Japan, where the decision-making authority may be widely delegated, ultimate responsibility still rests with such an individual and he feels it very strongly.

REDEFINING THE MANAGER'S JOB

formance. They could ensure that new commitments of financial assets, from whatever source, are made prudently and productively; that old assets are redeployed promptly when they are no longer acceptably productive; that proper provision is made for the long-term vitality of the enterprise; that the market position and reputation of the firm is not allowed to deteriorate; that personnel are employed with maximum utility; and that the environment is not abused. If they realize that they are legally liable for ensuring performance in these broad dimensions and understand their responsibility to ensure that they have sufficient information to perform such surveillance, we have come a long way and we can probably get there under existing law.

The board can of course be misled; they can be misinformed; information can be withheld. However, if the relationship is clearly understood, then any such misdirection on the part of the executive officer is clearly culpable and approaches a kind of fraud. If he is caught at it, not only should he be fired, he should be prosecuted by the board itself or, failing that, by a class of stockholders. With both the directors and the executive officer subject to possible litigation, you might expect them to be very careful in their interactions. If, then, as a backup mechanism, there is the possibility of some sort of censure and potential ostracism by the professional community of managers, that might be enough.

Certainly the mood of the courts and the regulatory agencies is moving in this direction. It is not a foolproof system. It is clumsy and untidy. But the important thing is to establish the expectation and acceptance that the manager will be held accountable for the consequences of his actions. Once that principle is generally acknowledged, a self-policing system might work. Without it there is no system.

However, if we are to have a strict accountability system, the management information specialists have a large task ahead. We need a virtual revolution in the way records are kept. Present accounts are so encumbered with the excrescence of historical artifact and distortion deliberately introduced in the pursuit of public policy that it is almost impossible to get two economists to agree on even what aggregate profit in the economy is or even whether it is going up or down. You get books of account for the City of New York or for Cleveland that are simply unauditable—or the Penn Central that goes broke almost overnight and the directors claim they could not see it coming.

It will indeed be a big job to figure out a system that is meaningful. It will be a much bigger job to get it adopted—even in a generation. However, it must be done eventually if we are to get an effective grip on the conduct of human enterprise. Obviously there is some vague awareness that something is awry. Accounting conventions are being questioned and some are being reconsidered. That is encouraging. It would be more encouraging if the proposed modifications tended to address the central problem of the foundering ship more directly rather than merely shuffling around the deck chairs.

CODA

The optimum system of management has not yet been devised. It must be developed and improved in a continuous process. But it must be developed in the context of its proper function of producing pre-agreed-upon results with the minimum commitment of available resources.

There are few if any "natural born" managers. They must be developed, trained. But their training must address itself to their central task, which is to produce something of value with maximum expedition. Much of so-called management development today is irrelevant. More is trivial. Some is quite simply

REDEFINING THE MANAGER'S JOB

technical. Very little approaches the central, particular role of the manager.

We no longer can indulge in the luxury of colorful crapshooters and glamorous gunslingers in positions in which they whimsically exercise great power. Nor can we permit congenial incompetents to preempt those positions of power and so forfeit the opportunity for more productive enterprise.

The axial principle of management is functional rationality—to adapt a phrase from Daniel Bell. It deals with the dynamics of cause and effect. It must become more rational if it is to become more efficient. It must abandon venerable incantations and archaic conventions. The logic of all organizational processes must be examined afresh to eliminate nostalgic bias and habitual inconsistencies. Management must operate in the "economizing mode," whether the term is used in the vulgar sense or in the technical jargon of the socio-economists.

Some observers detect an antirational trend in the current social ambience. Whether this heralds a new era of prevailing mysticism or is merely a transient efflorescence, those who would aspire to fulfill the function of managers have no alternative to rationality. Their effectiveness as managers will be directly proportional to their mastery of rational processes. If society does tend toward antirationality, it may make the managerial task more difficult but it will not alter this basic relationship.

Even an antirational society must husband its resources, and in the coming centuries must do so with ever more skill and precision. It must be acknowledged that during the nearly 500 years of European presence in North America the management of resources has not been ideal. The abundance of resources relative to the needs permitted a good deal of inefficiency and outright waste. Yet the productive accomplishments were much greater during that period than they were on the continents of Africa and South America, where the re-

THE FEAST OF REASON

sources were just as plentiful but the tradition of rationality was absent or inoperative.

In the transcendental cultures of most of the Asian continent, as the primeval resources base was eroded, society retrogressed to a resigned stagnation. Europe, almost as old, with declining resources but with a rational orientation, recovered from the Middle Ages and continued its vital evolution.

The mandate to manage applies to all purposeful endeavor. It is not a peculiar need of a "capitalistic" society, unless capitalistic is taken to mean capital-intensive, a characteristic of all industrial societies. It does not apply uniquely to "business," since it is clearly evident that more and more resources are employed outside the profit-making segment of the economy. It is not even limited to the realm of tangible resources, since in an increasingly complex society we have ever-increasing need to augment the impact of our intellectual and artistic resources.

This book introduced itself as "Utopian." As such it is inherently optimistic and assumes that management will become more rational and hence more effective. The alternative of dissipated resources, disaffected people, and deteriorating institutions is, if not unthinkable, too painful to contemplate.

APPENDIXES

IF WE EXTRAPOLATE AN INCREASINGLY RATIONAL APPROACH TO MANAGEMENT SOMEWHAT FURTHER INTO THE FUTURE, WE ARRIVE AT SOME ADDITIONAL RADICAL CONCLUSIONS. THESE APPENDIXES DEAL WITH A FEW OF THOSE PROBABILITIES

APPENDIX A
MANUAL SHIFT

Capital-intensive industries have long since learned that one of the most straightforward ways of increasing the productivity of assets is to work them as many hours as possible. However, even in companies that routinely run their plants 24 hours a day 350 days a year, the management seems perfectly content to leave a substantial part of its assets idle more than 75 percent of the time. We are all familiar with this situation, but it seems that no one ever gives it a second thought. Companies are now paying as much as $35 a square foot per year* for office space in midtown Manhattan—capitalizing that at seven times rental gives you an investment of close to $250 per square foot. With the increasing automation of office functions, furniture and equipment could very easily run that up to around $400 per square foot. In one of the glass boxes that corporate headquarters seems to favor, this can run up to a sizable investment. And it is used usually about six or seven hours a day five days a week.

A resource-conscious manager is certain to be pained by such a situation. He will not be happy until he finds a way to work those resources more productively. The solution is obviously a double or even a triple shift for office functions. The harbingers of this movement are already with us. Almost all computer centers are now run around the clock. Occasionally we are beginning to find certain input functions to the management information systems extended to an additional half shift or even a whole shift, particularly in the busy season of cyclical businesses. Order processing and traffic are obvious candidates for this procedure.

Interestingly enough, this situation came about not be-

---

*There is no way to keep this figure up to date, but the principle is clear.

REDEFINING THE MANAGER'S JOB

cause the users of the data processing equipment were uniquely perceptive about the opportunities to work office-type assets harder but because data processing equipment has been so commonly rented rather than purchased. The actual owners of the rented equipment could see quite clearly that a second or third shift on the equipment would represent marginal income to them, and so they stimulated multishift use by scaling their rental charges sharply downward for use on a second or third shift. This very simple and commercially reasonable action on the part of the owners forced the users to recognize the simple arithmetic of the situation, and seeing the situation in those simple terms, the users quickly found ways to take advantage of those bargain additional shifts.

But the same opportunity obviously exists for the electric typewriters and particularly for the new word-processing machines. It even applies to the desks and filing cabinets. Sooner or later people will undoubtedly realize this.

If we accept the proposition that head-office people are employed to produce some results—and there are those who would dispute the reasonableness of that proposition—then the prospect of doubling or even tripling the output of a $20-million head-office building must be attractive.

There are practical problems, of course. One of the most difficult is undoubtedly that so-called white-collar workers are not accustomed to shift work. One straightforward response to that difficulty is already used in some computer shops, which is simply to have people work three 12-hour shifts end to end. The ultimate expression of this tactic is to have two 12-hour shifts a day and run the shop six days a week with a total of four workforces. A workweek of 12-hour shifts is very attractive to some people, particularly with the enhanced interest in leisure time. It gives everybody a four-day weekend every week. Fatigue is a factor, but on the other hand it does cut down absenteeism.

APPENDIX A

It must be ackowledged that such eccentric work schedules for office personnel are still a rarity. Almost certainly it will be necessary to offer shift premiums to induce any substantial number of office workers to change their work habits. However, if there is an opportunity to double the output from $75,000 per person in fixed investment, these shift premiums could be quite substantial and still be justified.

There are petty problems that will be annoying but not insurmountable. One of them is the simple matter of a personal work station. Having someone else work part of the time at "my desk" will require some adjustment. However, it has been done for years in production shops operating on multiple shifts, and analogous provisions are obvious. Just as the machine tool operator has his own toolbox that he locks up when he leaves the plant, the desk worker would have his or her own bank of desk drawers for exclusive use.

Getting the external community to adapt to this kind of schedule may be more of a problem. Public transportation schedules could be awkward if this practice were adopted widely in a short period of time. However, shift work in offices is likely to be phased in over many years, in which case the adjustment in schedule would be accomplished quite painlessly. Think what it could do for rush hour on the subways both in terms of personal comfort and in spreading the use of transportation equipment over a greater part of the daily cycle. The considerable gains that could be realized in utilizing these public assets would accrue directly to the general economy. And think of what it could do for the road traffic patterns in areas where automobiles are the major form of travel to work.

A still bigger problem will be the matter of personal safety, particularly in the metropolitan centers. Unfortunately, it must be admitted that there are a lot of places in the United States where it is just not safe to be coming and going to work at odd hours. This is a general social problem that will have to

REDEFINING THE MANAGER'S JOB

be solved outside the management community. On the other hand, it must be solved or the cities won't survive. Spreading the activity in the downtown districts over a larger portion of the day may in itself make some contribution to the solution, but better lighting and a quantum jump in police effectiveness is also obviously going to be required.

Extending the office working period will have significant consequences over and above the simple increase in efficiency in the use of assets. One effect would be to damp down the office building boom. This will be tough on the construction industry, but in an era in which the use of materials is being examined ever more carefully, any reduced consumption of bricks and glass and steel for this purpose must be considered a social plus.

In an office that is operating 12 or 16 hours a day and possibly six days a week, we would expect the velocity of paper shuffling to increase substantially. Orders would be much more likely to be posted on the same day they are received than they would in a seven-hour shop, and bills are very likely to go out at least a day sooner. Letters dictated today are likely to be typed and mailed today rather than held over when the shop shuts down at five o'clock. There are benefits for everyone in this. Delivery performance would be improved. Inquiries would get faster responses. And there would be a reduction in accounts receivable as the float is reduced.

Since we are now talking of 10 or 20 years into the future, how does all this mesh with the "communications society" that we are told will become important by that time? Actually it fits very nicely. No matter how far we progress with data transmission links, remote printouts, visual displays, and picture phones, not everyone is going to work at home. There has to be a center of an enterprise somewhere, and certain functions are going to have to be carried out in, or at least coordinated from, a central location. Some person is going to have to perform

APPENDIX A

those functions, which means that some people will always have to "go to the office."

It seems most likely that the middle manager specialists and others who make particularly intellectual contributions to the organization will be the ones working increasingly in a remote area. But it is just that sort of person who is most likely to benefit from, enjoy, or even demand the flexible working hours that we are told will become increasingly common. To be assured that there is somebody available at the other end of all that sophisticated communications gear during most of the normal waking hours would be a particular convenience to these kinds of people if they choose to work early in the day or late into the night. They too could benefit from the possibility of having their inputs processed and returned to them overnight by a second shift.

Will it work? Well, the three-day workweek certainly has attractions, particularly for families with two working parents and children at home. Even conventional shift work can have some attractions for that sort of family. The long office day is certainly compatible with the concept of flextime. There is the possibility of reducing the time and energy consumed in transportation to and from work. There is increased efficiency in the use of municipal facilities. However, the prevailing consideration will undoubtedly be the increasing automation of office functions and the consequent increase in the capital intensiveness of such functions combined with the energy-related escalating costs of constructing and operating office buildings. We just will not be able to afford to let those assets lie idle 133 hours a week. The multishift system will have to work.

APPENDIX B
THE CONTRACT SOCIETY

Item: Middle managers who do not want to be told how to do things. They want to be held responsible only for results, with a minimum of "Mickey Mouse" procedures.

Item: Compensation systems directly related to individual performance.

Item: Fluid organization structure and professional morale rather than organizational loyalty.

Item: Competition based on performance among alternative sources of support services.

Item: Negotiation of acceptable standards of performance between superior and subordinate.

Add those all together and you get an approximate description of a contractual relationship within the components of an organization as differentiated from a hierarchical administrative relationship. In fact the term "contractual" is arising with increasing frequency in the management literature. If this relationship is evolving de facto, why should it not eventually become also de jure? There are very few reasons why it shouldn't, and since there seem to be many reasons why it should, the chances are very strong that eventually it will.

The antecedents are readily apparent. Engineering and constructing undoubtedly have the most venerable history. Some large organizations obviously maintain in-house capability in these areas, but most commonly these functions are contracted from outside suppliers. The independent distributor and trucking company has been with us since before memory. Contract research-and-development organizations go back into the thirties and since World War II have become a thoroughly established institution in the industrial community. Advertising and public relations have been purchased from

APPENDIX B

outside groups virtually since their inception. Placement services and executive recruiters take over part of the personnel functions. In recent years there has been a flood of outside services entering the marketplace. Contracts can be and commonly are written to do market research, accounting, data processing, maintenance, planning, and almost every other staff function you can define.

The precedent is there, all right. The forms of the relationship have been long established. The classical "make or buy" decision is now quite clearly present for those responsible for staff functions as well as for those in manufacturing, and in many cases it has been available, although perhaps not so widely acknowledged, for some time.

What is changing and what will continue to change in the future is the nature of the make-in-house options. If detailed supervision is going to be resented, if compensation will have to be quantitatively commensurate with performance, if increased personnel mobility makes organizational loyalties irrelevant, then many of the pluses for in-house services are eliminated. The comparison then becomes strictly one of cost/benefit—price for performance. In that kind of competition, in-house groups do not fare so well. In instances where contract services are long established, it is readily apparent that they are successful because their client customers cannot afford or are unable to attract first-class talent for their permanent organization. This is certainly true in advertising and is at least relatively true in all other business service industries. The simple fact seems to be that the individual who chooses to make his way providing personal specialized services makes more money as an independent than as an organization captive—that is, he does if he is good at it. And even if he is not good at it, he lives a more liberated lifestyle. Freedom to choose one's lifestyle is becoming a transcendent value for many people, particularly among intellectual workers.

REDEFINING THE MANAGER'S JOB

A few examples of service functions actually disassociating from a parent organization to become independent entities come readily to mind. Travel departments become travel agencies. Insurance departments become insurance agencies. Maintenance and security are often hived off if the unions will permit it. Office buildings are sold off—completely legally—to a group of employees organized as a real estate company to provide an investment vehicle in the form of a real estate company. Law departments become law firms.

There will be more of this sort of thing in private industry. There already is a great deal of it in government activity. Inevitably a lot of eyebrows go up when a government bureaucrat resigns and forms a company to do under contract what he used to do under civil service. However, a reasonable case can be made that this is the only way anything ever gets done in the government. It is the contract organizations that do the actual work. Their counterparts in the agencies negotiate the contracts and distribute the reports, but their contributions are often not substantive. This same sort of thing could happen in private enterprise if the social climate shifts sufficiently. The only kind of person who may be willing to accept extensive organizational discipline will be the kind of person who is content to stay in the civil service.

On the other hand, there is an opposite option. From the individual performer's point of view, if he can obtain the same kind of performance contract, or establish the same kind of relationship within the organization, what is his motivation to form an independent enterprise? Say he is a regional sales manager. He and his salespeople are compensated strictly on sales performance. He has virtually complete control over his marketing expense budget. He has considerable pricing flexibility. He has hire-and-fire authority over his people. His compensation is directly related to the net margin he produces. Wherein is he different from an independent distributor?

APPENDIX B

Take a plant manager who really manages his plant. He controls his materials supply, scheduling, personnel, and maintenance. His compensation depends on his unit cost of production. He must meet quality standards. He must manage his inventory in such a way as to deliver more or less on demand. But so must a contract supplier.

Computer-controlled production enthusiasts who speak about "customized production at mass-production prices" point out that a computer-controlled system can easily be told to make some special changes in the 404th item coming down the assembly line. To do this with a human-controlled production line would be an invitation to chaos. Some have pursued this possibility a step further and suggested that, in the future, entrepreneurial types will be able to rent time on an assembly line to produce specialized variants of standard products. More realistically, perhaps, in-company teams would have the capability to try out experimental ideas quickly, at little cost, and with virtually no additional fixed investment. In either case the opportunities for a results-contract kind of relationship are enhanced.

As the very evident trend toward negotiated relationships in organizations progresses, the substantive differences between "make" and "buy" narrow to the vanishing point. The make-or-buy decision will be made increasingly on the basis of secondary considerations. The dollar-heavy company will build its own capital-intensive plants; the financially lean company will look for someone else to put up the money. Faced with the possibility that the personnel of his regional sales organization might emigrate en masse to a competitor, the sales vice-president will be highly inclined to call on the services of an independent distributor with a proven staff of gung-ho young tigers. When the controller finds that the operating units, exercising the options afforded them along with their explicit accountability for results, are going outside for most of their operations research analyses, he will certainly suggest that consideration be given to disbanding the staff operations research group.

There has probably not been an individual interviewed to head up a staff support group in the last ten years who has not been told, "You understand, of course, that you will have to sell yourself to the operating units." This is almost certainly true, but under those circumstances why not sell yourself as an independent contractor and be assured of commensurate compensation?

The centrifugal effect of the "contract society" will never be completely pervasive. These are real economies of scale, but they are mostly in production, and even there they can work both ways. Witness the consortia formed, when permitted, to operate gigantic units to supply intermediate raw materials to several manufacturers. Consider further the organization that can afford a research department of 50 people, but has the option of using a 2,000-person contract research firm.

There are advantages to centralized purchasing and centralized financing. The geographical and political scope of the multinationals requires some single integrative structure, but even some of these, usually the biggest, encourage arm's-length transactions between their subsidiaries.

Note, too, that the very largest undertakings are never accomplished by a single entity using all in-house capability. The multibillion-dollar construction jobs are invariably done by a confederation of contractors. The big defense contracts always involve myriad subcontractors. Did anyone ever consider a single, comprehensive organization to put a man on the moon? The argument that large undertakings demand gross, integrated organizations is invalidated by simple observation.

It has been contended that the contractual work relationship is attractive only to the aggressive, entrepreneurial type. This is just not so. The imaginatively lazy will welcome the op-

APPENDIX B

portunity for less demanding work schedules and for freedom from supervisory hassling. The neo-Leonardo who wants to do a lot of different things will find the contract arrangement most accommodating. Even the craftsman who wants a protective organizational umbrella to shelter his self-satisfying pursuit of his craft will welcome a long-term contract that assures him of just that. The Japanese style of lifetime employment seems to be remarkably conducive to developing this type of competence. It really makes more sense to sign a long-term contract with the CEO's chauffeur who has specific duties than with the chief financial officer who is responsible for producing useful initiatives.

The nature of the chauffeur's future duties can be predicted with great certainty. The nature of the demands to be made on a policy-level officer will most likely change with changing circumstances and require new and different skills. The contract relationship will be least welcomed by the type of person who gets his kicks out of bossing people around. He will become a victim of organizational obsolescence.

More than ten years ago the telephone company grasped the principle of the "contract for results" concept when it arranged for certain employees to "own" a whole telephone book and be solely responsible for its production.* For large cities an individual may "own" a letter of the alphabet. Subsequently, the phone company extended the concept to other activities. A lot of so-called "job enrichment" proceeded in this vein.

But the practitioners never carried it to its logical conclusion. They were so concerned with eliminating the "alienation" of the workers and so anxious to "motivate" them to concen-

---

*R. N. Ford, "Job-Enrichment Programs at AT&T, *Harvard Business Review*, Jan.–Feb. 1973, p. 96.

REDEFINING THE MANAGER'S JOB

trate on a boring job that they never saw the positive economic possibilities of giving real substance to a make-believe relationship. Why not take the quotation marks from around "own" and actually contract out the preparation of the book even though it is done on the company premises?

Once the contractual mode of management becomes widely adopted, the reflexive urge to integrate can be expected to attenuate. In the first half of this century European companies seemed to Americans to have an almost obsessive desire to be self-sufficient. However, given their limited national markets, often one of the few ways they could expand their activities was to take a bigger slice of the action from raw material to consumer product. With the coming of the Common Market and the internationalization of many businesses, the options expanded and the degree of vertical integration declined.

American companies seldom could evoke the European rationale. More commonly they spoke of "controlling" their materials supply or their marketing channels. As that control weakens, the only reason for integrating either forward or backward will increasingly be that the distribution or the supply function offers greater return on resources than does the integrator's segment of the production chain. There certainly are such instances. However, in integrating by acquisition, the acquisition price will reflect the return possibilities of the acquired company, not its nominal asset value. Consequently, the return on the purchase price is likely to be not too much different from that of the acquiring company. Why buy a cow if you can get milk at a reasonable price?

The rise of what Norman Macrea of the London *Economist* has called "confederation of entrepreneurs" may well lead to the dismemberment of some large organizations. Historical experience in breaking up such giant firms as John D. Rockefeller's Standard Oil, the I. G. Farben, and the Japanese Zaibatsu strongly suggests that this could have a vitalizing effect

APPENDIX B

both on the organization's growth and on its economic effectiveness. In any case, the whiz-kid managers of the next generation are likely to be those who make big organizations grow smaller even during boom times while at the same time enhancing efficiency and profitability.

As the mechanism of control moves away from strict supervision and becomes performance against commitments, the integrative structure becomes superfluous. If, further, the temper of the times leads the more competent people to resist organizational strictures and favor more personal responsibility and flexibility, there will be a qualitative advantage to the contractual mode.

A number of external trends support this transition. The existence of increasingly sophisticated communications equipment is almost a necessary precondition. The tendency of economic activity to disperse away from the large metropolitan centers is already well established. Even the shift toward disperse energy sources such as solar or geothermal may be a factor. Most technological trends favor a federal network rather than a centralized monolith.

Not insignificant in putting a premium on organizational flexibility is the accelerating rate of strategic change within enterprises. But the primary driving force in the United States will be the insistence of younger managers on a rational, satisfying context within which to make their professional contribution.* These factors taken together could create a distinct economic advantage for the new style of management, in which case the Darwinian mechanism of natural selection will accelerate its propagation.

---

* Interestingly, a very extensive analysis of the future of Europe made by a multinational team of more than 200 scholars came to the conclusion that changing economic relationships alone are very likely to force Europe into a decentralized, subcontracted mode of production. See Peter Hall, *Europe 2000*, Duckworth, London (1977).

APPENDIX C
THE STRATEGY BOARD

Jim Hunt yawned as he walked over to his conference console. As Strategy Officer for Unisym International, he had a bigger control/display board than the other officers. He asked himself the same old question:

> ... do the boys really believe I can pull any number they want out of this big black box? ... probably not ... but they sure would like to believe in magic.
> ... one of the best systems going anyhow ... information systems gang claims it's always getting better ... pretty hard to hide anything in it—or at least we hope so ... but look at Acme and its Brazilian sub ... got taken for a real ride ... completely snowed the control system and got away with it for years ... situation finally blew and staggered Acme, big as it is ... worst of all, got both the Brazilian and U.S. governments on their tail, not to mention the LAFTA bureaucrats ... their external affairs reps will be eating crow for years before they get that one smoothed over ... what if one of our divisions took us that way? ... would have to shuffle plans all over the world to fill the gap ... could be happening in heavy chemicals ... if it is I won't have to pick up the pieces—too busy sending out résumés ... faith, Jamie. ... Amos's control systems geniuses talk very brave ... claim they have it airtight ... cross your fingers and hope for the best.
> ... right now better check the circuits before everybody else comes in.

"Harold, you fellows set up out there?"

"Aren't we always, Jim?"

"Oh, come off it. Last week's special performance analysis on the Western Division was a shambles."

APPENDIX C

"It wasn't that bad."

"Hell it wasn't. Half you couldn't see, and what you could see you didn't believe because there was so much noise in the transmission."

"Well, we were a little shorthanded. A couple of the boys didn't get in last week."

"Harold, you've got to keep those guys in hand. They're not just making pretty graphs and pictures. We're trying to figure out what the company's doing from those exhibits."

"Jim, what am I supposed to do? Good electronic-display people are hard to come by. If I lean on them too hard the whole crowd will walk out."

"You're breaking my heart! Seriously, see if you can keep them sharp for the Strategy Board meetings anyhow. I hate to look like an ass with the whole top brass in attendance."

> ... Tuesday Strategy Board sessions ... wonder if there isn't a better way to run a company ... so much time wasted ... everybody wants his kind of details ... the ego-mechanics have been telling managers for 50 years that wanting their special toys is a sign of immaturity ... guess they think it doesn't apply to them ... Billy Rowen and his sea stories ... how it was in the old days and who did what to whom ... trouble is they're fascinating stories, except they don't get a multibillion-dollar business run ... the old man could save a lot of time if he would bring them up short once in a while ... guess that just isn't his style ... think he enjoys a little freehand talk himself once in a while.
>
> ... would be nice if the machines could do it all ... chew up inputs and deal out optimal solutions ... but they say management is action under uncertainty ... for that I guess you need people ... sure are inefficient ... Jamie, all that math has seeped into your soul ... you still want to design the people out of the system.

REDEFINING THE MANAGER'S JOB

... where does Jamie Hunt fit into this system? ... God, I hate that "Jamie" bit ... thirty-five years I'm plain old Jim ... make vice-president and I get a baby name ... they've already got a Jim on the Strategy Board, Jim Ware, logistics officer ... so Zweibach, always the diplomat, says "why don't we call you Jamie so we'll know who we're talking about?" ... guess it's a small price to pay ... junior has to accommodate, but I could do without it.

... so where does Jim/Jamie fit in? ... says in the book I'm a "full-voting, policy-making member of Unisym's management team" ... generally get a fair hearing, I guess ... most of the time I feel more like a secretary, traffic cop, information clerk ... like part of the console ... so I didn't come up through the divisions ... so I have a doctorate in "systems" that didn't exist when they were in school ... so Ware has a doctorate in economics on top of his engineering papers ...where would that have got him 30 years ago? ... so Sybil has an MBA and Zweibach has his doctorate ... actually in philosophy, of all things ... you'd think sometimes that systems management was some new hairy academic theory instead of something that has been around for half a century.

"Oh, hello, Sybil. How are you this morning? You look ravishing, as always."

... and, as always, the first one in ... wonder if she's just an early riser or if she's still a little feminine-defensive ... hard to imagine why ... she made it delivering the goods ... Sybil Shearer, Wooster College, Harvard MsBA ... should be master of marketing ... or should it be mistress? ... anyhow, she put the learning systems division on the map ... salesman, director of marketing, general manager ... in what? ... ten years? ... fifteen years? ... she's a strong one in this group, too ... no chatter, always

APPENDIX C

has her facts straight, good strong logic ... maybe just very careful ... more defense than offense ... old man always stands up if she comes in after him ... I'm sure that bugs her ... well, we all have problems ... ah, and here comes Unisym's technology czar himself.

"Hi, Larry, how's our resident artist? Get any chiseling done on that chunk of granite over the weekend? Not that you don't chisel enough on the contract officers during the week!"

> ... Holstead sure is getting hung up on that stone cutting of his ... must have ten tons of rocks in that studio out at his place ... just rocks to me, but some people say it's pretty good art ... keeps him in shape anyhow.
>
> ... wonder if his boys are really going to come through with that new ground-effect vehicle motor ... science and technology people always seem to think they're the only ones in the industry with a good idea ... always going to do it first and better—until someone comes out of left field and beats us bowlegged ... and Larry, of course, always backs them ... suppose he has to, but it sure is hell trying to factor loyalty or optimism or whatever it is into a cost/benefit model ... and then there's Billy Rowen.

"Billy, before we get started, are your people going to have those return-on-personnel figures ready for next week or should I leave them off the agenda for another couple of weeks?"

> ... guess a lot of people thought Old Man Powers had really been sold a bill of goods when he made Billy resources officer ... responsible for return on all assets of whatever kind ... know-how, trademarks, consumer franchises, maybe ... but a finance man in charge of personnel? ... murder!

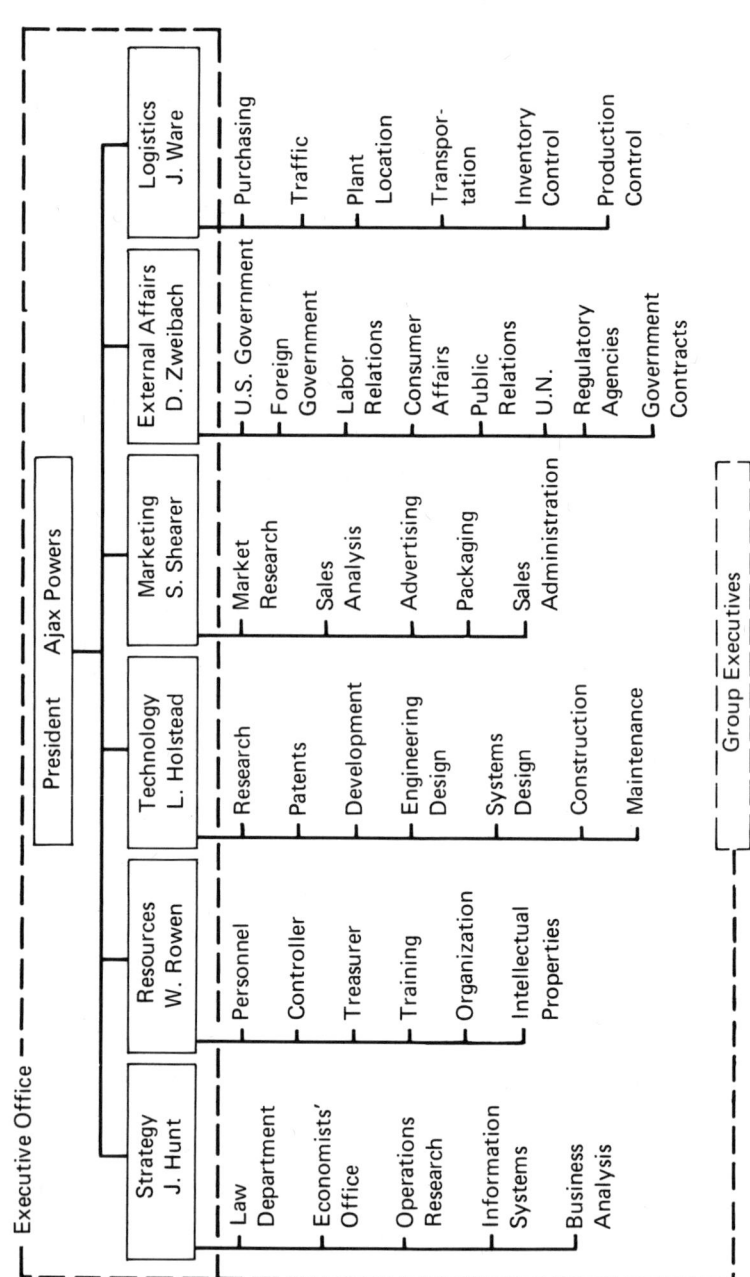

APPENDIX C

> ... but it's working ... Billy keeps track of every piece of talent we've got just like he does every dollar and lira and yen and zloty ... and if we're not getting a good return out of somebody, he gets him moved just like he'd pull a cash balance out of Deutsche marks and get it into yen if the interest rate was higher ... he may not love them but he sure doesn't waste them ... and he keeps them pretty happy, too, because he's not going to let a productive asset disappear off his books if he can help it ... oops, here comes the old man!

"Morning, Ajax."

"Gentlemen, Sybil, Billy, Larry, Jamie—we're missing Jim Ware and Dean Zweibach."

"Jim should be here any minute—in fact, he's just coming in now. Morning, Jim."

> ... he may be logistics officer, but he sure has trouble getting himself to the right place at the right time ... must be late three out of four meetings.

"Dean had some kind of crisis in Spain over the weekend and took off on an unexpected trip to see the Minister of Industry. I don't know if he'll be able to make the meeting."

"Well, let me say once more that I don't like to have these meetings with less than a full team. We're a small group, intentionally so. If one of us is missing, we always leave loose ends. I realize there are some matters that must be handled face to face, but I hope you will all try earnestly to be available on Tuesdays if at all possible. Now, Jamie, what's the first...? Dean, where are you? I thought you were in Spain."

"I am, Ajax. I'm in the Madrid office. I had them patch a video circuit through the New York board. A little expensive, but when Ajax Powers says 'Be at Tuesday strategy meetings,' Dean Zweibach, External Affairs Officer, Minister Plenipoten-

REDEFINING THE MANAGER'S JOB

tiary, with and without portfolio, is present at Tuesday strategy meetings."

"All right, Dean, we're impressed. What's the problem with the Minister?"

"Oh, he's unhappy because we filed intention last week to merge our French, Italian, and Spanish engineering companies under a European Community charter."

"You predicted that he might not like it. Is he going to give us trouble?"

"Well, he can stop us as far as the Spanish company is concerned, since Spain is only an associate member of the community and isn't bound by the common corporate code."

"Will he?"

"I don't think so. He would offend the people in Brussels, which he doesn't want to do right now. Anyhow, he knows we could always fold up in Spain completely, and he'd still have to let us work there out of France or Italy under the terms of the association treaty."

"Did you point that out to him?"

"Not really. Everything was very circumspect and gentlemanly. Nobody threatened anybody, but I think we came to an understanding."

"Well, let's keep it cool over there. He could put pressure on our friends at Alcazar, you know, and queer the joint venture in Thailand."

"Dean, keep us posted.... All right, Jamie, let's move on to the agenda. Do you all have the staff papers transmitted to you Friday?"

Jim Hunt looked at the faces in the six viewing screens. He could hear the sprinkler going in the back yard and the faint barking of the beagles in the kennels, but he felt completely divorced from ordinary time and space. The seven of them functioned almost as a collective intelligence. And yet they were not in any one place, or they were in seven places simul-

APPENDIX C

taneously. From his console he could probe into the vitals of operations in hundreds of other places. His computer in New York City could talk with other computers in Keokuk or Karachi and ask them "What is going on? What has happened in the past week?" It still spooked him a little even after two years. When he was in the Analysis Section—and particularly later when he headed up the Information Systems group—he used to feel pretty smart when he could make the patterns come out of the numbers like pictures in a developing tray.

But it was an intellectual, abstract excitement, even though he knew that the networks he designed and manipulated connected real activities of real people. This incorporeal omniscience at the Strategy Board was different. The sense of power was awesome and yet unbelievable. They called it a "real-time" information/control system; but when he walked the few steps from his breakfast table to the study/office Unisym had had built onto his house, it was like stepping into a time capsule. It wasn't real at all. It was no time, no place. He wondered if Zeus had ever really sat on Mount Olympus.

The first item on the agenda was always the operations review. Jim's fingers played over his control console with the detachment of a skilled organist as he called up the familiar charts. The boss was talking.

"Jamie, those figures are still only projected to 2004. I thought we were going to move out to 2005 this month."

"Programming hung up, Ajax. They want to feed in some new algorithms when they make the changeover and they hit some bugs. We should have it next week."

"Well, don't let them foul up the series. If we get a discontinuity in this data base, we'll never know what's going on. Check it yourself, Jamie, before it goes on stream. I never trust these data mechanics.

"By the way, is Information making any headway on getting us ten-year projections instead of five?"

REDEFINING THE MANAGER'S JOB

"Not really. They say the confidence level is still so low that it would be worse than nothing."

"Keep them on it, will you? The way things move around here, five years in the future is practically history. We've got to get a grip on a longer term."

... on with the routine analyses ... usual comments ... Billy still worried about exchange buildup in China ... why doesn't he get it out of there instead of "viewing with alarm" every week? ... Sybil's got a cost/price squeeze in the heavy-chemicals division ... wonder if we should be in that business? ... better start a divestiture study, but it will be awfully hard to sell to the old timers ... Ware still beating the drum about transportation costs now being greater than conversion costs in the manufacturing divisions and no reversal in sight ... we know you're important, Jim; cool it, will you? ... Dean not saying very much ... wonder if he's tired ... or hung over ... he has these quiet spells, though ... for a top negotiator he can be a remarkably quiet man ... and Larry has something to say about everything ... we'd get on a lot faster if he had a quiet spell once in a while ... Ajax mostly listens ... but when he wants to talk, that little gesture of the hand, even over the view screens, sure shuts everyone up.

"Jamie, before we go on with the regular agenda, I'd like to discuss the Maintenance Service concept again. I've talked to a lot of people since the last time it came up, and I think I can see how to make it work. Can we take the time?"

"I'm sure we can, Ajax. Some of the later items can be held over if we have to."

"You all know the concept. Unisym has operations all over the world. Each installation has a maintenance staff. I think overall they are about the best around. But most of the time they are merely standing by for a breakdown.

APPENDIX C

"Everybody else has more or less the same situation, but in some of the smaller plants it's terribly uneconomic. If we could set up a network of bases around the world to supply maintenance for a fee, a lot of plants, our own and others, could eliminate their captive departments."

"But, Ajax, we've modeled this strategy a half dozen times. By the time we get the special equipment in, and the spread of talent we would need, and the scheduling system and everything, there just isn't enough left to make it attractive to the customers and leave us a decent return."

"That's just the point, Billy. We can get a premium for the service; we don't have to price it below the level of existing costs to make it attractive. The operating people I've talked to are frantic trying to keep staffed with highly skilled people scattered around in twos and threes all over the world. They can't recruit them, they can't keep them happy, and they are fiddling around with 30 or 40 national unions all the time. We could recruit worldwide, train them at our Institute in Puerto Rico, locate them in attractive places where there is some intellectual environment, and deal directly with the international union headquarters. Dean, you did say you thought we could get them covered by an international labor contract, didn't you?"

"Oh, I think so. We'd have to balance off the workforce racially—and maybe nationally—and you can bet Luther will stick us with some pretty fat living and transfer benefits, but it can be done. It's just a matter of whether we can afford the ticket or not. We'll end up with unit labor costs equal to about the highest anywhere in the world, you may as well count on that."

"But you could do it?"

"Well, Ajax, you know you never know with these kinds of negotiations. A lot of factors could enter that have nothing to do with Unisym. And of course you know Luther has to contend with his elected Council and Chamber, and you're never sure how they will jump—but, yes, our relations are pretty good and the odds are we should be able to get an international contract from them."

"Larry, have your people gone any further with the equipment and operations thinking on this?"

"Just the preliminary studies, Ajax, but they look pretty interesting. We've sampled some probability maintenance routines, and there are some ideas on airmobile maintenance shops that look promising."

"What about the recruiting and training side, Billy? Could the Institute handle it?"

"Oh, we could set up to handle it at the Institute all right, but we haven't done anything yet because we haven't got any specs from Larry's Systems Design gang."

"O.K., let's put a study team together on this and see if we can't find a way through. I'm sure there's an opportunity here. Billy, Larry, Jamie, will you get together and set up a task force? And Sybil, better get them somebody from Market Research. Let's set a six-month decision date. Assume a premium price structure and shoot for a breakeven in about three years. Who has a good man who's hot to head up the team? Anyone in Maintenance or Systems? How about somebody from your Economics group, Jamie? Get some nominees together and we'll sit down later in the week and pick one. I'd like to brief the man myself, since this is sort of a hobbyhorse of mine."

"Now let's get back to the agenda."

"Hey, fellows, before we go on, how about a break? My kidneys are getting too old for these nonstop meetings."

"All right, Billy, let's take ten minutes. But please, everybody, clear your circuits by 11:15 so we can get started again promptly."

Jim cut out of the conference circuit and punched the coffee button on the console.

APPENDIX C

... call the secretarial office and take a quick look on the tube at the morning incoming ... Carol can retransmit hard copy of the stuff that looks important and route on the rest.

... time to look over the transmittals dictated yesterday ... turn the key in the lock switch to put the authorized signature on the originals in the office.

... Seidel might like a shot at the maintenance network study ... she's about ripe for a major task force lead and has a lot of background in maintenance cost ... get Carol to fax through her folder and maybe talk to her tomorrow.

... still a couple of minutes before the screens light up and the wheels begin to turn ... this maintenance package sounds risky, but it could go ... if it does it will change a lot of lives ... people will be moved around all over the globe ... a lot of production economics could be changed ... certainly a lot of other organizations ... Dean's people would certainly have to scurry around to get all the new residence visas and the permanent travel visas, but if the ICL gives its blessing the rest will be just paperwork ... what a weird institution, the International Congress of Labor ... Werner Luther is more of a sovereign than most heads of state ... doesn't really come under anybody's jurisdiction, though he does make a curtsy once in a while toward the U.N. and the ILO ... does have his troubles, though ... legislative chambers of the ICL full of real monsters ... reps from all over the world and from all sorts of local outfits ... we talk about Dean's "state department" ... bet Luther's political department is the largest diplomatic force going ... ah, here comes the home team ... better cut myself in.

"Everybody feel better? Where's Jim Ware?"

REDEFINING THE MANAGER'S JOB

"He was trying to get a call through to Broken Hill. He's probably still talking."

"Well, let's start anyhow. Larry, guess you're up on the Cleveland disposal systems contract. What's the problem?"

"Temporarily, at least, we've got bad troubles. HUD is holding up progress payments because their auditors don't want to let us expense the basic systems design work. They claim it's a facility investment and should be capitalized."

"How much is involved?"

"A lot more than our profit's likely to be."

"Oh, for heaven's sake! I don't know why we stay in this big government work. They want us to maintain this urban systems capability, but they keep pestering us with all their regulations and trying to take all the profit out of the work. Why don't you tell them to get off our backs or we won't take any more prime contracts?"

"Jim, they've heard that story before, and they ain't impressed. We make money on our government business. The margins may be small, but the ROIs are pretty good."

"Sounds like the margin on this one is going to be negative."

"We'll come out whole in the end, but it's going to take a while to unwind it. When you're dealing with a $200-billion operation like HUD, once some son of a bureaucrat puts a piece in crosswise it's a hell of a job to get things unstuck. Back in the seventies when I was a project engineer, I used to think the DOD guys were hard to live with, but they were just bucking for brownie points. Now that HUD's the big cheese, they've got a lot of do-gooders in there that I swear are out to see we don't make a nickel, although they'd never admit it."

"So what do we do? Play patty-cake? Get tough? Drop out? Dean, what's the atmosphere?"

"We've got a lot of old friends in the Office of Waste Disposal and I think we can get them to call off the hatchet men, although the auditors don't work directly for them, you know.

APPENDIX C

Anyhow, this is part of the government contract business; and if we want to stay in it, we have to expect this kind of thing once in a while. The crux of the matter is I don't think we can possibly back out of this one or any other HUD contract. John Q. Public expects us to do this sort of thing. If we act less than enthusiastic, the public members of our board will start to scream bloody murder and we'll have everybody—the SEC, the IRS, the FTC, and the whole blooming alphabet—buzzing around our ears."

"All right, let's be good boys, then. But, Dean, put this one at the top of your list because it's costing us a hell of a lot of money, and give us a weekly confidential memo on the state of negotiations. Try to get some kind of special adjustment for the delayed payments. And, Billy, give us a weekly fix on just how much this hang-up is costing us. But don't put anything on tape that could end up as Exhibit A. Let's all remember the Truth in Business Act."

"Now let's move on. Sybil, what's with the western regional sales force? Haven't you been exercising your irresistible charm on their bargaining agent?"

"They want to change their employment status to a direct participation basis."

"But they have a union contract. Shouldn't Dean be handling this?"

"I don't think so, Ajax. There's a policy question here. What they want is a single net performance contract covering the whole group. They're taking the position that we've done it with research and engineering groups and some of the central staff sections for years, and they want the system extended into field sales."

"But don't they understand that you have to hire some of these specialist groups as a team—they don't function individually? That isn't true of salesmen."

"Maybe so, but a couple of other companies have made these kinds of arrangements with sales groups, and the boys

REDEFINING THE MANAGER'S JOB

and girls have got the wind up. They claim they could go as a group to some other company and get such a contract. What I think they actually mean is that if they dropped the marginal producers, the cream of them could cut a deal with a smaller company. They could make a pretty attractive package under those circumstances, and they might well be able to do it. In fact, I bet they've had a nibble somewhere."

"Syb, I told you at the time: You let the camel in the tent when you made a group contract with the advertising department."

"But Jim, we had to. They were going to set up their own agency, and with almost everybody else in advertising on a group basis we could never have staffed another department from scratch on an old individual contract basis."

"Sybil, that's just the difference. We could do without an advertising department and use all outside services if we chose to. As it is, even over and above media charges, we spend 90 percent of our advertising budget outside. The same with research, engineering, and the others. We don't provide more than 10 to 15 percent of our RD&E in house. The rest we contract from the professional outfits who for most purposes are cheaper and better qualified than anything we could maintain for ourselves. In that situation the captive groups are always competing against the outside market, and we have a club over them. With a sales force, that wouldn't be true."

"That may all be so, but I don't think these people are bluffing—not 100 percent anyway. So we'd better make up our minds because if we go along with them, the thing will go through the entire organization like wildfire."

"Syb, just what do they want anyhow?"

"They want a net price on company products, Dean. They would set their own margins and divvy up among themselves what was left after selling expenses. A little more complicated, but that's the guts of it."

APPENDIX C

"Would they accept take-or-pay volume quotas?"

"Maybe."

"Who hires and fires?"

"They do, except if we terminate the whole group."

"Wow!"

"Look, it isn't really different from what Jamie does with his operations research team or Larry with his whiz kids in molecular mechanics."

"Yes, but those guys don't get tangled up with our customers and stir up the market."

"Well, the argument is that the customers will not be affected by the change at all. The salesmen will still be employees; they will still be subject to overall company policy; they are just taking over the direct compensation system. It won't increase our selling expense, and we'll save a lot of administrative cost and headaches."

"It's a pithy argument."

"Scares hell out of me."

"It's nothing but an old-fashioned distributor set up with fringe benefits."

"Well, we're on the spot. How long can we stall them?"

"Couple of weeks. Any longer than that and they'll start to get nervy, no matter what we do. This isn't something they just thought up in the last couple of days."

"All right. Jamie, get a lawyer on it. Billy, we need to know just how much of this sort of thing is going on and where. Mostly California, I bet. Find out if any sales groups have changed companies en masse and what happened. And give some thought to how we would control costs under such a setup. Dean, do you think you might be able to find out for us who, if anyone, is trying to seduce that crew? Good! We'll schedule a full half day to thrash this out week after next. I have a sinking feeling that this is the way the world is going—or at least this country—but I don't like it."

REDEFINING THE MANAGER'S JOB

"Well, gentlemen—Sybil—it's after 12:00. I think we should break for lunch. Shall we reconvene at 1:30? Sorry, Dean, I guess it's a little early for dinner in Madrid, but you shouldn't have one of those heavy Spanish dinners anyhow if you're going to stay awake after the break. You can have a sophisticated midnight supper, instead, after we quit for the day. Try a McDonald's enchilada to tide you over. Jamie, can you defrost a tray to eat at your console, so we can discuss some things over lunch?"

"Sure, Ajax, give me ten minutes and I'll see you back here."

... the old man still thinks I'm his assistant ... for two years now he has been stalling about getting a replacement ... guess it's a compliment in a way, but I wish he would move on it.

... morning went pretty well ... not too much chaff ... the old man still calls the shots, though ... he's a gentleman and he listens, but when he gets a notion it's grim death ... he is going to get his worldwide plant maintenance system come hell or high water ... probably will work, but the growth isn't there ... manufacturing is growing so much slower than the rest of the economy ... down to 25 percent of GNP now in the big countries and still losing ground ... but he still thinks a company mostly makes things ... probably too late to change him now ... lost youth and all that ... when he was making his reputation you still had manufacturing VPs and they were pretty powerful guys sometimes.

... wonder if he'll give up the chair at 60 like he's supposed to ... who would go in? ... Billy is as old as he is ... Dean I don't think wants it ... Larry would take it, but I think he'd just as soon not ... Jim might take it ... Sybil? ... me? oh, hell, why worry? ... that's a couple years yet, and lots can happen.

APPENDIX C

> ... got to hand it to Dean ... quiet guy, but always seems to know when and where to push the buttons ... likes to be a little mysterious and offhand, but maybe it's better we don't always know exactly what he's doing ... likes to joke about his "state department" but it's really not that much of a joke ... couple hundred people ... full-time staff at the International Congress of Labor ... delegation in Brussels and a group at LAFTA ... whole stack of people in Washington and I don't know how many other capitals ... plus his flying squads ... wonder when he'll set up a representative to the Vatican.

"O.K., Ajax, ready to go."

> ... tea and clear soup ... wonder what would happen to that guy if he really let go and started to eat.

"Jamie, I've finally given up trying to find a replacement for you inside the organization. The men I would like don't seem to be hot to be an 'assistant to' and the ones who want it don't seem to have the horses. Anyhow, I've decided to go outside. I've contacted some of the professional representatives we know, and they've sent me some candidates' résumés. I've asked for copies to be sent to you, and they should be coming out of your facsimile printer now. There are about 20 in all; but if we can pick out the dozen or so most likely ones, I'd like you to try to arrange to interview them later in the week. You know the job and you know me so you should be able to screen them as well as I could—maybe even better. Short-list about three and arrange for them and their reps to see me as soon as it can be fitted in."

"The résumés are about what you'd expect: name, education, age, and sex—I'm surprised they still give us that—chronology of job experience, honors, hobbies. As usual the reps guarantee the facts and warrant no significant derogatory background. Frankly I still have trouble getting a feel for peo-

REDEFINING THE MANAGER'S JOB

ple from the skinny résumés we get these days, but I guess it's better than the puff sheets we used to get and then have to go snooping around to find out if half of what the guy said was true."

"The first couple there are from Cady. He usually has good men, so we should look these over carefully."

"Ajax, this man Kuesell apparently worked at FPC for an old classmate of mine. His credentials sound impressive, and I could get a quick rundown on him from Dave Fulton."

"O.K., but be sure to do it on a very personal basis. If the reps get the idea we're snooping around behind their backs, they'll report us for unfair labor practices—or worse yet, blacklist us—and then we'll be in a real fix. Let's get Kuesell in anyhow."

"Ajax, how about this Canaran? He looks right on as far as experience goes."

"Yes, you'd better talk to him, Jamie; but he's represented by John Wagner, and Wagner is just impossible. You can't talk sense with that man. If we did take on Canaran we'd probably have to try to get him to change his rep."

So on they went through the stack of forms, trying to translate a single sheet of bare-bones chronology into a flesh-and-blood person with whom they might have to work very closely for many years. By 1:15 they had pulled out eight "possibles," and Jim called Carol, his duty secretary, on the direct line, gave her the names, and asked her to contact the reps and arrange one-hour appointments beginning at 10 A.M. Thursday, packing them as tightly as possible during the day and evening. He would stay over till Friday morning if necessary. He shut off the voice circuit and carried his dirty tray back to the kitchen.

. . . Carol is a nice young kid . . . wonder what it's like to be single and live in New York City now that it runs pretty much around the clock . . . do you ever get used to it not ever being dark now that the vapor lights are

APPENDIX C

operating over most of the town? . . . it was only parts of midtown that had the skylights when we moved out of town . . . maybe you get afraid of the dark again like a kid.

. . . remember when some of the top men still had secretaries right by their offices who would come in when they called? . . . must have been kind of nice and friendly . . . almost like an extra wife . . . guess I was just born too late . . . but there wasn't nearly so much romping on the divans, though, as the old timers like to pretend . . . makes good stories but probably mostly just talk.

. . . hope Billy didn't have more than two martinis with his lunch or we'll hear lots of talk . . . old man's back on screen already.

"Hi, Jim. Have a good lunch? Gentlemen, Sybil, if you're all ready, let's get back at it. Billy, what are we going to do for office space?"

"We are about to run out at the 57th Street building. We looked into moving some more activities into the satellite offices up in Harriman, but most of the subprofessional people probably wouldn't move and we have a lot of trouble keeping that place staffed as it is. And we would have to build up there anyhow."

"Any chance of putting on a second shift in Harriman?"

"Not in that labor market, I don't think—even if we doubled the shift premium."

"That's what we said when we went to 24-hour offices in the city."

"Yes, but the clerical people just aren't there in Orange County, and anyhow Harriman doesn't run around the clock like Manhattan."

"Can we get more space in the city?"

"Sure, but it will cost like the devil. You've got the figures there in the staff paper."

"So you're proposing a seven-day workweek?"

REDEFINING THE MANAGER'S JOB

"Well, sort of. Look, Ajax, ever since we went to shift work in the offices, we've been on a four-day week with three-day weekends, right? And we sold the shift concept by shortening both the total hours and the days in the workweek, right? And it wasn't all that hard to sell once the town was lit up and cleaned up around the clock. In fact, because we were early, we even got some favorable publicity as enlightened employers and good citizens for spreading the transportation load, et cetera. And we tripled the capacity of our offices overnight—no pun intended. Now if we play this right, we can be heroes again and save a big piece of money. Instead of working four days on and three days off, we put them on four on and four off, with alternating crews."

"You mean you would have six shifts?"

"Yes, but let me finish. The effect is to reduce the average workweek from 32 to 28 hours. In return the people have to learn to live on an eight-day cycle that progresses one day of the week each week. It's the same kind of tradeoff we made when we went to four days, three shifts. Our payoff comes from almost doubling our office capacity at zero investment, and with prime space going for up to $50 a square foot that's not small potatoes."

"But six shifts—what chaos!"

"Look, we've already crossed that bridge. If we can keep a continuous operation going for three shifts, we can do it with six. And remember how we speeded up office operations when we went to three shifts, in spite of the confusion. We gained a little on receivables, we picked up a little on the cash account, and we sure speeded up order processing and traffic. We ought to make some gains from this system, too. Those three dead days out of every seven sure bring us to a screeching halt now."

"Boy, Billy, I dread the thought. That means three whole new sets of supervisors. You'd never know where to find anybody. It would take a big education campaign."

"Look, Ajax, it's not difficult. Aldol downtown has done it

APPENDIX C

in part already, and they claim the people love it. We don't have to do it all at once. Convert over by departments, just like we did to shifts. Heck, the data processing groups are running seven days now, and they manage. You want return on your assets. Here's one way to get it. The figures are all there."

"Sure, Billy, but this isn't something we have to decide today. Talk to your behavioral sciences people in personnel and see what they think. Maybe then we can pilot it through them and call it a behavioral research study so we don't get everyone all upset until we know what we want to do. Dean, is there any talk around the unions about anything like this?"

"Only the usual stuff about a 30-hour week that I know of."

"Well, get your antenna out and see if you can find out what their reaction is likely to be, but for goodness sake don't let them guess that we are seriously considering it. Okay, so let's see if we can get through the rest of these items fairly fast. We have performance contract renegotiations coming up with the group operating officers pretty soon, and I would like to start developing our position today if possible. Jim, where are we on that Japanese refinery?"

"Coming down the home stretch, Ajax. Treasury has O.K.'d it. MITI in Japan has cleared it, which means among other things that the manufacturers' syndicate has given its blessing. All we need now is an endorsement from GATT and the chop from the International Union and we can go out for bids. Dean says another 30 days—right, Ambassador?"

"GATT's no problem. This thing was cranked through the Asian Planning Authority, so GATT will just sprinkle holy water on it as it goes by. I don't know what's with the labor people. They've been acting very cagey the last couple of weeks. I don't know whether they're going to try to horse-trade with us or whether they want a lever to get something out of somebody else, maybe Mitsui. Anyhow, Dick Christy, my permanent rep at the headquarters, says he's practically sitting on their door-

REDEFINING THE MANAGER'S JOB

step every day, so I guess we can't do anything but just wait. If it doesn't come through in 30 days, we'll have complications we don't know about yet."

"O.K. Are any of these other agenda items ready for action now? If they're just other status reports, we can get that out of the staff papers. Are there any extraordinary items we should take up? Good! Then let's talk a little about the performance contract reviews. Jamie, could we have those summary displays for each of the operating groups back on the view screens?"

> . . . *now comes the really tough part of big management . . . negotiating with governments and unions, and customers and suppliers, is rough, but child's play compared to performance contracts.*

"Here's Group I. Looks as if McClintock is going to beat both his sales and profit forecasts again."

"He's always too conservative."

"Conservative, hell! He's the greatest con artist in the company. He comes in every year cry-mouthing like the world was coming to an end. And we end up rolling over on our backs and accepting a lot of deferred charges for promotion and facilities and what have you. Every year he hits us for a whopping performance bonus."

"I'm afraid you're right, Jim, and it really is immaterial whether he does it consciously or because it's his nature. Jamie, have economics pay special attention to his General Environment Analysis this year. And Sybil, tell market research we don't want another surprise market 'explosion' in Group I's area. Larry, I think we got taken a little last year, too, with McClintock's story of all that new superior technology the competition was just about to hatch. I don't say we panicked, but the seed was planted and not much really developed that

APPENDIX C

hurt us. Let's give the inputs for Group I a little special attention all around this year. Let's see Group II."

"Looks like Alvarez will come in just about on target across the board. Now there is a conservative. Don't you think we could jack him up a little this year, Ajax? He's got some pretty good market franchises going for him. Is he losing share of market in many places, Sybil?"

"Yes, in quite a few, but he always argues that he doesn't want to buy the market."

"Well, it's a good argument and his return on investment sure looks sweet."

"He's got some pretty stable mature situations, too. Maybe that's exactly what he's good at. Billy, put a confidential study team on this, will you, and see if there are any go-go situations in Group II that we ought to consider shifting. Otherwise, frankly, I'm disgustingly tempted to sit back and just bask in those ROI numbers. And I know at least Billy agrees with me. Maybe we can needle a little more bounce into Group II, but I doubt we'll ever make a whizbang out of Alvarez and we've got plenty of other guys drooling for the cash flow he throws off. Let's see the numbers for Group III?"

"How's that for ROI?"

"Yeah, that's just the trouble. Harkins says it's just tight operations, but I can't believe he isn't skimping somewhere. Jamie, are Group III's businesses really that lush?"

"Not really. Harkins just seems to have fatter margins than anyone else in his industries in most cases, as near as we can determine. The Business Analysis gang can't spot anything way out of line. He's just a little leaner all the way through."

"I know. And Harkins is an old hand and has always had good operations. But if we run out of steam in that group in four or five years, which is about when he'll retire, we'll look awful silly after all the fat performance bonuses he's collected. Larry, I want to be sure we have a good feel for what's going on

REDEFINING THE MANAGER'S JOB

in his development groups—and don't let your natural optimism or professional loyalty or whatever it is put too rosy a glow on it. And, Billy, have someone check his personnel development program closely to see if he really has the people coming along. And everybody—Larry, your maintenance people, too—look a little carefully at the data on this group. We don't want to be overly suspicious—and I'll give Harkins the benefit of the doubt in most cases—but it's just too easy to milk an operation for a good quick performance report, even these days, and we don't want to get taken, even by our friends."

> ... so the battle begins ... eight group execs and each one a different situation, a different personality ... this we'll do the old-fashioned way in the big conference room down at headquarters ... just too tricky to filter through video ... the group exec with his staff and personal rep on one side, Ajax and the rest of us on the other, with the computer models offstage at the other end of the control consoles.
> ... all in the family, but sure has become what the lawyers call an adversary relationship ... all very friendly and gentlemanly, of course, but eventually there has to be that performance agreement with the two signatures ... so much sales, so much return on assets, such-and-such an organizational performance, these market shares, thus and so technical accomplishment, this production performance to be accomplished with so much new money, these people, these markets, and on and on.
> ... and then the compensation package with steep performance bonuses and penalties ... if a guy cuts a good deal for himself, either because he cons us or gets lucky, he can be a millionaire in one year in a company this size ... if he falls on his face he could end up eating peanut butter sandwiches ... motivation ... incentive ...

APPENDIX C

they've got it turned up to full gain at this level... and it's all on the table once a year.

... then the group exec has to go and subcontract it out to his division heads... and their compensation comes out of his gross... same process down through levels and levels and levels... no idea how many levels in most of the divisions... but that's why it has to be this way... you couldn't run an outfit like this the old direct chain-of-command way... hell, it would be complete paralysis.

... takes a certain kind of guy to be in those line operating positions... don't think I could do it... don't think I've got the nerve... sure, I used to negotiate a performance agreement when I had the infosystems department... still do in fact... but the leverage isn't there... the swings aren't as wide and the performance criteria aren't so clear-cut.

... not many of the operating guys make it up to headquarters jobs... guess most of them don't want to really... particularly if they get up to group exec... don't really have much to gain... and they're always looking for that big killing, that one big year that will set them up for good... well, "whatever turns you on," as they used to say...

"Gentlemen, Sybil. I wish you would all work over the numbers on Groups I and II this week and be ready to propose a performance package next Tuesday. If it turns out we all see the picture about the same, we should be able to draft our opening negotiating position with alternatives at that time. We'll try to take two groups then each week so we'll be set for the annual review season three months from now. I expect to be in my office the rest of the week; but if you can't raise me here, New York will know how to reach me. Have a good week. I'll see you next Tuesday, if not before."

REDEFINING THE MANAGER'S JOB

"Goodnight, Ajax."

Jim threw the master switch on the console. The viewing screens were dark. The readouts were little blind holes. He was alone again. Just an individual in the Pocono Mountains. Not plugged in.

> ... what did we really accomplish? ... the company keeps spreading out ... the management systems keep getting better ... the information feedback is fantastic ... but there seem to be more things that have to be negotiated, that can't be simply decided, controlled ... maybe that's good ... maybe it's some kind of institutional democracy working ... otherwise, who controls the controllers? ... government? ... there's only a couple of governments big enough to really put strong pressure on an outfit like Unisym ... and Washington is the only one that really tries ... in Russia the state industry leaders are the government so the question doesn't arise ... Japan? ... there the government uses the worldwide companies as an instrument the way people used to use armies, so the relationship is entirely different ... China? ... who knows, but you get the impression that anything can be arranged ... that leaves lonely old Washington and sometimes I think they are fighting a rear-guard action ... the stockholders? ... scattered all over the world, they're not owners, they're bank depositors—or more precisely, lottery players ... they don't even nominally elect all the board any more ... with public representatives, consumer representatives, union representatives, the board has become a debating society and essentially a public one at that ... sure, they can fire the officers, but how often does that really happen? ... so what are we? ... the executive body, the Strategy Board—a self-perpetuating priesthood serving a god called "optimal utility"? ... or

APPENDIX C

merely a switching gear through which negotiations among divergent interests are arranged?

... that's enough philosophy, Jamie ... you're getting too profound up here in the hills ... maybe we should move back into the city where there's a little more tangible reality, before I go completely rarefied ... it's so damned expensive, though ... maybe after the kids leave home.

... anyhow, got to go to the city to screen those candidates and their professional reps on Thursday for Ajax ... that means leaving here before 8:00 if I want to get in by 10:00 ... and $50 for the heliporter ... which I can't expense-account and can't even take for tax credit ... "transportation to and from place of employment is not an allowable business expense."

... but where is my place of employment? ... mostly here ... it's company equipment, company furniture, the company even built the room, so why shouldn't this be my base? ... those rules were made in a different time ... but try to get them changed ... don't know which would be tougher—the IRS or the accounting department ... furthermore they're not fair ... I go in at least once a week, which means that's over $2,000 a year I have to swallow ... some of those guys don't average once a month in the main office and Holstead almost never goes in ... so I'm abused.

... and now that rabble-rouser in congress, Aloutski, trying to make us pay taxes on company-furnished home offices as additional compensation ... that's ridiculous ... hell, I hardly ever use this room for anything but company work, and anyhow it would cost them to have an office for me somewhere, so why not here? ... he might get away with it, though ... there's a lot of people who still have to go into town four days a week, and they all vote.

REDEFINING THE MANAGER'S JOB

... maybe while I'm in New York I should stay over and see Reeves ... my performance contract is coming up for evaluation next month, too, and we should agree on a position ... he's a good rep, but like all these guys he sometimes thinks he's got to earn his percentage by pushing the employer around ... Ajax has been real good to me and I'd just as soon keep it nice and friendly ... I made all my standards this year and even a little more, so I should be in line for some performance bonus, but I don't expect a pot of gold ... not the second year on the job ... we do have to decide, though, whether to take it now or put it in the deferred kitty ... which reminds me, I have to ask Reeves what's happening to that Hong Kong stock he bought for me last spring.

... wonder if Reeves could wangle me a sabbatical year in four or five more years ... hell of a risky job to leave for a year, though—both for me and for the company ... probably better not try ... afraid I've moved up too high to indulge myself in that kind of income ... there's always a price.

... well, time to quit ... wonder what Mary's doing ... said something about going to New Hope to the theater tonight ... I think I'm in a nasty mood ... maybe she can get Perry Wilson to take her.

BIBLIOGRAPHY

Bagley, E. R., *Beyond the Conglomerates.* New York: AMACOM, 1975.
Battaglia, O. W., and J. J. Tarrant, *The Corporate Eunuch.* New York: Thomas Y. Crowell, 1973.
Bell, D., *The Coming of the Post-Industrial Society.* New York: Basic Books, 1973.
Bell, D., *The Cultural Contradictions of Capitalism.* New York: Basic Books, 1976.
Bell, D., Ed., *Toward the Year 2000.* Boston: Beacon, 1967.
Bennis, W. G., *Changing Organizations.* New York: McGraw-Hill, 1966.
Brown, H., *The Human Future Revisited.* New York: Norton, 1978.
The Center Magazine, "The Establishment and All That," Santa Barbara, Center for the Study of Democratic Institutions, 1970.
Churchman, C. West, *Challenge to Reason.* New York: McGraw-Hill, 1968.
The Conference Board, *Challenge to Leadership.* New York: Free Press, 1973.
Cornuelle, R., *DeManaging America.* New York: Random House, 1975.
Dean, J., *Management Economics.* New York: Prentice-Hall, 1951.
Drucker, P., *The Age of Discontinuity.* New York: Harper & Row, 1969.
Farmer, R. N., *Management in the Future.* Belmont, California: Wadsworth, 1967.
Farmer, R. N., *The Real World of 1984.* New York: McKay, 1973.
Friedman, M., *Capitalism and Freedom.* Chicago: University of Chicago Press, 1962.
Georgescu-Rocgen, N., *The Entrophy Law and the Economic Process.* Cambridge: Harvard University Press, 1971.
Hall, P., *Europe 2000.* London: Duckworth, 1977.
Heller, R., *The Great Executive Dream.* New York: Delacorte, 1972.
Jay, A., *Management and Machiavelli.* New York: Holt, Rinehart and Winston, 1967.
Kahn, H., *The Year 2000.* New York: Macmillan, 1967.
Kahn, H., *The Next 200 Years.* New York: William Morrow & Co., 1976.

REDEFINING THE MANAGER'S JOB

Kahn, H., *World Economic Development*. New York: Morrow Quill, 1979

Kahn, H., ed., *The Future of the Corporation*. New York: Mason and Lipscomb, 1974.

Kuhns, W., *The Post Industrial Prophets*. New York: Harper & Row, 1971.

Leavitt, H., et al., *Organizations of the Future*. New York: Praeger, 1974.

Macrae, N., "The Company Entrepreneurial Revolution," *The Economist*, December 25, 1976.

Marrow, A. J., *Behind the Executive Mask*. New York: AMACOM, 1964.

Merrell, V. D., *Huddling: The Informal Way to Management Success*. New York: AMACOM, 1979.

Paarlberg, D., *Great Myths of Economics*. New York: New American Library, 1968.

Parkinson, C. N., *The Law of Delay*. Boston: Houghton Mifflin, 1970.

Purdic, W. K., and B. Taylor, eds., *Business Strategies for Survival*. London: Heinemann, 1976.

Ross, H. I., *Financial Statements: A Crusade for Current Values*. New York: Pitman, 1969.

Stine, G. H., *The Third Industrial Revolution*. New York: Putnam, 1975.

Tavel, C., *The Third Industrial Age*. Homewood, Illinois: Dow Jones–Irwin, 1975.

Townsend, R., *Up the Organization*. New York: Knopf, 1970.

Tuccille, J., *Who's Afraid of 1985?* New Rochelle: Arlington, 1975.

Vacca, R., *The Coming Dark Age*. Garden City: Doubleday, 1974.

Zaleznik, A., *Human Dilemmas of Leadership*. New York: Harper & Row, 1966.

INDEX

academic institutions
  management training in, 92
  objectives set by, 78
  production management students in, 171–172
  role determination for, 44
accountability of management
  for capital allocation, 114–115
  in future, 222–225
  government imposition of, 61–64
  for planning, 125
  principles for, 59–61
  self-imposed, 65–67
accounting
  methods, viability of, 131–138
  net worth and, 131–133
  replacement-cost, 98–101
  two kinds of, simultaneous use of, 150–151
"acting" manager position, 200
advertising industry, power of, 50
Air Force, U.S., 92
alienation
  of middle managers, 13
  of production specialists, 14–15, 165–166
allocation of resources, see resources, management of
alternate use value, 143–144
American and Foreign Power, 95n
American Institute of Certified Public Accountants, 139
American Society for Testing Materials, 55

antitrust cases, 217
assets, 29–30
  alternate-use value of, 143–144
  conservation of, 95–96
  depreciation of, 98–104
  gross, 135
  intangible, see intangible assets
  production management and, 167
  replacement-cost accounting for, 98–101
  return on, 134

B-1 bomber, 92
banks, power of, 61
bargaining, collective, 24–25
Bell, Daniel, 92, 226
board of directors, see top management
bonuses, performance, 158, 196–197
borrowing, 29
bosses, multiple, 181
British Institute of Management, 59n
British Petroleum, 5
Buetow, Herb, 190–191
bureaucracy, 7, 216
Burton, Sandy, 141

Cabot, Sebastian, 75n
capital formation, 20–21, 114–115
capital gains, reinvestment and, 111, 113

275

INDEX

capitalism, 20–22, 227
capitalizing leaseholds, 134
cash flow
   depreciation, 101–103, 106–107
   discounted (DCF), 103–105, 136
cash flow rate of return, 136
CEO (chief executive officer), see top management
Chandler, Alfred D., 177
charitable foundations, self-liquidating, 95n
chart, organization, 175, 176
   organization tree as, 177–179
charters, see statement of purpose (management's)
chief executive officer (CEO), see top management
Chrysler Corporation, 60, 95
Churchill, Winston, 49
Cleveland, Ohio, 225
collective bargaining, 24–25
commercial organizations, independent, see contracted services
commercial properties, 7
communication, 205–209
   by implication, 209–210
   misunderstanding of, 210–211
   problems in, 207
   work shifts affecting, 234–235
communism, profit-making and, 5, 6
compensation
   bonuses and, 158, 196–197
   by contribution, 198–200
   as motivator, 190–191
   systems for administering, 193–195

competence of management, assessing
   by accounting, 130–138
   by discounted-cash-flow rate of return, 148–149
   human resources considered in, 153–159
   in public-resource use, 159–161
   by resource-use evaluation, 144–148
competition, disclosure of objectives and, 77
Comptroller of the Currency, U.S., 55
conservation of assets, 95–96
constructive motivation, 204
consultants, 185–187, 222
consumable resources, 35
contracted services, 185–187, 222
   disassociation from parent organization of, 237–238
   in future, 236–237
contract manufacturing, 222
corporate dividends, see dividends, corporate
corporations, 214
   charters for, 75
   in Europe, 5–6
   misconceptions about, 17–20
   multinational, see multinational corporations
   ownership in, 28–31
corruption, see crime, white-collar
cost of living, 23–24
credit unions, employee, 30n
crime, white-collar, 56–57, 61
   legislation concerning, 62–64
cultural lag, 68

276

INDEX

DCF, see discounted cash flow
decentralization of organizations, 236–243
 see also contracted services
Defense Department, U.S., 92
depletion, 137
depreciation
 cash flow, 101–103, 106–107
 of fixed assets, 99–101
 in return on investment, 135–136
depreciation reserves, 99–100, 113
development
 of managers, 225–226
 strategy for, 81
dictatorships, socialistic, 21
diffusion of costs, 24
directors, board of, see top management
discounted cash flow (DCF), 103–105, 136
 competence of management assessed by, 148–149
 return on investment compared to, 150–151
disinvestment, 102–105
distributors, 222
dividends, corporate, 101–102
 management and, 108–109
 reinvestment of, 111–112
 taxes on, 106–107, 109–111
double taxation on dividends, 106–107, 109–111
Drucker, Peter, 30n, 133, 177

earnings-per-share, 133
economizing made, 92–93, 226
education, 89, 214
 see also academic institutions

employee credit unions, 30n
employee pension funds, 30n
Employee Retirement Security Act (1974), U.S., 62
employees, see human resources
ENI, 5
environmental interaction statements, 161
Environmental Protection Act, 60
equity, 29–30
European Council of Management, 59n
expensing, 137–138

"faithful retainer" managers, 14
FASB (Financial Accounting Standards Board), 134n, 138–139
Federal Procurement Policy, Office of, U.S., 91–92
Federal Trade Commission, U.S., 55, 217
Financial Accounting Standards Board (FASB), 134n, 138–139
food brokers, 222
Ford, Gerald, 49
Ford Motor Company, 60
Fortune (magazine), 87
France, 63
franchised public utilities, 95n
Friedman, Milton, 43

Galbraith, John Kenneth, 56
Germany (West), 20–21
 Mitbestimmung in, 38
government
 "business management" in, 214–215

277

INDEX

government (*cont.*)
  objectives determination for, 90-92
  priority-establishment by, 49
  as regulator of management, 55, 216-217
  value establishment by, 47-49
Great Britain, *see* United Kingdom
gross assets, 135
grouping of staff, 180-181
growth
  in objectives formulation, 80-81

Harvard Business Review, 40, 172
harvesting mode, 81
Health, Education and Welfare, Dept. of, U.S., 179n
health care organizations, 214
  role determination for, 44-45
hierarchies, self-perpetuating, 53-54
"huddling," 176n
humanitarianism, managerial, 202-203
human resources, 7
  capitalization of, 154-155
  disinvestment of, 34-35
  evaluation of use of, 153-159
  grouping of, by interest, 180-181
  individualism in approach to, 192
  management of, 33-34
  production management and, 168
  return on, 162-163

I. G. Farben, 242
incentive programs, individualization of, 192-193
income, operating, 146
independent commercial organizations, *see* contracted services
India, Steel Authority of, 87
inflation, 23-24
  depreciation and, 100-101
infraresources, *see* public resources
insurance
  clerical malpractice, 59n
  liability, corporate, 64
intangible assets, 32-33
  accounting for, 151-152
  production management and, 168
  return on, 162-163
Internal Revenue Service, U.S., 63, 103, 217
inventory profit, 97-98
investment allowance, 136n
investment spending, 82, 138, 147
Italy, 114-115
IT&T, 95n

Japan, 199
  accountability in, 223n
  compensation in, 190n
jargon, 20
job descriptions, 175-176
job enrichment programs, 241-242

Kahn, Herman, 213
knowledge workers, 221-222
Kristol, Irving, 56

INDEX

labor, cost of, 24–26
lag
  cultural, 68
  managerial, 68–69
laws
  broken by business, 56–58
  social responsibility and, 42–43
  on taxation, changing, 109–111
  on white-collar crime, 62–64
leaseholds, capitalizing, 134
Liberia, 5
Likert, Rensis, 153–154
"line"/"staff" dichotomy, 183–185
Lockheed, 61, 92

McLuhan, Marshall, 206
Macrea, Norman, 242
malpractice insurance for clergy, 59n
management
  accountability for, see accountability of management
  asset-use determination by, 144–149
  autonomic quality-control structure of, 56
  categories of business and, 4–6
  checks on, 54–55
  competence of, see competence of management, assessing
  conventions of, dangers in, 15–16
  defined, 3–4
  directors of, 36–38
  governmental regulation of, 55, 216–217
  intentions of, see objectives, setting
  as national activity, 8–11
  ownership and, see ownership
  planning by, 123–125, 128–129
  of production function, see production management
  professionalism in, 58–59
  of resources, see resources, management of
  review sessions by, 187–188
  social responsibility of, 40–43
  value judgments by, 44–47
  see also middle management; top management
management by objectives, 13–14
management by results, 3
  objectives-setting in, 83–85
"management up" concept, 127–128
managerial lag, 68–69
manual shift, 231–235
manufacturing, contract, 222
market, value establishment by, 49–52
market economies, 21–22
Mary, Queen of England, 75n
matrix-type organization, 181
Mautz, Robert K., 139
middle management
  alienation of, 13
  planning by, 126–127
migration of population, 221
Mitbestimmung, 38
moral utility of product, 40

INDEX

motivation
 cash bonuses as, 158, 196–197
 challenge as, 203–204
 constructive, 204
 incentive programs as, 192–193
 of production management, 168–172 *passim*
 productivity as, 11–14
 promotion as, 201
 salary as, 190–191
 see also compensation
multinational corporations
 charters for, 75
 currency-fluctuation accounting by, 139–140
 flexibility of, 220–221
 regulation of, by governments, 219–220

negligence, accountability for, 63–64
net worth, 131–133
New York (city), 29, 35, 225
non-profit enterprise, 5
 depreciation of fixed assets in, 101
 misconceptions about, 17–20
 objectives determination for, 86–93
 ownership of, 31–32
Northwestern Railroad, 96
not-for-profit enterprise, *see* non-profit enterprise

objectives, setting, 77–78
 growth and, 80–81
 in non-profit enterprises, 86–93
 in planning, 121–122

priorities in, 79
results considered in, 83–85
statement of purpose in, *see* statement of purpose (management's)
structure for, 123–125
survival and, 94–95
by top management, 82–83
objectives tree, 123–125, 177–179
Occupational Safety and Health Act (OSHA), 217
officism, *see* bureaucracy
operating income, 146
organizational span of control, 187–188
organization chart, 175, 176
 organization tree as, 177–179
OSHA (Occupational Safety and Health Act), 217
ownership
 components of, 29–30
 power of, 28–29
 statement of purpose by, 74–75
 by stockholders, 30–31

Packard, Vance, 50
Park decision, 62
Parkinson, C. Northcote, 181*n*
Penn Central, 29, 225
pension funds, employee, 30*n*
pensions, retirement, 198
P/E (price/earnings) ratios, 134
performance bonuses, 158, 196–197
planning, 116–119
 advantages of, 128–129
 basis of, 121–122
 objectives in, 121–125
 writing in, reasons for, 119–121

280

INDEX

plans, written, 119–121
population migration, 221
price/earnings (P/E) ratios, 134
pricing, transfer, 150
priority establishment
  by government, 49
  for objectives, 79
production
  management as means of, 4
  management of, see production management
  objectives in, 81
production management
  alienation of, 14–15, 165–166
  new practitioners of, 172–174
  responsibilities of, 167–172
  top management and, 166
production specialists, see production management
productivity
  as motivation, 11–14
  of office functions, increasing, 231–235
  of personnel, resource commitment for increasing, 157–158
professionalism, 58–59
profit, 130
  indicated, 135
  inventory, 97–98
  net, 132
profit-making enterprise, see corporations
promotion, 200–202
public resources, 7, 35–36
  effectiveness of management's use of, 159–161
  production management and, 168
  return on, 162–163

public school system, 89
public transportation, 233
public utilities, franchised, 95n
purpose, statement of, see statement of purpose (management's)

Rand, Ayn, 66
Rationalisierungskuratorium der Deutschen Wirtschaft, 59n
rationality in management, 8–11
regulation of management
  by government, 55, 216–217
  top management and, 217–219, 223–224
reinvestment of earnings
  by corporations, 113
  responsibility of management for, 114–115
  by shareholders, 111–112
remuneration, see compensation
replacement-cost accounting, 98–101
reserves, depreciation, 99–100, 113
resource(s)
  alternate use value of, 143–144
  assessing manager's use of, 144–149
  borrowing, 29
  capital as, 20–21
  consumable, 35
  human, see human resources
  management of, see resources, management of
  in non-profit enterprise, 88–93
  office function, maximizing productivity of, 231–235

INDEX

resource(s) (cont.)
  public, see public resources
  types of, 7
  waste of, 226–227
  see also assets
resources, management of, 7, 215
  inflation and, 23–24
  in market economies, 21–22
results
  management by, 3
  as motivation, 11–14
  for non-profit enterprises, 88–93
  in objectives determination, 83–85
  organization oriented toward, 176–177
retirement pensions, 198
return on assets, 134
return on equity, 131–133
return on individuals, 162–163
return on infraresources, 162–163
return on intangibles, 162–163
return on investment, 130
  discounted cash flow and, 150–151
return on resources, 162–163
review sessions by management, 187–188
Richardson, Elliot, 84–85

safety, personal, 233–234
salary, see compensation
sales personnel, 156–157
Schlesinger, Arthur, Jr., 56–57
school system, public, 89
Schumacher, E. F., 222

Securities and Exchange Commission, U.S., 55, 63, 76, 138
security as motivator, 204
self-liquidating charitable foundations, 95n
self-perpetuating hierarchies, 53–54
shareholders, see stockholders
Shenandoah Oil Company, 95n
shift, manual, 231–235
social cost, distributing, 51
socialistic dictatorships, 21
social responsibility, 40–43
Soviet Union, production quotas in, 196
span of control, organizational, 187–188
specialization, 13
  grouping by, 180–181
spending, investment, 82
staff service function, 170–171
Standard Oil, 242
Stanford Research Institute, 32n
Stanford University, 32n
statement of purpose (management's)
  disclosure of, 76–77
  initiation of, 76
  for private enterprise, 74–75
  for public enterprise, 74
Steel Authority of India, 87
stockholders, 29–31
  dividends for, see dividends, corporate
  reinvestment by, 111–112
  return on equity of, 131–133
strategy, see objectives, setting
supervisors, multiple, 181
survival as objective, 94–95
Sweden, 5–6

282

INDEX

task force organization, 179–181
 administration in, 182–183
 leadership in, 181
taxation
 on corporate dividends, 106–107, 109–111
 exemption from, 32
 expensing and, 137–138
 on fixed-asset investment, 102, 103, 106–107
 fraud in, penalties for, 63
 legal avoidance of, 150
teachers, 15
termination of employment, 202–203
Three Mile Island crisis, 69
tolling, 222
top management, 126–128
 accountability to, 223–224
 changes in future for, 217–219
 compensation correlation coefficient for, 191
 compensation for contribution of, 198–199
 objectives-setting by, 82–83
 production management and, 166
trading companies, 222
transfer pricing, 150
transportation, public, 233

uncapitalized intangible assets, 32–33
underdepreciation, 100
unions, 24–26, 157
United Kingdom, 5, 21, 63
United States
 population migration in, 221
 production management in, 165

value establishment
 by government, 47–49
 by management, 44–47
 by marketplace, 49–52

Wanamaker, John, 50
white-collar crime, see crime, white-collar
World Council of Management, 59n
W. R. Grace, 96

Yale University, 92n
Yugoslavia, 5, 6

Zaibatsu, 242
zero-base budgeting, 144
"zero-base" organization, 179
zero-growth situation, 112–114